W9-BJC-460

Also by Fay Vincent

The Only Game in Town: Baseball Stars of the 1930s and 1940s Talk About the Game They Loved

The Last Commissioner: A Baseball Valentine

WE WOULD HAVE PLAYED FOR NOTHING

★ ★ ★ ★ ★ ★ ★ ★ ★ ★ ★ ★ ★ ★ ★ ★ ★

BASEBALL STARS OF THE 1950S AND 1960S TALK ABOUT THE GAME THEY LOVED

The Baseball Oral History Project
Volume 2

FAY VINCENT

Simon & Schuster Paperbacks
New York London Toronto Sydney

Simon & Schuster Paperbacks
A Division of Simon & Schuster, Inc.
1230 Avenue of the Americas
New York, NY 10020

First Simon & Schuster trade paperback edition April 2009

SIMON & SCHUSTER PAPERBACKS and colophon are registered trademarks of Simon & Schuster, Inc.

For information about special discounts for bulk purchases, please contact Simon & Schuster Special Sales at 1-800-456-6798 or business@simonandschuster.com.

The Simon & Schuster Speakers Bureau can bring authors to your live event. For more information or to book an event contact the Simon & Schuster Speakers Bureau at 866-248-3049 or visit our website at www.simonspeakers.com.

Designed by Nancy Singer

Manufactured in the United States of America

10 9 8 7 6 5 4 3 2 1

Library of Congress Control Number: 2007045170

ISBN-13: 978-1-4165-5342-7
ISBN-10: 1-4165-5342-8
ISBN-13: 978-1-4165-5343-4 (pbk)
ISBN-10: 1-4165-5343-6 (pbk)

All photos courtesy of the National Baseball Hall of Fame Library except photo on p. 252, which is courtesy of Associated Press Photos.

To the estimable Marvin Miller—
whose contributions to baseball continue
to be ignored by those blinded by their own ignorance.
With respect, regret, and apologies.

CONTENTS

INTRODUCTION

Some ten years ago, a friend gave me a set of tapes of interviews Larry Ritter had done as the basis for his captivating book, *The Glory of Their Times,* and I was enthralled to listen to old-time ballplayers talk about their days in baseball in the early part of the twentieth century. This book, the second in a series, is a direct product of that chance encounter with the superb work that Ritter had done.

My decision to try to emulate Ritter led to some forty-five interviews of ballplayers and to the deposit at the Hall of Fame in Cooperstown of the videotapes of those interviews, with the hope that over time fans of our wonderful game will be able to see these fine players tell their stories. By preserving these tapes we preserve the essence of what makes baseball unique.

At the outset of this Oral History Project, my friend and mentor Herbert Allen encouraged me and helped me to finance the effort with a generous grant. The Hall of Fame receives the author's share of the proceeds from this book, and has graciously begun to find ways to make the tapes available to fans and students of baseball. In doing the interviews, I have been assisted by good friends Claire Smith, the eminent baseball writer; Dick Crago, the longtime announcer at Dodgertown in Florida; Leonard Koppett, the late sportswriter; and Jon Pessah. My editor at Simon & Schuster, Bob Bender, and I edited transcripts of the videotapes to create this manuscript. We tried to faithfully record the comments of the interviewees, correcting minor grammatical mistakes and occasional errors caused by the inevitable lapses of memory after several decades. Thanks also to Jim Gates and Pat Kelly at the Hall of Fame for their help with the introductions to the ballplayers and the photographs, respectively. And, once again, I acknowledge the enormous contribution of my colleague George Cooney, whose production crews have ensured that our videotapes are highly professional. My thanks to them and to all the others who have worked with us to make this such a rewarding undertaking.

My great pal Bart Giamatti, the scholar and former commissioner, often claimed that the history of baseball was an oral one and that baseball stories were at the heart of the appeal of our game. If so, these stories that you are about to uncover are sure to delight you as they have me. To hear players such as these talk about their love for the game and about their earliest baseball memories is a treat, like a neverending ice cream cone. It cannot get any better. Read on and have fun.

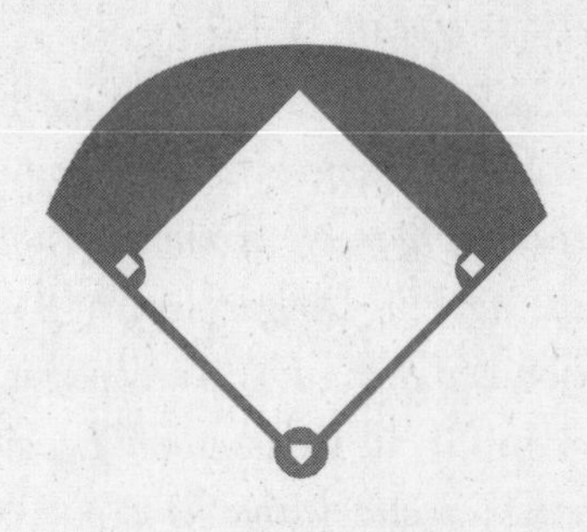

RALPH BRANCA

Ralph Branca spent a dozen years in the big leagues. Using his strong right arm he posted eighty-eight career wins, was named to three All-Star teams, and won a World Series game at the age of twenty-one. But all that was forever obscured, right or wrong, when he gave up "The Shot Heard 'Round the World."

According to two future Hall of Famers, Branca was expected to be a star when he arrived in the big leagues in the mid-1940s. "He was real fast and there was a wide sweep to his curve," said New York Giants manager Mel Ott in 1945. "There was a slight deception to his delivery that had a tendency to throw the hitters off stride. He's a fine looking young pitcher." That same year catcher Al Lopez said, "Branca showed us a real fastball and a sharp curve. He has a chance to be one of the best right-handers in the National League."

As a twenty-one-year-old in 1947, Branca matched his age in victories, finishing with a 21-12 record and an impressive ERA of 2.67. Eddie Dyer, the St. Louis Cardinals manager that year, said, "I've seen Ralph when he's been a match for just about any pitcher. Give him a little time to develop consistency—learn to pace himself, for instance—and you're going to see one swell pitcher." Branca never developed into the star so many had predicted, since an injured back forced him to retire in 1956.

On October 3, 1951, the twenty-five-year-old Branca of the Brooklyn Dodgers entered the third game of a three-game-playoff against the New York Giants in relief of Don Newcombe. With one out in the ninth inning, two men on base, and the Dodgers leading 4–2, Branca threw one strike to Bobby Thomson and then saw his second pitch hit into the stands for the homer that won the Giants the National League pennant.

The event remains unforgettable thanks in part to Giants announcer Russ Hodges's famous call: "Branca throws. There's a long drive . . . it's gonna be, I believe . . . The Giants win the pennant! The Giants win the pennant! The Giants win the pennant! The Giants win the pennant!"

In his reminiscence here, Branca talks about the relationship that he developed with Thomson over the years, and he discusses the recent revelations that the Giants were stealing the Dodgers' signs during the 1951 season, including the playoffs.

I grew up in Mount Vernon, New York, four blocks from the Bronx line. I come from a family of seventeen. I have two older brothers, one who's still alive. And they got me into baseball. My first recollection is my oldest brother, Julius, was playing with a local team, sandlot ball. And he was playing the outfield. The field had a slope to it. He played left field and he turned to go back and he hit the hill and, bing, right down. And he broke his nose. And I remember being six years old. I didn't really remember, but he told me. It was 1932 when I was six. And I remember sitting next to him and how proud I felt to be sitting next to my brother. My brother Ed was not quite as good a ballplayer. He could play softball; he had some ability. He was the fastest runner in the family. They were like second fathers to me. So they bought me my first glove. My brother Jules was also a catcher. So we would pitch to him in the driveway. And my brother John,

Ralph Branca

who is a year and a half older, my two younger brothers Al and Paul, we all were pitchers. They all went to Class B. John, Paul, and Al all went to Class B and organized ball. I was different from anybody else because I was six-three. I could throw harder. They threw probably about 85, 86 mile an hour curveballs. They knew how to pitch. I remember pitching to my brother Jules in the driveway. And Ed and Jules would take us to ball games. I guess they were Giant fans because they took us to the Giants most of the time, and once in a while to Yankee Stadium. So I became a Giants fan. We had a little field right next to our house where we played softball at night. As I grew up, I'd go down and play ball all day. We'd go down at nine o'clock and play till like noon. Go home, have a sandwich and glass of milk, and then go back and play. And then go back home, let's say, five o'clock, whatever, and have dinner, and then we'd play softball next door. So it was baseball sunup to basically sundown.

Because I was a Giant fan, my heroes were Mel Ott and Carl Hubbell, and Hal Schumacher, who was a good pitcher. But Hubbell was the king, and Hal was Prince Hal. Hubbell was a really great left-hander. I remember sitting in the bleachers in the Polo Grounds and watching his screwball go the other way and marveling at it.

I went to a tryout when I was sixteen. My brother John was the star that year. He won all the games, and I won two of them. So we went together as a team to tryouts. We went to the Polo Grounds, Yankee Stadium, and a place in Coney Island where we went to try out for the Dodgers. I never threw a ball at the Giants tryout. We went to the Yankees tryout, and I didn't know what they said, but later on they said, "Too young. Get in touch with him next year." And then when I went to Brooklyn, to Coney Island, they liked me. They said, "You got any other pitches?" "Yeah. I have a drop." And they said, "What's a drop?" So I threw this. "Oh, that's an overhand curve." Because it went twelve to six. I threw a flat curve also. But they liked me and had me throw a batting practice. And, of course, I guess I got pumped up. And then I just thought maybe I have a chance.

I graduated in June of '43. I signed with the Dodgers the following year, June 1944. During 1943 they had these V12 and A12 programs. The Army was A12, and the Navy, I guess, was V12. I had wanted to go in the V12 program. I was going to be a pilot. I passed all the tests, and I had pretty good marks. But I had had asthma as a kid. And I had a punctured eardrum. So when I went for the physical, they rejected me. I still thought I would be drafted when I turned eighteen the following January, January '44, but the Army again rejected me. So I never got drafted.

There was another kid from Brooklyn named Billy DeMars. We went to Olean on the New York Central, and we slept together in an upper berth because that's all they could get for us. So we slept together in an upper berth, two seventeen-year-old kids. Billy turned out to be a great shortstop, and he coached for years and years and years in the big leagues. And a very nice guy.

I didn't want to do anything ever to embarrass my family, especially my mother. So, you know, I just—well, you know *Jack Armstrong, The All-American Boy*. And I used to listen to that show on the radio. And one of the shocks was when I got to the big leagues to see guys smoking. I mean, that floored me. And, of course, as a rookie I sat on a bench my first year, in '44. I was sitting next to Paul Waner. I sat next to him about two innings and then I walked down to the end of the bench. There were a couple of older pitchers there. One of them was Frank Wurm. And I said, "Does Paul Waner drink?" They laughed. "Did you hear what the kid asked? Did you hear what that kid said?" My first road trip, we go to Boston. We stayed at the Kenmore Hotel. And Paul Waner's my roommate. Well, in the morning he reaches under the bed. He takes out a bottle. They had these round tumblers, and he filled it about that high and said, "This is my orange juice." I said, "Okay." But he said, "Don't tell anybody." I said, "No, I wouldn't say a word." But that was a funny experience. The first road trip I took, Paul Waner was my roommate.

The Dodgers were versed in fundamentals and mechanics; not necessarily mechanics, but fundamentals. You had to learn the game. You had to learn how to bunt, you had to learn how to cover the bases, you had to learn game situations, what do you do. And I think players talked about the game more often. I mean, you rode the train, and what did you talk about? You talked about baseball. We sat in the dugout during rain delays and talked about baseball. Sat in the locker room during rain delays, and talked about baseball.

My first appearance in a game was June 11, 1944, in the Polo Grounds. I remember walking from that bullpen and it seemed like I was on a treadmill—I kept walking and walking. And believe it or not, I struck out the first three guys. I got Mel Ott to pop out. My boyhood hero. Threw a fastball inside. It was the eighth-place hitter, the pitcher, and the leadoff man. But I struck them out, my first three hitters.

Here is what I consider the moment that I realized I could play in the big leagues. We're battling the Cards, 1946. I'm twenty years old. And the Cardinals come in and somebody's a half game ahead or behind. So Leo Durocher, our manager, announces to me that I'm to pitch to one man and then he's going to bring in Vic Lombardi because the Cardinals will load up their team with left-handers. And, of course, I warmed up, and I was going, "Sacrificial lamb, my butt." I get them out in the first inning on five pitches. I walked off, and Leo said, "Hey, kid. Keep throwing like that. I'm keeping you in." Well, I ended up pitching a three-hit shutout and I struck out nine. I think I only walked two guys. And in the next game, I pitched another shutout. And so I think, well, he got me so fired up that I really was throwing hard that day.

In '45, I was always around the plate. I would walk guys, but I was never very, very wild. I mean, I would miss by inches and probably was basically more wild high than any other place. That comes from mechanics sometimes, where you try to overthrow or else you rush to the plate and your arm can't catch up with your body. It's a timing sequence, and so when you get too far out in front with your body, your arm just doesn't catch up, so you're wild high. But I was around the plate mostly, but probably walked as many men as I struck out. I threw a changeup. I had a straight change. But my curveball, I threw hard. I mean, I threw straight over the top. I gave up the flat curve and threw an overhand curve, and I threw it hard. I threw a lot of fifty-five-footers because I threw it as hard as I could.

Clyde King and I roomed together. He was very, very bright, and so we would talk baseball, talk a sequence of plays and the plays that happened. And it's funny things like a man on first and then some guy popped the bunt up, and I trapped it and threw to first. Clyde looked at me, and he said, "I thought I would be the only one who would think of that." But I trapped the bunt and threw to first for a double play. Infield fly rule wasn't in play at that time. But Clyde King and I talked pitching a lot.

There was no pitching coach. That wasn't in vogue then. So pitchers taught one another, and then I tried to watch other pitchers and see how they pitched.

Getting to Ebbets Field—I tell the story, people won't believe it. I lived in Mount Vernon, four blocks from the Bronx line. I used to walk a couple of blocks to catch a bus to go to 241st Street and

White Plains Road in the Bronx, and I would take the Lexington Avenue subway line to Grand Central. Then I would take the shuttle over to catch the BMT to Brooklyn, and get off at Prospect Place. I didn't have a car. I was making $400 a month the first year in '44, and $600 a month in '45. And so I lived at home. I went home every night, but that's the route I took.

I pitched well in '45, but I wanted a raise to $6,000 from $3,300. And Branch Rickey never answered me. I guess I made a blunder. I was on the U.S.O. tour and I arrived on the West Coast and called home, talked to my younger brother Paul. He said, "Your contract came." It was like January 20. I said, "What's it for?" "Same number." I said, "Send it back." I guess I was supposed to write a letter or call Rickey. But the front office people told me that he got ticked at me, so he wouldn't contact me. And so I went down to spring training only on March 17, 1946. I had worked out at NYU, and I signed for $5,000. My spring training consisted of three innings, five innings, seven innings. That was my spring training. Because, you know, I was twenty years old.

In 1947, the first game we played was an exhibition game against Montreal, our Triple-A team. I pitched against Jackie. I threw him a fastball down the middle, and he grounded out. And I guess he went back to get his glove because by the time I was crossing the foul line, he said, "Thanks, Ralph." I thought, What is he thanking me for? Does he think I threw a ball down the middle so he can get a hit? Later on, it dawned on me he was thanking me because I didn't sign the petition, which I guess he knew about. Some of the Dodgers, when we were in spring training in Panama, had a petition going around that they didn't want to play with a black guy. I played with blacks my whole life as a kid. So when Jackie came along, it didn't mean anything to me because they lived next door to me.

Jackie and I were close. I know he cites it in his book that in the middle of June we were playing in St. Louis. And he's playing first, and for some reason I was sitting in the front row; they had a double-decker dugout. Normally, the pitchers sat in the back and the position players came in and sat in the front. I was sitting in the front row for some reason and there was a short pop, it wasn't very high, and Jackie came, hell-bent for leather to catch it. And as he caught the ball he tripped over the mound—they had the warm-up mound right in front of the dugout. He tripped and instinctively I stepped up out of the dugout and tackled him. I caught him on my shoulder; he was bent over, stumbling. He sure as hell was going to go right into the top of the dugout, and I caught him on my shoulders like a tackle, a full-hit tackle the way you play football. But he cites that in a book and he said that it meant that we both had "Dodgers" on our uniform and that we were teammates. Jackie and I always got along because he was a competitive guy, and I think I was very, very competitive. I hated to lose. But, you know, if I'd lose, I'd lose fairly. But we were very competitive. I don't know if it was that year or the next year, but we were both in the shower. I had pitched and we were both in the shower. And he had an abrasion, which we used to call the strawberry—you know, without sliding pants, you'd scrape yourself. An abrasion, a contusion, whatever you want to call it. So he's sitting there and I say, "You know, Jackie, you don't get strawberries." He said. "No? What do I get?" I said, "You get black raspberries." So he looks at me, he shakes his head, and he says, "You know, Ralph, only you would think of it and only you would say it." That's how close we were. He laughed at me.

God, people would insult him, hooting and hollering, you know. And Ben Chapman, manager of the Phillies, was very vociferous. I mean, they threw black cats on the field; they'd throw watermelons on the field. And Ben Chapman would say, "Hey, boy, I need a shine, come over here, give me a shine." "Hey, boy, how come you ain't picking cotton?" "Hey, boy, come over here and let me rub your head."

I remember one time in Cincinnati. It was a hot Sunday afternoon and there were a lot of blacks in the stands. He popped up and they screamed and yelled. He turned and he got on their case, said, "What are you yelling at? I popped up. Learn this game. Stop acting like fools." And that would be Jackie. But, see, I loved Jack, because he didn't give a quarter, didn't ask for a quarter, wouldn't give a quarter, didn't want a quarter. He wanted to prove that he could play ball, he was equal.

I loved Gil Hodges. I roomed with him for a while. Gilly was a stand-up guy in his quiet way. He didn't say much. He made the switch from catcher to first base. He was originally a shortstop. They made him a catcher, then he went to first base. He and Jackie got along and would gig one another because Gilly had this dry sense of humor. His first year, Jackie played first base. But they knew Jackie was a natural second baseman. They thought maybe he had more range at second base, so they moved him to second. But the move really revolved around Campy.

When Campy came up, then they could replace Hodges as catcher, put him at first, and move Jackie to second. And that was the move they had plotted all along. That really sealed it. And then Newcombe came. The acquisition of Newcombe and Campy really pushed the Dodgers into being a class team.

The Yankees had the most success because they won the most pennants and World Series. The Dodgers, starting in '47, would've, should've, could've. They could have won nine out of twelve years. And the Giants won two years. But the greatest thing about it is that to me, it was the golden era of baseball. That golden dozen or thirteen years was really terrific, especially in New York, because the fans in New York were being treated to seeing excellence almost every day. And we go from after the war in '46, when the Red Sox and Cardinals played in the World Series. Then outside of '48, there was a New York team represented in the World Series every year. And I think that the round-robin conversations between the Giant fans and the Dodger fans and the Yankee fans—who's better, who's not, and the Willie, Mickey, and the Duke stories, and, of course, Joe D. It was Joe D, and the Giants for us. The Giants were a tough team. They had a lot of home-run hitters, they had Johnny Mize.

And the team we had. Basically, we had Carl Furillo, Duke

Snider, and a left fielder, and then we got Andy Pafko. And the infield was set once we got Billy Cox. It was Hodges, Robinson, Reese, and Cox. That was the team. The left fielder changed occasionally until Pafko got there. And the pitching staff was Carl Erskine, Don Newcombe, myself, Preacher Roe, and then we had Rex Barney one year and Erv Palica. Had a lot of hard-throwing guys on the Dodgers. And the Yankees staff. They had Spec Shea, Vic Raschi, and then they got Allie Reynolds. Reynolds was very, very tough. Joe Page was great out of the bullpen. Gene Woodling played great for them. Joe Collins at first base. Joe and Moose Skowron and Phil Rizzuto at short, and Gil McDougald and Bobby Brown and Bobby Richardson, Billy Martin—all tough. And they had pitchers that were spot pitchers. They had Johnny Sain for a while. He came over from the Braves. I think that was in '51. And they got Mize over there; he was there in '49 with the Yankees.

In 1947, I led the league in starts; I had 36 starts, I relieved 7 times. And I like to say, "It doesn't count the times I went down and warmed up and didn't get in. The guy got the last out." I was second in strikeouts behind Ewell Blackwell, who had 193. I had 148, that was second. Now they strike out so many more guys, don't ask me why. I was third in the league in ERA. Spahn led it, I think, with 2.33; Blackwell, 2.47; and I was at 2.67. I pitched 280 innings. I gave up 251 hits, walked 98, struck out 148. I never missed a start. I was making $6,500. So when I went to contract, being twenty-two years of age, I didn't know how to negotiate. I went in and just picked out what I thought was a fair figure: $15,000. And then Rickey said, "No, you walk too many men and you didn't complete enough games." Well, I completed 15 out of 36. But we had a bullpen that was conducive for me going seven hard innings. We had Hank Behrman and Hugh Casey. And I remember Eddie Stanky saying, "We got two guys down there." I roomed with Eddie. He said, "You go hard seven innings and let's see what happens." But I did complete 15 games, though. And Rickey said, "No, you walk too many men and you didn't complete enough games." I settled for $12,500. He should've just said, "Kid, you're worth it," and given me the money. I couldn't leave the club. If I didn't sign the contract, I'd sit at home because there's no free agency. I couldn't bring an agent with me who could argue better than I could. And my choice was either accept it or sit at home. So I accepted the $12,500.

I ended up 12-5 at the All-Star Game in '48. In 1948, Tommy Brown and Billy Cox were playing catch, warming up before infield practice in St. Louis. I'd just beaten the Cardinals 1–0 the night before. I was playing pepper, back of home plate. The next thing I know, I got hit on the leg and I went down. Dr. Harold Wendler came out. He looked at it, and I said, "Should I do my running?" because you had to do your running. He said, "You can run." Well, the upshot of the whole thing was that the leg got infected; the lining of the bone got infected. Then it went to my arm, and I won only two games the last half of '48. I think it cost the Dodgers the pennant because the Braves ended up beating us, and I think, had I stayed there and done just what I did the year before, won nine games in the last half, I think we would have won the pennant.

I think doing the running hurt me because I think if I'd gone to the locker room and not run and put ice on it, I might have solved that problem. I pitched up in Boston after this, and we took a train to Philadelphia. And I remember my leg got swollen up. They called it periosteomyelitis; the lining of the bone got infected. They had to drain it. I still have the scar from when they cut and put a drain in. But I was in the hospital like two weeks.

That leg infection hung on in the next year and into '50. Finally in '50, the last half of '50, August, they put me in the bullpen, and I threw every day. I used to warm up every day like I was going to go in, and my arm got strong again. And that's why I started 1951 as the stopper. Not the last guy, the closer. I was going to pitch the seventh, eighth, and ninth because that's what relievers did in those days. And my arm got very strong. I started out 1951 as the reliever. I think I was 1-1 on May 28. I wasn't pitching much. We were either winning big or losing big. They started me in St. Louis. I kind of turned the season around, because I won 3–2. The funny part of that game was I pitched seven innings and it rained. Now we have a half-hour, forty-minute rain delay and I go in, take a shower, got new oil on my arm, new uniform, new sweatshirt, and went out and got the last six guys out. Now, I cannot visualize a guy doing that today—coming from the bullpen, where the most they pitch is three innings, to go seven innings and then go back in. Just the other day, it happened. A guy got rained out, they took him right out, they brought in the reliever. It's a whole different philosophy.

I think today's pitchers, pitching every five days, going six innings, don't throw enough in the game or in between, to keep their arms strong. Inch by inch, they get out of shape. It's like they're looking for the finish line quickly. If I'm going to run a marathon, I'm not going to run sprints to practice for it. I'm going to run marathons. If I'm going to pitch, I'm not going to use a machine off the wall, I'm going to use my arm. I'm going to throw. If you have proper mechanics, you're not going to hurt your arm, especially without pressure. I could go in spring training and throw twenty minutes of batting practice, go on the sidelines and throw half an hour and my arm would never get tight. As soon as I pitched two innings in a game, my arm would get tight because there's tension and pressure, and you're throwing the ball harder. Now you have to throw strikes, so it's more pressure, and you're throwing harder because you're facing a hitter. I think you got to throw. Today's players, with the way they can train all year-round, there's no reason they can't pitch every four days. Nothing's going to happen to their arm if they have good mechanics. If you have poor mechanics, I don't care what you do; unless you get your mechanics right, you're going to get hurt. So if you have good mechanics—and they have video machines that you can look at a guy and see what he's doing and make a comparison. They never took a movie of me to show what I did when I was going good and what I was doing when I was going poorly.

• • •

Campy was a happy-go-lucky guy. Loved to tell stories. You know, built like, well, we'll say short and squat, but he could throw, had a quick release. And he was a good hitter, had a lot of power. And he was a good guy to be around, because he was always on the up. Really, I don't ever remember seeing Campy being down.

I didn't like the target he had because I was a low-ball pitcher, and I always wanted to have a knee-high target. Campy gave a big target. And I used to tell him, "Get over, get down," because he straddled the outside corner of the plate. I liked to pitch inside because I was sneaky fast. But, you know, Carl Erskine loved him. He called great games for Erskine. He called good games for me, too, but I just think, as a part of the team, he was a good guy to have in the locker room. He's a good guy on the bench. He never gave up, and he had a great attitude. He said, "To play this game, you got to have a lot of little boy in you." Which means you have to have fun playing, which I think is a great attitude.

At first, Campy and Jackie were very close and then somehow they went on a barnstorming tour and Campy thought that he didn't get paid enough and Jackie made all the money. And they got a little separated with that, but I think they respected one another. Jackie

Roy Campanella

was feisty and fiery, and Campy was placid and an easygoing guy and jovial. And Jackie, I guess because of who he was, being the first, was a little more serious and more competitive. But overall, they got along. The other guy in that triumvirate was Don Newcombe. And Newcombe and I were very close because for some reason, big guys had to work harder to stay in shape than the little guys. I'll never understand that reasoning. But we would play pepper and then we'd go do our running and we would run together. And I'm going to say we'd run twenty laps from the foul line to center field and back, twenty times. Then the other pitchers would come out and run. There'd be the starting pitchers and the bullpen. Well, they'd run like ten laps and Newcombe and I would run the ten laps with them, but we've already run twenty. We talked about pitching. He's a different type of pitcher. We both had good fastballs but his curveball was very small. He had narrow curveballs, almost like a slider today. I thought it was a great pitch because it almost looked like his fastball, but it just broke sharply at the end. He had a great year in '56. He was 27-7, won the MVP and the Cy Young Award. I saw him recently, and he's in good health and doing well.

Carl Furillo was a hard-nosed guy. I can't say "a loner," but he wasn't gregarious. He just had a few friends that he stayed around with. But he could play. He had a lifetime batting average of .299. He had a great arm and played the Ebbets Field wall like a sergeant. And he knew what he was doing. He knew where the ball was going. He got out of baseball, and he thought that the Dodgers screwed him, to be blunt. He had had a bad calf, and they wanted to send him down to the minors so he could rehab. Actually, they had a baseball camp in Dodgertown for kids. And they wanted to send him to Florida, where there were trainers to work on his calf and get him back in shape. But he refused to accept going down to the minors, so they released him. I remember I've heard him tell the story that Charlie Dressen said that if he ever got released, Charlie would take him. I think

Carl Furillo

Charlie was managing Milwaukee at that time. But Charlie didn't pick him up. So he was angry, thought that he got blackballed.

Jackie, Pee Wee, Hodges, and Campanella were the real leaders on the team. Erskine was a class act and very intelligent. He would be, like, next in line. I was player rep for a while, then he became player rep. He has an innate sense of what's proper.

If I was to pick my center fielder, I would've picked Mickey, because he was a switch-hitter. He hit from both sides. Unfortunately, he hurt his knee early on in his career, so you don't really know if he could have been even a little bit better. Truthfully, I think Duke was the best outfielder of the three of them, Mays and Mantle. Duke got a great jump on the ball, charged the ground ball, and had the best arm of all three. Not only was he stronger, but he was more accurate. And he played in the toughest ballpark. Of course, Yankee Stadium and the Polo Grounds, you could run forever and never worry about a wall, whereas Duke had to worry about running into a wall. And he had to play the wall in right center because it was at an angle. It went down and angled out. And the scoreboard was another angle. And the screen was another angle. So, maybe I'm prejudiced, but I think Duke was the best outfielder of them all.

Joe D was so graceful. I mean, you didn't realize how fast he was because he looked graceful. I watch video clips of him now and you realize he was really running hard, but when you saw him play, it looked like it was easy. But he played the hitters very, very well. He knew how to play the hitters. And he made everything look easy because he was so graceful. As an aside, I'll tell you my Eddie Lopat story. Eddie Lopat got traded from the White Sox to the Yankees. Now, with the White Sox he was a .500 pitcher, which is very good because that was a mediocre team. Guy's pitching in his first game in Yankee Stadium. He said, "I'm a little bit nervous." He said, "I got the bases loaded. I got three and two on the hitter. So I just took a breather. I went to the mound and looked out to center field. I'm rubbing the ball up and Joe D was playing straightaway. So I throw the pitch and the guy hits a screamer to left center." He goes, "Oh, no." Then Joe D catches the ball. He's like, "I couldn't wait for him

Joe DiMaggio

to get to the dugout." He got to the dugout. "How the H did you get over to the left side?" He says, "I knew you had to come in with the pitch, so I just moved over twenty feet." So Joe D, he sensed what was going on with the game and moved over. But I know that in '47, they said, his arm was hurt. We got the report, but I know he had an accurate arm, decent—and I know he was very graceful. And hitting in Yankee Stadium when left field was 402 on one side of that bullpen and 415 on the other side of the visiting bullpen. Too tough for Joe, that's a long way to hit at straight left. Had he been playing in Ebbets Field, he probably would have hit a lot more home runs.

I pitched Joe inside. As I said, I was sneaky fast, so I pitched him inside, fastballs inside. And I won the highest compliment. In 1947, we played an exhibition game in Louisville, and Larry Goetz was an umpire traveling with the Dodgers on the train. We went from town to town on the train, and some night I saw Larry at dinner on the train. He said, "You got some compliment today, kid." I said, "Really?" He said, "Joe D said you have the best stuff he'd seen in all spring." I had pitched a two-hitter for seven innings. He got one of the hits, one of the few hits he got off me.

Tommy Henrich. I love talking to Tommy. He's a raconteur, and he's very, very, talented. Mr. Dependable, Mr. Clutch. And I remembered him telling me a story. Don Newcombe was in a 0–0 game in the World Series and he got behind him. Tommy said, "He's going to throw me his curveball." And, of course, he looked for it and hit a home run and beat Newcombe 1–0 in the first game of the 1949 World Series. Henrich told me that in spring training, he never tried to pull a ball until the last week of spring training. He said, "I always try to hit it the other way. That made me wait and look at the ball."

You have to get into a hitter's head, how to pitch, what he expects, and try to confuse him. If you get a guy out on a curveball the first two times, and now you've got a man on first, he thinks you're going to try to get him out on that curveball this time, somehow, you want to say, no. Curveball, he fouls it off. Fastball, you waste, or he fouls it off again and then he gets a ball you wasted. Now you throw him a fastball, see, 1-and-2, and he takes it. He says, "Now he's coming back with the curve." And you just throw him a fastball and they go "Uh." They just flinch on it. And so you have to be thinking with the hitter. And each hitter's different.

Robin Roberts had great mechanics. He would almost coast. He would throw the ball—I'm going to say 88, 89 miles an hour, but if he got in a jam, whoa, he'd just reach back, he'd go to 93 or 94. He had a good curveball. And, I mean, he pitched forever. He'd give up five runs in the first three innings, you'd figure they knocked him out, but at that point in time Philadelphia wasn't fighting for anything, you know, so they leave Robin in. It's 5–0, next thing it's 5–5, next thing, Robin had won the game, 6–5. Because he was a battler. And as I said, he always had a little reserve that he'd go to to get guys out. He'd put that extra zip on the ball.

Richie Ashburn was one of those punch hitters. You know, he didn't have power, but you couldn't strike him out. He'd slap at the ball. He could pull it if he wanted to. If he got it inside, he'd hit it. He could fly. Good outfielder and didn't have the strongest arm, but Richie was a good competitor.

Stan Musial was a tough out. I mean, no matter where you pitched him. If you pitched him inside, he'd pull. You pitched him outside, he'd hit it the other way. The most success I had was changing up on him. Because he had that kind of crouch-coiled stance. But he hit the ball where it was pitched. And those fans in Brooklyn were such great fans. They used to give him a standing ovation. He got more cheers than the Dodgers because they respected his ability.

There were some good defensive catchers that couldn't hit, like Del Rice with the Cardinals, a great defensive catcher. But he couldn't hit, couldn't run. I mean, a race between Del Rice and Rube Walker, you would have needed a calendar to time it. But Rube was also a good catcher, a good defensive catcher, a good caller of pitches, sequence of pitches. At first base Johnny Mize could hit. Wasn't the greatest of fielders. Ted Kluszewski could hit, wasn't the greatest fielder. I think Hodges was the greatest right-handed-fielding first baseman of all time.

In 1951, the Dodgers were rolling along. We were thirteen and a half games up, and we went into the Polo Grounds around August 10. You know, there were seven weeks left in the season, and it looks like a lock. You just have to play .500 ball and you're going to win. You got a thirteen-and-a-half-game lead. And we went in and we got beat three games in a row. I remember the first game was a night game; Erv Palica started and gave up a few runs. He said he had a sore arm, but Charlie Dressen insisted on pitching him. And we end up losing the game 4–2. The next day, I lost 3–1. And the next day Newcombe lost, I believe it was 2–1. We got beat three straight games, so the lead immediately went to ten and a half. And then we just struggled. The hitters really didn't hit that much. I think Jackie and Duke are the only two guys who hit their average in the last seven weeks. But the pitching staff, Charlie went to not using everybody on the staff. Instead, I think he overused Newcombe and myself, because we would start and relieve, and also Erskine and Preacher. Clyde King was our reliever, and Clyde pitched a great first half, and then he came up with a sore arm, so he wasn't quite up to it. Clem Labine had come up, and Clem had great stuff. He had a sinkerball, and he had a great curveball. And he hung the curve one day and the guy hit a home run, and I think Charlie put him in the doghouse, and he didn't pitch until the second game of the play-offs, when he pitched a shutout, beat the Giants 10–0. I think he could have used Clem more often down the stretch.

Going into September, we had thirteen pitchers on the roster because they brought up guys from the minor leagues. And Charlie

Dressen should've given some of the staff a little rest, given us an extra day rest here and there. Because I think we went downhill starting late. I pitched a shutout on a Friday night. We had a doubleheader Sunday, doubleheader Monday, and he asked me if I could pitch on two days' rest. And fortunately—unfortunately, because I had a no-hitter going, and I knew I had a no-hitter because Furillo had thrown out the opposing pitcher on a soft line drive to right field. Furillo's playing him shallow, threw him out at first. I went, "Uh-oh, no-hitter." It was twilight. I said, "If I ever pitch a twilight game, they're not going to hit me because they can't pick me up in this twilight light." And I went to the ninth and I shook Rube off and the guy got a base hit. And then I got the next guy out and next was a Baltimore chop. Metkovich hit it, Cat Metkovich. I pitched a two-hit shutout.

This was against Pittsburgh. Then I pitched against Sal Maglie and lost 2–1. There's a play that nobody ever talks about. Only Dick Young mentioned it in his writing. Dick Young was a very bright guy and a good writer. We had men on first and third. Jackie was on third, and I believe Duke was on first. And Pafko hit a one-hopper right down the line and Bobby Thomson was playing even with the bag. Bobby was playing third base at the time because Willie Mays was now playing center field. And he dove to his right and caught the ball on his knees and Jackie instinctively went back to the bag. Don't ask me why, but he went back to the bag. Thomson tagged him, and while on his knees, he threw to first, a double play, and I lost to Maglie 2–1. This was in September. Nobody ever talks about that being a turning point, but I think it was. They all talk about that play in Boston, where Campy blocked the plate. What was his name . . . Bob Addis. He never got to the plate and the umpire called him safe. Campy threw the glove in the air and the umpire said, "If that comes down, you're out of here." So Campy got thrown out and we had to make a switch. Hodges went to catch, Jackie went to first, and Wayne Terwilliger took Campy's spot in the batting order. And sure enough, in the ninth, Terwilliger came up instead of Campy and he made an out and we lost the game. That's the day that Preacher Roe kicked in the umpire's door. I did not do that to umpires, but Preacher did. That's the other turning point that they all talk about. But the Giants made a great run. They went 37-7 the last forty-four games of the season, which is unthinkable.

End of July, beginning of August, and the Giants are way behind us. Hank Schenz had been with the Cubs, got traded to the Giants. And he happened to mention to Herman Franks, one of the Giants coaches, that he had a telescope from the Navy that you could expand and you could see a fly on a chimney 300 feet away. Herm says, "I got to see that." So he brought it in and somehow, some way, they devised a scheme of setting up this telescope in the Giants clubhouse at the Polo Grounds. The clubhouse was in dead center field; there were steps on either side of this open space where you went up to the clubhouse. On the top level was Leo Durocher's office. So they had this scheme to hook up a buzzer system. Now Herman could sit on the far side of Leo's desk in the shadows and he could look right into home plate. They set this telescope up and could see right into home plate and catch the catcher's signs. But they hooked up a buzzer on Leo's desk. Hank Schenz sat with him. Hank Schenz played in one game the whole last half of the year, because he was there buzzing the buzzer. They were looking at the catcher's sign. With nobody on, catchers put down one sign. They put down one, two, three, wiggle, whatever the signs are. And if they gave the sequence of signs, Herman being an ex-catcher, would know what they were calling. So Herman could do that, and he would buzz. The buzzer sounded in the bullpen and in the dugout. Sal Yvars was a reserve catcher. He sat down there and he had a towel in his hand, and he'd leave it still for a fastball, wave it for the curve, and flip it over his thigh for the changeup or the slider. There was a buzzer in the dugout. And the guys would yell "Sock it." S, straight; "sock it," fastball. Then, "Be ready." B, second letter of the alphabet; "be ready," curveball. If they yelled, "Sock it," the batter knew a straight ball was coming. "Be ready," it was a curve, and "Watch it" was a changeup or a slider, a pitcher's third pitch. The next inning, they'd go back to the bullpen and this time, Yvars would have a ball in his hand. He would hold it still for fastball, throw it up and down for a curve, and then back and forth with each hand for the third pitch. So they called all the pitches. And they won sixteen games in a row. Sal Yvars has said that they would get five, six runs ahead and they wouldn't give the signs anymore, because they're afraid somebody would discover it. And he said sometimes Alvin Dark and Eddie Stanky knew that a curve was coming and they'd make a futile swing like they got fooled, just to try to fake everybody out. The Giants players get ticked at Yvars, because he does talk a lot, but Sal was straightforward, and he talked about it for years. He was the only guy who mentioned that they stole the signs. And then, of course, January 31, 2001, that big article came out on the front page in the *Wall Street Journal* written by Josh Prager, telling the whole story.

So the Giants admitted that they stole the signs. Well, back then, Bobby Thomson was reluctant to say that he got the sign on that pitch. He got them during the year, and he got them that game, but that time up, he says his mind was elsewhere. He was just concentrating on getting a hit. Well, to be truthful, I find it hard to believe, because if you're used to doing it for seven weeks, you're going to do it in that situation. I'm not taking anything away from him. He hit what I thought was a real good pitch. He hit a fastball up and in. And I know I threw a lot of high fastballs that got hit for home runs, but none that were up and in. I mean, out over the plate, right over the middle of plate, yes. So he hit it, and I give him credit, because he hit a tough pitch, but I say—and he's been a friend of mine for years—I say, "I give him credit for hitting the pitch, but this should not have been a play-off." That's my contention. It should not have been a play-off. The Dodgers should have won by fifteen games or twelve games or whatever. And we could have coasted in to the World Series, got our pitching staff back in shape, and it wouldn't have been in tough shape had we had a big lead. We could have beaten the Yankees in '51, because the Giants were up two games to one and it rained, and instead of pitching Sain, the Yankees pitched Allie Reynolds. He won 6–2. That turned the Series around. The Yankees ended up beating the Giants. But I think if the Dodgers could have gone in that Series, I think we had a really good shot at beating them. I'd like to believe that we would have beaten them.

In that deciding game of the play-off, Game 3, I was the number one man in the bullpen. I had pitched Monday, and pitched eight innings, and then Clem pitched the next day, beat the Giants. I was number one in the bullpen and Newcombe was starting. Newcombe had pitched a lot. He had pitched as much as I had, start and relief, and, in fact, I think that was the year he pitched a doubleheader and did very well. But Newcombe was pitching, and I was in the bullpen. It's 455 feet away, and we were just watching the game and it was a close game. Suddenly, we had a 4–1 lead. And my arm was so stiff that I started to loosen up in the sixth inning. I never sat down. I just kept throwing until my arm loosened up. And I have no excuse, because when I walked in, I was throwing as good as I possibly could. My arm was really back to being in a good shape. I pitched on two days' rest back in August and my arm was not quite as strong. A little rubber had gone out of it, and yet I was effective. I just didn't think I had real live rubber in my arm. So I was throwing very, very well. And I remember talking to Jackie and Pee Wee before the game. "You got butterflies? Anybody got butterflies?" And they both laughed. And now I walk in from the bullpen and I see them right at shortstop, saying, "You got butterflies?" So they both laughed at me. The score was now 4–2. Whitey Lockman had doubled and Don Mueller had slid into third and broke his ankle, so there was a lull in the action. And they carried him off the field and replaced him with Clint Hartung as a runner. The score is 4–2, men on second and third, and Thomson, the winning run, is up, the bottom of the ninth. But that's another thing that nobody talks about. We had won the coin toss, and don't ask me why, but Charlie Dressen decided to play the first game at home. Maybe he got input from the office or whatever, but we played the last two at the Polo Grounds. And I'm saying, "Why?" That's so ludicrous to me that he made that decision, because we should have played the first one in the Polo Grounds and the last two at home. Thomson hits the home run. Sayonara. If they didn't have last at bat, who knows?

Anyway, the Giants had come up in the bottom of the ninth losing 4–1. They got a run in. And there was another play in that game, another turning point. Hodges was just holding the man on with one out, and he was playing like, you know, halfway or three steps behind the runner. The runner was not going to steal. It was Alvin Dark. He was not going to steal. Mueller's the hitter, and Hodges should've been playing back to get the second out, get one sure. If Hodges plays back, he catches the ball; it was hit to his right. He went to his right, Jackie went to his left, it went off the tip of his glove, went behind Jackie. Now they got first and second and one out. Monte Irvin popped up and Lockman hit a double. Now it's a run in, second and third, tying run's on second, winning run at the plate, and I get called in. And as I said, there was a lull in the game, because Mueller had broken his leg. So when I got to the mound, Dressen said, "Get him out." Rube Walker was the catcher. And unfortunately, I didn't say, "What signs are we using?" or maybe we would have changed the signs or something.

Campy had hurt his thigh and couldn't play, so Rube caught. The first pitch I threw him, you couldn't zero it any more dead in the middle of the plate. It was right there, dead in the center of the plate. I was really relaxed and could throw the ball hard. Now, the next pitch, I want to go up and in. And so I threw him a fastball up, and it was up and in. And Thomson will say I didn't get it in enough, but I have looked at the reruns, I looked at the pitch, it was in enough. He just stepped in the bucket, anticipated I was going to pitch him up and in. Because, to be truthful, he hit a home run off me in the first game in Brooklyn. And when it went up, I said, "That's an out." And then I watched Pafko start to drift back. And that ball cleared the fence by inches. So he knew I pitched him up and in, because relative to the end of 1951, I really think I had good success against Bob. He anticipated. He hit the ball, with an uppercut swing, and I knew it was going to go down. I knew. It was like an overhand curveball, and all I kept yelling was "Sink, sink, sink." And the game was over. And I don't even remember that I picked up the rosin bag and threw it down. I didn't remember until I saw it on television.

I was feeling that I cost the team the pennant. We lost, and here we had it cinched. We all were going to get in the World Series, a chance to win, a chance for glory. You don't even think about the money, because you're just thinking about wearing the World Series championship ring. And then that was all gone. I mean, that just flew away, and it was hard to believe. I see the picture of myself walking off the field and Jackie standing and making sure Thomson touched all the bases. And I guess he was in disbelief himself. And so, you know, we got to the clubhouse and there's some memorable pictures of me in the locker room. And all I could say, you know, was "Why me?" I probably was the last guy in the locker room, because I just sat, I guess, stunned.

Branca in the clubhouse after giving up the home run to Bobby Thomson

When I got to the car, now it was like October 3, so I was getting married seventeen days later to Anne. I got to the car and her cousin was there, Father Pat Rowley. He was the dean of campus ministries at Fordham. And, of course, I got to the car, parked in the right-field parking lot. I said, "Why me? You know, I love this game so much. Why me?" And he said, "God chose you because he knew your faith would be strong enough to bear this cross." And I know that's Jesuit philosophy. What he said made a big impact on me, because I realized that the Dodgers sent in their best pitcher. And he was a better man that day that hit the home run. And so, you know, baseball is a game where you've got to learn how to win and you've got to learn how to lose. You win graciously and you lose graciously.

The other guys were all afraid to say anything to me. They were very cautious around me. But there was always a pat on the shoulder and hugging, and Jackie said, "Hey, if it wasn't for you, we wouldn't be here." And so, basically, I look at the season, and when I reflect on it, I know I was a reliever until May 28, and then I started five games in a row, because the pitching staff was not doing that well. And I pitched four complete games, won them all. In the fifth game, I was losing 1–0 after pitching seven innings. So I pitched 43 out of a possible 45 innings. It ended up that Hodges hit a home run in the ninth inning, and we won that game, 2–1. That kind of settled the pitching staff down. And we had good pitching. Preacher Roe went 22-3. Newcombe, I don't know what his record was. Erskine. And myself. But at one point, in June, July, and August, I was 12-5. I went 11-4 in those three months. I lost to Maglie 2–1. I lost to Robinson 3–2. Every game in September, I got one run, the team got one run until I left. I left in the fifth inning, sixth inning, one run. We didn't hit. We just didn't hit. And I think the pitching staff got worn out. We got Johnny Schmitz in a trade, and Pafko, and Terwilliger, and Rube Walker. Pafko did not hit that much. He tried to pull the ball after he got to Ebbets Field. They all see that short fence and they want to pull it. Pafko was a straightaway hitter. And I've seen other guys who've come to the Dodgers, traded, and then hit the ball to right center and right field. Honestly, you see those short points, you want to hit home runs. And Pafko fell victim to that. He tried to pull the ball too much.

I saw Thomson the very next day. I went to Yankee Stadium, the opening of the Series in Yankee Stadium. One of the photographers asked me to pose for a picture choking him, so I saw him the next day. Maybe I should've really choked him. But, yeah, we posed for the picture, and then I didn't see much of him. I think that first year I went back to NYU. Anne and I were married, and I went back to NYU for some classes. And then spring training started. The unfortunate part of my whole career was that I hurt my back in a screwy accident off the field. And I really was never much of a pitcher after that. I struggled all the way. My back got thrown out of whack. My pelvis got tilted, the left side went up an inch and a half, and I really never pitched effectively after that. I may have pitched in good games here and there, but I was never consistent.

Bobby Thomson

• • •

I don't think anybody could have visualized that this moment would live as long as it has, but when you reflect back, you see that, first of all, the Giants came from a long way back, whether they got aid or not—you know they got aid. Even with the help, they won 37 and lost 7, so the Giants came from a long way back. That's history. The New York media—New York was the capital of the world. It was the intense rivalry between the Dodgers and the Giants.

So everything went into the mix, the last game. It all boiled down to that one point and with, as I said, the great rivalry, them coming from so far behind, the last of the ninth, there's no more tomorrows, and Russ Hodges's call—all go into the mix of why it's still remembered.

People say, "It made you famous." I say, "No, infamous." I said, "If I have my druthers, you know I would have liked to have struck him out and struck Willie out because that was my job." Willie was on deck. I don't want to live on that moment. It defines my whole career. And if you look at my career, the youngest guy ever to start a play-off game, one of the youngest to start a World Series game, first game World Series, one of the youngest guys to start an All-Star Game, one of the youngest guys ever to win 20 games or more, and yet, because of injuries, I should have won 20 the next year. I know I was 12-5 at the All-Star break. I should have won 20 the next year. But because I got hit in the leg, I didn't win 20.

It'll never happen again—three New York teams finished in first place one year, 1951. That will never ever happen again. But I think that that was such a golden era for baseball. Maybe the rest of the country doesn't feel that way because it was all basically New York. New York dominated.

Joe Black came up in '52 as a reliever. He went 15-4 and then started the World Series. He beat the Yankees in the first game. Joe was a big, heavy guy. He probably weighed 225 or more. He had a moderate fastball. He had a small little curve that looked like a fastball and just broke two, three inches, which I think is a great pitch. In fact, I think Mariano Rivera throws what I call a spiral that breaks two or three inches, not really a slider, it's a fastball that spirals and breaks just a little bit. So it's thrown as hard as a fastball. It's a tough pitch. You got to gauge it. But Joe had a great year. And then he had a funny finger that . . . I don't know, it was nerve damage that he couldn't control. And he said Charlie Dressen tried to teach him to change his motion. He said he never got back to his basic mechanics. And from there on, he just didn't really perform well and went downhill the rest of his big-league career.

In the middle of '53, I was traded to Detroit. I roomed with Teddy Gray. Good little left-handed pitcher and a class act. Teddy and I were very, very close. In '54, I guess we were on the road, maybe our first road trip, and he said, "You know, I have to tell you something. You know, I was sworn to secrecy, but I have to tell you." And he told me that some guy who had been on the Giants had been traded to the St. Louis Browns and told him the story about how the Giants used this buzzer. So then he went through the whole thing about this mechanical device, the buzzer setup, how Herman Franks called all the signs, and that's how come they won all the games. I think it's one of the most despicable acts in the history of the game, to go on and win the pennant. I'd been a goat for two years now, and why? There shouldn't have been a play-off game. And I'm saying, well, it wasn't really all your fault that you lost, because they cheated. That made me feel a little bit better.

It leaked out before but it always died. In 1962, 1963, I was doing shows with Howard Cosell after a Mets game, and a story came out of Arizona that the Giants used a buzzer system to steal the signs. I didn't want to talk about it, but Howard and the producer just kept hammering at me. Then I finally succumbed and said that I knew about it and how they did it. And they said, "Why don't you want to talk about it?" I said, "I don't want to cry over spilled milk. It's sour grapes, and I don't want to be a sore loser." And I never had any conversation with anybody. It was just like natural for me to say, "No, I'm not going to talk about it." And don't ask me why I did that, because sometimes I get introduced to somebody and Anne's standing next to me, and the guy'll say, "Oh, Bobby Thomson." And I just turn and walk away. And he said, "Oh, I said something wrong?" She answered, "You certainly did." Or I'll say, "What am I supposed to do now, faint because you mentioned Thomson?"

I can tell you two incidents. I'm with the Giants farm club in Minneapolis in '55 trying to make a comeback. And I'm warming up in the bullpen in Omaha and some guy is yammering at me while I'm warming up. And I got to yammering back at him. So Alex Konikowski and Allan Worthington, two relievers with the Giants who were at Minneapolis then, said, "Come here, we have to talk to you." So we walked. The dugout was right at the end of the stands, and the clubhouse was right behind the dugout. So they said, "We're going to tell you something that will make you feel better." I said, "You're not going to tell me anything that I don't know." "No, no, no. You don't know this." "No, I know what you're going to tell me." "No, you don't know this." I said, "I know what you're going to tell me." "No, you don't know this." "All right." So when I told them I knew about the buzzer, their mouths dropped. "You know?" So they didn't say anything because I never told anybody that. I never talked about it. But then I played in a golf tournament with a friend of mine who knows Sal Yvars. He said, "Sal was talking about a week later at Shultz's garage, how they stole the signs." And so Sal was at the golf tournament, and Phil Mushnick from the *New York Post* was there. And Sal told how they had stolen the signs. So Phil said, "Is that true?" I said, "Yeah, that's a true story." "So why don't you just talk about it?" I said, "I'm not going to talk about it." And he wrote about it. But it died. All those stories died.

People have said to me, "Well, everybody stole the signs." I said, "You steal them on the field, that's one thing. But when you do what they did, that's despicable. It's immoral." And it wasn't illegal to do what they did because there was no rule against it but it was immoral.

Still, Bobby and I have a good relationship. I think he's quite a little bit different. It's still a good relationship, but it's a little different now. He's a good guy. He means well. He's a humble guy, and I get along with him.

I was with the Yankees in '54. I was just starting to throw a screwball. Of course, I threw a screwball to Ted Williams and he grounded out at second base. Yogi laughed. And then I pitched against him in Boston, had him struck out, but the umpire blew it. I threw a fastball, and Ted blinked, and the umpire blinked, then he called it a ball, but I really had him struck out. I didn't pitch against him that often, watched him again, all the games against the Yankees. But, you know, Ted had an ego thing that he had to pull a ball; he was going to defy the shift, and, well, he could do it. As a hitter, you had to wait, wait, wait, and he had such a quick bat he could do that. Guys got a quick bat now. You look at Gary Sheffield, he's got such a quick bat, a good hitter. But all Ted had to do is bunt ten times a year or hit the ball to left field to overcome the shift. He gets up 500 times. He does that and it's 20 points on his batting average. And he calls pitchers dumb? Ted is not going to like that.

Compare the Yankees and Dodgers? It was pretty close between Yogi and Campy. First base, I got to give that to Gilly over the Yankees. Second base, Jackie; shortstop, Rizzuto. That would be a great argument, Rizzuto and Reese. You can go back and forth that Pee Wee had the better arm, if you go on who had better arm, but Rizzuto was quick; he got rid of the ball quicker. And both could hit; they could bunt, they could squeeze, they could do all the fundamentals very, very well. Third base, it'd be an argument there, but pretty close at third base. The outfield? Snider and DiMaggio, when Duke finally got to play the outfield probably steadily in '48. But he was young and DiMaggio was an established star, so the Yankees probably get that one. The Yankees also had Gene Woodling and Hank Bauer. Enos Slaughter played for them a little bit, too. Those were very good teams.

The Baseball Assistance Team was formed in 1986. It was started by Peter Ueberroth. He was approached by Equitable Life Insurance. They wanted to get into baseball as a sponsor, and Peter said, "Well, you have to do something for charity." And John Carter, who was then CEO, came up with this plan that they would have an old-timer's game in every city, and they would donate $10,000 for each game into this fund that BAT would disperse. BAT was first the Baseball Alumni Team, then it became the Baseball Assistance Team. We would help needy people in the baseball family. First, it was just major leaguers, then it became umpires who were in the major leagues, then it became players in the Negro League, now minor-league players with three years of experience. Warren Spahn asked me to come to one of the meetings. So I went to the meeting and just listened. I wasn't on the board or a member, and I said, "Well, we need a president." And I got elected.

We're finishing our seventeenth year. BAT has probably given out, I'm going to say, $10 million. I was president, then I vacated that position, let Joe Garagiola be president and I became chairman. But I've run the dinner. We have a fund-raising dinner every January at the Marriott Marquis in New York, and we've raised anywhere around $500,000 to $600,000 a year. So over the fourteen dinners, we probably raised, well, $7 million to $8 million. That's been a joy to me, because the first seventy-eight guys we helped, I happened to look at the chart and I said, "Holy smokes, I played with this guy. I played with that guy." And there were like ten guys that I played with, who'd been on my team, even a guy I roomed with for a short trip, on that list. But it's all anonymous. We never say whom we're helping. The only way people know is if that guy comes forth and goes public and says, "I want to thank BAT for saving my life. I want to thank BAT for all they did for me." But it's always done anonymously and as discreetly as possible, but it's a great feeling to know that I was in there in the beginning, and I'm still there. And I forgot one other thing—we even helped the women from the ladies' league.

The game is not better now. The game is now entertainment. I see guys playing the game and they try to make easy plays look hard, trying to make the highlight film or play-of-the-day films. And I look at it, I say, there's no team effort. They don't really care whether the team wins or not as long as they perform, because they go to arbitration, it's based on their stats. They make so much money that the $300,000 you get for the World Series doesn't amount to much. My first World Series, I was making $6,500, and if we won, I would've doubled my salary. I lost. We got $4,700. I think that they change teams so often that sometimes you're rooting for a uniform and not a team. Guy's your teammate and the next year, he's playing for another club. Do you want to knock him down? He was your buddy on this team. I think because of the union, the strong bonds of union, they don't knock anybody down anymore. They knock over the catcher. I don't understand it. The catchers got all the equipment, they try to knock him over. But especially fans today say, "Players are bigger and better. It's a much better game." Then I go, "Time—do they run any faster? No. Do they throw any faster? No. Do they know all the fundamentals? No. Do they play as a team? No."

I mean, we really stuck together. Maybe it was the train rides and being together all the time that there was a camaraderie and a friendship and a closeness that pervaded our association, that we really were friends, we really pulled for one another, and I just think it's too much individual and too much an entertainment sport now.

To me, baseball is losing its place in American history, in the American spotlight, because you're losing the young fans. The fan base is scattered. Football has grown, basketball has grown, there was no track and field fifty years ago, pro tennis was small. Even the women's leagues have all changed that. Baseball should go to a plan to get new, young fans. Play day games on the weekends. Sitting in the upper deck for a dollar per person, a family can go for $4. You give them a ticket. That one ticket, they get a Coca-Cola for a dollar, they get a hot dog for a dollar or a dollar and a quarter, and everybody gets one. And once that's through, if you want to buy another hot dog, it's $4. If you want to buy another Coke, it's $4. But the family can go and park in a certain spot for a dollar. So a family of four can go for $15. Build up a fan base and do it every weekend. Have fans come to the ballpark. You got empty stands in the upper deck against so many teams. Just fill it with young fans and build up a fan base.

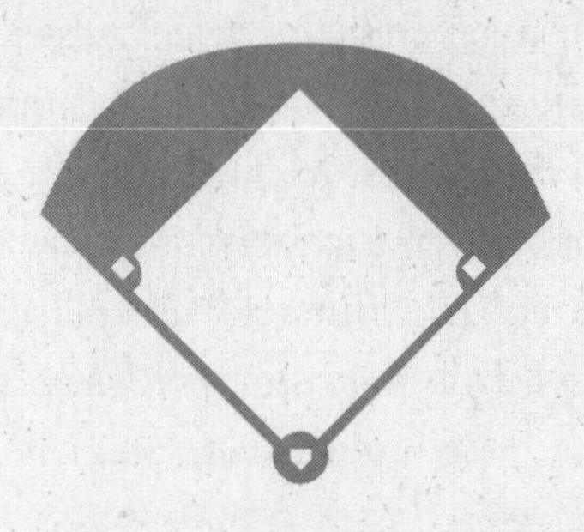

BILL RIGNEY

Bill Rigney was a baseball lifer, one of the few among us able to spend most of his adult life doing something he loved. Whether it was as a player, coach, manager, broadcaster, scout, or executive, his high regard for the game was always evident to those fortunate enough to cross his path.

"The fascinating thing about baseball is that everyone knows it is a business and you have to win and you have to draw fans and you have to be successful, but you still have fun along the line doing all that," Rigney once said. "I don't think I ever woke up one day in my life that I didn't want to go to the ballpark."

Rigney's more than six decades as part of the national pastime's landscape included a stint as an infielder with the New York Giants from 1946 to 1953, where his ability as a bench jockey overshadowed his ability on the field. When his playing days were over, he managed in the big leagues for eighteen seasons with the New York and San Francisco Giants, the Los Angeles and California Angels, and the Minnesota Twins. Though he never skippered a team to the World Series, he was named Manager of the Year after leading the Los Angeles Angels, in only their second year of existence, to a surprising third-place finish in 1962.

Pitcher Jim Coates once said of Rigney, "He's the greatest I've ever played for, and I played for Casey Stengel and Fred Hutchinson, among others. I'm fighting for a job and may be cut next week. If so, I'll leave satisfied that I've received a fair shake." Jack Sanford said that Rigney gave the game back to the players, adding, "He always gives you the best of it. I respected the man when I was pitching against his teams and I respect him even more now." Lew Burdette, who played the last two seasons of his eighteen-year big-league career under Rigney, said, "He commands total respect and that's the greatest tribute you can pay the manager or coach of a professional team."

Even those from opposing dugouts could see the influence Rigney had on his players. "You do not have to be told that Rigney commands the respect of his players," said Red Sox Hall of Famer Carl Yastrzemski. "That's evident just watching his team play. And it's especially evident in close games when Rig seems to draw that extra effort out of them."

Rigney spent the final twenty years of his life working in the front office of the Oakland A's. Upon his death in 2001, Giants owner Peter Magowan may have summed up the life of Rigney best when he said, "Baseball and the San Francisco Giants have lost one of their greatest treasures. Rig was a baseball man through and through."

I guess when I was ten or twelve, I really had the bug, the love for baseball. I used to cut out the box scores of the Giants, any paper I could get that had the box score and put them in a scrapbook, so I kind of knew what was going on in the major leagues. I never dreamed I would ever get there, but at least I was going in the right direction. And I can remember, you know, Mel Ott being the manager and Mel Ott being the player, and the Giants were my team, but for what reason, I have none. It could have been the Cardinals, it could have been the Brooklyns, but the Giants were the team that I followed closely.

The Pacific Coast League, when I finally got there, I thought it

Bill Rigney

was heaven. You played a week in every city. You had some great towns to go to. You had Seattle, Portland, Sacramento, San Francisco, Los Angeles, and San Diego, and you were a week there in each town. Of course, it wasn't so good if some club had a good pitching staff. It wasn't a lot of fun, then, because you had to face those same guys twice, but what I learned from the Coast League days was that a lot of major-league players were coming back to the Coast League because of the weather. The weather was perfect for those aging arms, and they loved it out here. As a matter of fact, some of them were making as much or more money than they made when they were in the major leagues. So it was a learning league for me, because I got all this information for nothing from all these players that had been in the major leagues for a while.

I played in the first major league game I ever saw. That was opening day in '46. I started with Oakland in '38. They sent me to Spokane, then I did Vancouver, and then I did Bellingham, then I did Topeka, Kansas, and finally made the Oakland club in '41. I played every game, played 177, I think that was every game, and then the next year I played 180 and never missed an inning.

I was really the only young player that the owner had to sell, because the rest of them were all former major leaguers, and all had a few years on them. If he was to sell a player, it would've been me, and it eventually was. The Giants finally made the deal while I was in the service.

When I got to New York, I was staying at the New Yorker Hotel. I walked up to Times Square. I couldn't find the New Yorker Hotel on the way back, which was about eight blocks away. I remember coming down from West Point, remember how they had the West Point games against the Cadets, and I got to the Polo Grounds about 10:00 at night and everybody's carrying their own bag. I walked into this gorgeous clubhouse; you know, it went down three levels, and I got down to the lower level. I'm looking around at the names on the lockers and there is Mize and there's Rigney right alongside Johnny Mize.

So I got my stuff in my locker and now I've got to see the ballpark. We were in center field, the clubhouses were in center field. So I walked outside, and I walked down the steps. It was a big horseshoe, all the night lights were on and it was just breathtaking. Now the butterflies are really starting to do their thing with my stomach. And I know that tomorrow I'm going to be the shortstop and there's going to be forty or fifty thousand people there. You think you can handle this at eighteen, so it was a moment that I'll never forget because it was my first introduction to the major leagues. This is what the major leagues were about. I can remember the next day when we ran out on the field. And I said, if there's a Lord in heaven, let him hit the first ball down to me so I'll get it over with. Well, the batter hit it right through the box and I went over and sucked it up and threw him out, and I said, "Hey, this looks like it's got a chance, you know. Hey, I may be all right up here." And then I went up, I was leading off. I went up to hit, and Oscar Judd was pitching for the Philadelphias, and he had a screwball. I had hit against him at Sacramento; he was at Sacramento when I was in the Coast League.

And I worked the count to three and two and he threw me a

screwball—strike three ring him up, and I thought, well this is the major leagues, huh. No fastballs, no walking, screwball three and two. I never forgot that. I finally got him a couple of times, but it was the biggest thrill of my life, other than my marriage, the first game on the Polo Grounds.

We came through Danville, Virginia. We played an exhibition game against the Indians and Mize hit a home run in the ninth inning to win the game. And when we came in the dining car, Eddie Brannick, our road secretary—the most dapper, typical elegant New Yorker I ever knew, I don't think he ever wore the same pair of shoes two days in a row ever, zero—at any rate, he said to Mize, nice hitting, Big John, nice going. Eddie always had those silk ties on, so John said, Gee, what a good looking tie, and Eddie said, You like it? He peeled it off and said, Here, every home run that the guys hit this year, I'm going to buy them a tie.

So at any rate, if you hit a couple of home runs, the next day there were two ties in your locker. Well, then, we went on a spree where Willard Marshall and Johnny Mize and Walker Cooper and even Rigney got in on the act. We didn't see Eddie for about two or three weeks. All of a sudden, there was a big box came into the clubhouse and they opened it up and there was twelve ties for Mize and eight for Marshall and four for Rigney. He kept count.

It was a powerful club. Boy, we could put runs up there in a hurry. I remember Fritz Ostermueller with the Pittsburghs pitched a no-hitter for six, a shutout for seven, and got beat 9–8.

In 1947, we didn't have a lot of pitching. We did get Larry Jansen that year. He ended up 21-5. He had a great year. Dave Koslo was a fair left-hander, but those were the only two real decent pitchers I thought that we had until Sal Maglie came back. When Mag finally came back from Mexico, we had three pretty good pitchers. And then Chub Feeney got Jim Hearn, and now we had four pretty good pitchers, and now we felt we could go at the Brooklyns.

One day in 1948, we're in the ninth inning in Pittsburgh, and Ralph Kiner's hitting with a man on. Johnny Hopp singled or something, it was shocking, he got a base hit, now Kiner's up. I'm playing third; here comes Stony Jackson from the dugout for Mel. We all gather around there, and he says, "Otty says don't give him anything to pull." All right, he goes back to the bench. He no sooner sat down than Larry Jansen threw one pitch and Kiner hit it right over the scoreboard. We lost 4–3. I think that's the game that broke Otty, that one right there. We played the second game of the doubleheader, and we won big, 10–3. But I think Otty had had enough. The next day, who walks in the clubhouse, unbeknownst to all of us, but the Lion. Leo Durocher walked in.

Things changed soon as the Lion walked in there. Everything changed. The pace got a little bit higher. Good enough wasn't good enough anymore. That's what I think I learned from Leo, that it's never good enough; it'll only be good enough if you win.

You couldn't help but like Ott. I think he'd have been better off if he had hired someone tough. He had all of his pals as coaches. He

Leo Durocher

Mel Ott

should have gone and got a couple of tough guys, you know, guys that would say, "No, Mel." 'Cause these guys all said, "Yes, yes, yes." I remember just before we were going on that trip, I was the first guy in the ballpark every day. I came in the clubhouse for an afternoon game about 9:30, 10:00. We had lost the night before, and Otty is sitting there in his office with three empty bottles of milk, one empty bottle of Scotch, and I remember, and nobody knows this, he said, "Do you think we'd be better off if I resign?" And I said, "I don't know what makes us better off. No, I don't think it would be better if you resign. I think you could kick butt a little bit." I said, "I think that's what I would do if I were you, I'd just be a little tougher." At any rate, it was ten days later he resigned and we got Leo. He couldn't be a little tougher; that wasn't his nature. When the Lion came from Ebbets Field to Coogan's Bluff, everything got different.

We knew we had a man in charge that was in charge. There was no doubt about that. And when we got Eddie Stanky and Alvin Dark, we knew that this club was heading for the winner's circle. The goal was the winner's circle now.

The famous August 1951—thirteen and a half games behind. Maybe this has nothing to do with it. And I'm sure if the Brooklyns looked back on it, they'd say, "Oh, you're full of bull." But they swept us the series over there, and that got us twelve and a half or thirteen out. This isn't a story I'm telling out of school; this is a story that should be told. The two clubhouses in Ebbets Field were right alongside, but there was a door locked here and a door locked here, so there wasn't any access. Well, after they swept us, Jackie Robinson opens up their door, he's got a bat and he's beating on our door.

And I'm sitting there across from Stanky and Dark and Henry Thompson and Monte Irvin, and I remember Jackie saying, "Leo, Leo, how do you like it? I can smell Laraine's perfume all the way in here." Leo then was married to Laraine Day, the actress, and now we'd just lost three straight and we're not in a very good humor, but we have to take this because it's true—not the perfume part, the three losses. And finally, we could hear Branca singing, "Roll out the barrel, the Giants are on the run, the Giants are done."

And years later Newk, big Don Newcombe, finally said, "Ralph, you were singing that. Now, the fact that they heard it wasn't in the agenda, but that damn Rigney remembers anything if he hears it once." So, at any rate, finally Stanky said something to Jackie about sticking that bat, and there was a big quiet. And finally Jackie backed off, but it seemed like that one game kind of triggered everybody. And right after that we started the sixteen-game winning streak.

That night at the end of May in Philadelphia when Willie Mays arrived, I felt that gave us a chance to win. This one player, just the enthusiasm that he brought, the ability that he brought to the table, and watching him play, and watching the pace of the team jump up a little bit, with him in center field. And Bobby Thomson went to

Willie Mays

third base and Whitey Lockman went to first base. Leo played everything he could play. And it worked. All of a sudden, the team started winning, and then we didn't know how to lose. And I will say this about the manager, all those games, they were all 3–2, 4–3, 5–4. There were no walkaways; you had to manage. And he did a great job. He brought us back and he wouldn't let us quit. I learned an awful lot about managing from him that year. Hey, we're still in this thing; come on. Mays filled that big gap in center field, and Bobby went to third base, Monte Irvin went to left field, we had Don Mueller in right field, so we had our good solid attack. You have to have a little luck, too. Nobody got hurt; we went right down the wire with this same club.

There were no dumb plays, no pitcher screwing up, making a bad pitch at the wrong time. Everybody seemed to get into it. I think the Brooklyns must have felt this a little bit, because years later I talked to Pee Wee Reese about it. He said, "We knew you were coming. Even though we played well, we played over .500. You guys were, I think, 37-7 in the last 44 games. There was nothing we could do about it; we were just going to have to go at you one more time." And then when Jackie hit the home run off Robin Roberts, here we go again. And you know it's funny, when we got onto Ebbets Field that day, Mr. Big Mouth, Jackie, was in the batting cage hitting, after the banging on the wall with the bat. So Wes Westrum and Lockman and I walked behind the cage, and I said, "Jackie, turn around, you'll never guess who's here." And he wouldn't turn around. That was the first play-off game.

It was that year, in '51, that I knew I wanted to manage. I watched Leo and I watched Charlie Dressen and I watched Al Lopez and I watched all my favorite guys manage, like Walter Alston.

In 1955, I was managing in Minneapolis, Triple A. I was trying to win the pennant and the Junior World Series. It was during the Junior World Series, I was in Charlie's restaurant and Tom Sheehan came in, the news bear. And he said—matter of fact, I was in the men's room—and he came in and stood alongside me and he said, "Well, I wasn't supposed to tell this, but you're the new manager of the Giants." I said, "Tom, I'm trying to win this thing here for these guys. I don't want to know about that." If that happens, it happens, but I was trying to get through the Junior World Series, which was important to the Minneapolis team. But that's when I first heard it. He said, "Leo's gone and you're the manager." Couldn't he have waited another week to tell me this? And as it turned out, we did win the Junior World Series.

Carl Hubbell used to keep telling me, he said, "Hey, just hold the line here, do as good as you can do, because you're going to have another good team coming up here in about another three years." So, in other words, see if you can last three years. Well, it was amazing. I thought it was going to be the best thing that happened to me; here I was coming home to manage a major-league club, the San Francisco Giants. It was the highlight, probably, of my career, being able to come home to San Francisco and be the manager of this club.

Opening day at Seals Stadium, it was a gorgeous day and festive and we were playing the Dodgers, and everything had wound into a nice tight ball. Then when Ruben Gomez shut them out, it was just a day to remember. My first game, there was a whole bunch of firsts. And, of course, Willie; Willie being Willie, that's all we needed. And I remember Ty Cobb coming out to the game. We were taking batting practice one day. I looked over near the dugout, and I saw this fellow standing there. And I turned away, and I said, Wait a minute, that's got to be Ty Cobb, because I knew he lived in Atherton. So I walked over and I said, "Ty, Bill Rigney." He said, "I know who you are." And I said, "Come on down here." He loved Mays. He liked to watch Mays hit. I said, "Well come on and get behind the cage here." I said, "Come on let's go, I'm the manager, you're with the right guy." So he walked behind the cage, he watched him hit, he watched those balls just jump off his bat. He said, "By George, what a player, he could have played with us." He said, "He could have played with us." But he came to a few games. I said, "Anytime you want to come here, you're welcome to use my box." He never did call or anything like that. They tell me he was at a few games.

I left the Giants during the 1960 season. Expansion had come to baseball. My friend Chub Feeney called the Angels president, Bob Reynolds, and said, "Rigney will be perfect for you."

I got introduced at the first luncheon in Palm Springs by the cowboy, Gene Autry, who said, "Well, my job is to introduce the new manager." And he said, "We tried to get Casey Stengel, but something came up that we couldn't get Casey, so we settled for Phil Rigley." And Gene had had a few vodkas. At any rate, it worked out. And, of course, you know, the next year, 1962, we caught lightning in a bottle.

Walter O'Malley said, "You got a lot of general managers awful nervous, my friend." I ran into him at a nice restaurant in L.A., and afterward he said, "Geez, what a job you did." And I said, "Well, little luck here and a little there." "No," he says, "I watched the whole thing. That was the best job I've seen anybody manage." It was a little too soon, that's all. But what it did do for us, it bought us some time as far as getting people, getting fans, and getting a farm. We didn't have a farm system, and Chub was so good about that.

• • •

The managers who stick out in my mind as being really difficult to manage against? I think of the White Sox, Al Lopez. Of course, Al had such a good team. He was a good manager. And the team at Baltimore, you know, they finally came on after they got Frank Robinson and, boy, they had a whale of a team. And Earl Weaver was such a good manager. Alston, Weaver, Al Lopez.

I never got a chance to see Gene Mauch manage much. I knew he was a good manager, but I never got a chance to see him because he was either in the other league or he came in the American League after I was gone. But I thought those other guys didn't miss a beat.

After the Angels, I went back to Minnesota. But now it's a major-league team, and a pretty good one. Maybe the best team I had, you know, with Rod Carew and Tony Oliva and Harmon Killebrew. And we won 98 games. And then Baltimore beat us with Jim Palmer and Mike Cuellar.

After Minneapolis I said, "Well, I think I've had enough. I've had enough changing pitchers." As much as I still loved the game, I got to a point where I asked, "Is this all worth it now?" I'm in my fifties, I guess—1970, '71, '72. Yeah. And I just said, "Hey, that's enough. I'm going to go home." Eventually, I got an offer from the Angels to do some color commentary on their TV broadcasts with Don Drysdale.

Don and I did the Angels TV games for a couple of years and I enjoyed that. During that time, the Haas family bought the A's and I got to know Roy Eisenhart, the president of the A's. Roy asked me, Would I be interested in coming with them? And so they hired me to do some TV broadcasts and to be a consultant. And working with Walter Haas and Roy Eisenhart, Tony LaRussa, that's as good as it gets. Couldn't get any better than that. Those were wonderful years.

As a kid, I watched the Giants, watched the Detroits with Charlie Gehringer, whom I later got to play for in the service. I picked good players to watch. I want you to know that. I didn't just pick anybody. But then when Horace Stoneham was a big factor in my life, when I finally became a Giant and got to know Horace and Chub Feeney and Carl Hubbell, the whole organization, I think what I liked just about best of all of the inside of baseball was the farm directors and the job that they did. I thought that was the interesting part. I could see why people stayed in baseball; let me put it that way. I loved it because I loved baseball and I loved to manage. I loved to play and I just loved being part of the national pastime. And then I realized you're not alone here.

All those other guys feel the same way as you do. And I said, "That's why some organizations win and some don't win." And I saw how much it meant to Hub and Chub and Horace. You know, this was their life, too; not only my life, but it was their life, too. And I got to appreciate what this business was all about. We were all lucky to be able to play it, able to manage it, and able to get a job and remain in it, which there weren't a lot of.

I thought one of the worst things I did or one of the things I didn't do—and I regretted it all my life—is that opening day in the Polo Grounds on the eighteenth of April in '47 when Jackie Robinson hit his first home run, I didn't walk over to him and say, "Hey, I'm Bill Rigney. I just want to shake your hand and wish you the best of luck because it's not going to be easy for you, but I wish you the best," and leave it at that. And I regretted it all my life that I didn't do it, because I knew I was too late, you know, after I got to know him.

You know, just reading about it, you knew how tough it was going to be for him. Why I didn't do that, I don't know, because he was standing right there. All I had to do was walk over and say, "I'm Bill Rigney. I'm the shortstop for the Giants. I just want to wish you good luck." Big deal. But I regret that.

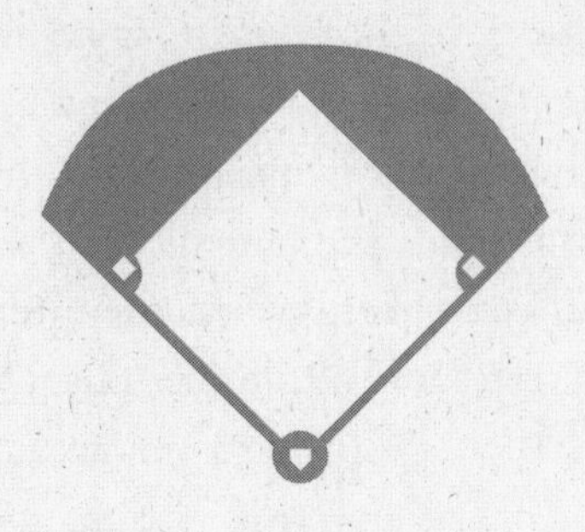

DUKE SNIDER

Edwin Donald Snider was known as "Duke" to the Dodger faithful, a graceful center fielder and powerful slugger who called Brooklyn's Ebbets Field home for more than a decade. As Hall of Fame executive Branch Rickey once said, Snider played baseball with "all the pleasing skills."

Snider, along with Willie Mays and Mickey Mantle, was part of a magnificent triumvirate of center fielders who played for the New York City baseball teams in the 1950s. While the question of who was the best among the trio is often debated, it cannot be refuted that Snider led all batters in home runs and RBIs during the 1950s.

"Anytime you mention Snider with Mays and Mantle, you're putting him in pretty good company. To me, all three were tops in their field—legitimate superstars," said longtime Dodgers executive Buzzie Bavasi. "Duke had the four fundamentals. He could run, throw, field, and hit. He had no area in which he was lacking."

Longtime Dodgers teammate Pee Wee Reese, who witnessed Snider's defensive prowess in person, once stated, "The greatest catch I ever saw was one made by Snider in 1954, when he climbed the wall of Connie Mack Stadium like a mountain goat to take an extra-base hit away from Willie Jones of the Phillies."

In an eighteen-year big-league career (1947–64), spent mostly with the Brooklyn and Los Angeles Dodgers, as well as short stints at the end of his playing days with the New York Mets and San Francisco Giants, Snider had 407 home runs, 1,259 runs, 1,333 RBIs, 2,116 hits, and a .295 batting average.

"There never was, and still isn't, any doubt in my mind as to Snider's ultimate place among the truly great hitters of the game," said Hall of Famer George Sisler, a onetime Dodgers coach, early in Snider's career.

The eight-time All-Star, who hit 40 or more home runs five consecutive years, is also the only player to hit four home runs in two different World Series (1952 and 1955). A major reason for the success of the Dodgers, Snider's 11 home runs and 26 RBIs in his six World Series appearances are the most by a National League player.

After Snider did not receive the required number of votes for election to the National Baseball Hall of Fame in his first years of eligibility, none other than Mays sang his fellow center fielder's praises before his eventual induction in 1980.

"When I played for the Giants in New York, all the fans ever did there was to compare me and Mickey Mantle and Duke. It created a lot of arguments and I don't know if anyone ever won," Mays said. "All I know is that Mickey and I are both in the Hall of Fame and Duke is still waiting to get elected. It's about time he was voted in. He belongs."

I started playing softball when I was in the fourth grade in elementary school, fast-pitch softball, not the rocking-chair softball that they have going today. I played fast softball. And I pitched. I think that taught me to have a fast-quick bat when I went into hardball. I went on, went into high school, and started playing regular baseball, and started playing pretty well. My father started putting the baseball bat on my left shoulder. He wanted me to hit left-handed, he says, because most major-league ballparks are made

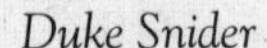

Duke Snider

for left-handed hitters. Their fences are a little bit closer, and first base is a couple of steps closer when you're running to first base from the left-handed batter's side of home plate. So that's the way I started.

At the age of fourteen, I was playing against grown men in Southern California, semipro baseball and holding my own. I wasn't excelling, but I was holding my own. I was still growing and getting stronger; and a couple years later, when I was a junior in high school, I pitched on the high school baseball team. I batted fourth in the batting order, because I could hit.

I became a baseball fan in Southern California. Major League Baseball was only as far west as St. Louis then, and I watched Pacific Coast League baseball when I was a youngster.

I liked the Brooklyn Dodgers because of 1941, when they lost the World Series. I was listening to it on the radio. It broke my heart when they got beat the way they did. Pee Wee Reese was just starting. He was the shortstop on the Dodgers, became captain of the team and a very good friend of mine. And Pete Reiser, who was a center fielder and a very good hitter. I was an outfielder, and halfway decent, but they became my favorite team.

There were three other teams after me: the St. Louis Cardinals, the Cincinnati Reds, and the Pittsburgh Pirates were all trying to sign me. But the scout for the Brooklyn Dodgers took the bull by the horn and came in one day, and he said, "I'm going to sign you." And it was during World War II, and I knew that after this one season—I was seventeen years of age at the time—I knew after I played one year of pro ball, I was going to be drafted into the military.

It's not going to sound like very much, and it wasn't very much, but I signed for a $750 bonus, and $250 a month salary. I remember when I went to spring training with the Dodgers at Bear Mountain, New York. We trained in West Point, in the field house. They put nets all around where we could take batting practice, because there was snow on the ground outside.

But there was no travel then because of World War II. The trains were all taken up. There weren't very many airplanes at that time. So we had to all come in to New York, and had our spring training in the field house in West Point. I was sent to Newport News, Virginia, for my first year in minor-league baseball. I found out what humidity was, because we had very low humidity in Southern California.

The difference between playing pro baseball and high school baseball is that you play a game every day. And it's amazing how good you can get when you play every day and practice every day. I didn't realize at that time that that was so important, to get an opportunity to play every day, and how good you could get at hitting the ball, catching the ball, fielding the ball, and what have you. Getting the instruction that we got in spring training, hitting instruction, fielding instruction, how to play the game. "How to play it the Dodger way" is what they would say in the meetings. "This is the way we do it. This is the way we want you to do it." So there's a big learning process involved, and you get the finer points of the game. You get to learn the game a lot better.

During spring training Branch Rickey would have meetings; all the prospects would be there. All the guys that were in the organization would be there, and he'd give us lectures on how to run the bases, how to play the outfield, how to play the infield, the whole bit. We'd get that in our lectures. And it's amazing how many guys went on in their careers to become managers in the minor leagues and major leagues from the Brooklyn Dodger organization, because of the way they were schooled in the organization.

I really enjoyed it. I had a lot of fun playing my first year of minor-league baseball. And then, I was drafted into the military, into the Navy. I was in the submarine part of the Navy, not the subs themselves, but I was on a submarine tender. We repaired the subs when they came back from the Pacific. We would repair the subs and get them ready, stock them and everything, get them ready so they could go back out on another tour of duty after their R & R was over. So that primarily was my duty, actually, to repair the submarines.

Whenever I could get off the ship, I played for the ship's team, and then we played the Marines. There's a Marine base right by the dock, where we were docked in Guam. And I hit this Marine team pretty good. I hit several home runs off of them. They finally took me aside one day and said, "Look, if you'd like to play for us, too, we'll get you a short haircut. We'll get you a short haircut and get you some dog tags and make you look like a Marine, and you can play for us." So I said, "Okay." And so I played for this Marine team as a Marine, and meanwhile I was in the Navy. I don't have anything cut short anymore.

Because of a military rule, I had to be kept until July 4 before I could be sent to the minor leagues to get more seasoning. I had just gotten out of the service the July of the year before, and I finished the season at Fort Worth. I went to spring training and I was on the Dodgers team. I knew I didn't belong, but I was there.

So Branch Rickey brought Gil Hodges and I into his office one day. This was in 1947, when Jackie broke in. Gil was the third-string

Gil Hodges

catcher, and I was the sixth outfielder on the club. Well, Gil and I were sitting in Branch Rickey's office, and he says, "You know, in about three years from now, you two guys are going to be leading this team in home runs, and you're going to be leading this team in RBIs." And Gil and I both looked at each other, and we got up and left his office after he talked to us a little bit more. And Gil said to me, "How—how can he say that, Duke?" He said, "I'm the third-string catcher and you're the sixth outfielder, and neither one of us gets to play. And yet three years from now, we're going to be leading the team in home runs and RBIs?" But that was the way Rickey could size you up. He knew exactly what I needed to work on. He knew exactly what Gil needed to work on.

And Branch Rickey was right. We were leading the team in home runs and RBIs, and playing the very solid defense for him.

I think the happiest moment in my baseball career was when I put on the Brooklyn Dodgers uniform. This might sound a little corny to you. But when I put the Brooklyn Dodgers uniform on and knew that I belonged in that uniform. And that didn't happen for a while because I needed to play more. I needed more experience. But one day I put it on and I said, "Hey, I belong in this uniform." Then, I was a major-league ballplayer.

I had four years of junior high school, which went through the tenth grade. And when I was in the ninth and tenth grades, Jackie Robinson was going to Pasadena Junior College, the first two years of college. I would go down to the junior college in Compton, where I was raised in California. I would go down and watch him play football on Friday nights when Pasadena would come to town. I would always go to the game and see Jackie play football. I'd see him play basketball a couple times during the year. I'd see him in the long jump. And I'd see him play baseball in those years. Then he went to UCLA, and I managed to have my dad or a friend take me to UCLA to see him participate in football, basketball, and baseball. So he became a sports idol of mine when I was a youngster growing up in Southern California. And I marveled at the way he could play baseball. He was not fast, but he could run. He could stop and start faster than anybody I've ever seen. He had a kickoff one time against Compton in football when he was at Pasadena, and he reversed his field twice, and the third time he came around he went for a touchdown, 80 some yards, but he actually ran about 175 yards, because he dodged everybody. I remember this, just like the way it was yesterday. I can close my eyes and picture it, in fact, the way Jackie would run the bases, getting the rundown play. There'd be six Phillies. They've got a picture down in Vero Beach, Florida, where the Dodgers have spring training. They have a picture down there of a rundown with the Phillies, and there's six Philadelphia players in the rundown with Jackie, and Jackie ended up scoring. That's the way he could stop and start.

Opening day, his first day. Opening day was my first day. And I'm sitting on the bench watching Jackie perform. It was such a thrill just to be in the big leagues. I was a rookie; he was a rookie, but he really wasn't a rookie. He had played in the Negro Leagues.

Jackie Robinson

I wasn't prepared to see what Jackie had to go through. I know that my first year I was seventeen years old, and I was in Newport News, Virginia. I lived in a private home. This elderly lady had a home, and she rented a couple of rooms out to a couple of us ballplayers. I would take the bus into the ballpark. I'd get on the bus, and I always liked to sit in the back.

I put my money in the little slot, I walk to the back of the bus, and I sit down. And there were quite a few black people back there, but that didn't make any difference to me. I'm from Southern California. I had buddies, black friends and Japanese friends, out in Southern California, and they were my best friends. It didn't bother me who was sitting there. I just sat back there, and I got dirty looks from some of the black people. I got dirty looks from some of the white people. Finally, I looked up, and it said, "Colored Section."

I didn't get up and move. I stayed there. But that was the first day of my bus ride. From then, I meandered up to the front and I sat in the front. The black people had to sit in their own section of the stands, and there were white and black drinking fountains. There was none of this in Southern California. And it kind of startled me, and it woke me up to what people were going through.

And then, I came up to the big leagues in '47, and all this turmoil about Jackie coming into the league. I wasn't surprised he was there, because I had seen him play. I knew he was a big-league ballplayer, and he was going to help them win a pennant one of these years. All the static that was in the papers and everything, and things—the profanity and the racial slurs that were hollered from the other team's dugout and things like that—I was startled, because I wasn't brought up that way.

I understood to a certain extent what was going on. They're still fighting the Civil War, these guys. And finally, I was embarrassed a few times. In Philadelphia one night, a big fat guy named Pete that had a gravel voice, he was on Jackie something terrible. I was embarrassed at what he was hollering at Jackie, truly embarrassed at what he was hollering.

And Jackie took it in stride. He just wouldn't acknowledge the guy or anything. He just played the game and ended up getting a couple more base hits—another ball game. But he was schooled well by Branch Rickey, and I know Rachel, his wife, did a wonderful job helping him through that situation.

I was there that day in Cincinnati when Pee Wee walked over. The fans were on Jackie pretty heavy, and Pee Wee went over and put his arm around him. And that sort of quieted the fans, because Pee Wee was from Louisville, Kentucky, and when he put his arm around him that shut a lot of people up because Louisville isn't very far from Cincinnati. A lot of Pee Wee's friends were there. I remember that very well. And Jackie to his dying day would thank Pee Wee for doing what he did.

There were three or four guys that passed a petition around in the clubhouse. They took it to each player, wanted them to sign it. The petition said, "I will not participate in a game that Jackie Robinson is in the lineup." And nobody signed it. Just the four guys that

Pee Wee Reese

took the petition around, they were the only ones that signed it. They brought it to me and I said, "What are you talking about?" I said, "This guy is an idol of mine. I'm not gonna sign that thing." I said, "I'm tickled to death to be on the same team with him." And Pee Wee said the same thing, and he didn't sign it. Everybody more or less just said, "Hey, he's here. He's going to help us win the pennant." That's the way we looked at it.

I will tell you the one thing that I remember more than anything else: Jackie comes into the clubhouse, goes to his locker, disrobes, and puts his baseball uniform on. And when he put that baseball uniform on, he put his game face on with it. You could see it in his eyes. You could see it in his eyes that he was ready to go out there and beat somebody. And that I think helped a lot of us in realizing what the game was all about.

I was a free swinger. You know, if the ball looked halfway decent, I took a cut at it. I wasn't up there to get a walk. I was up there to hit the ball, and I really didn't know my strike zone. Everybody has their own strike zone. I would swing at pitches eye-high and I'd swing at pitches, some of them almost in the dirt, things like that. So Branch Rickey took me to Vero Beach, Florida, brought me in from the Dominican Republic, where we had spring training in 1948. And I went into a batting cage and a pitcher would throw pitches to me. And I'd stand there without a bat in my hand, just like I was holding a bat, but I'd stand there like so and I would take every pitch and then I would umpire.

There would be an umpire there and a catcher; Branch Rickey and George Sisler and a couple of other guys would be in back of the cage. I had to call every pitch, and it was amazing how many times I was wrong, it being a strike or a ball. And I'd have to do that every day for a while. Then they would put a bat in my hand, and then I'd hit every pitch—curveballs, fastballs, whatever.

And after I had hit every pitch, well, I took some because they were definitely balls because it was live pitching. But after I'd hit the ball, I had to tell Branch Rickey, "That pitch was outside and it was about knee high." And it was amazing how wrong I was. I had to learn the location of the pitch, whether it was a strike or not. But they would emphasize to me, "Be ready to hit every pitch until you see it's a pitch you don't want to swing at."

They say in Little League a lot of times to the kids, "Don't swing at it until you see it's a strike." Well, if you tell a kid that, you take the aggressiveness out of him. They didn't want to take out my aggressiveness. They just wanted me to be more aware of which pitches were hittable and which weren't. It took a couple of years, but I eventually learned the strike zone well enough to get close to 100 walks some years.

I think I became pretty much a major-league hitter in 1948. I came back up from Montreal in August and started getting more hits and swinging the bat a lot better. But 1949, I had a decent year, hit .290 something and 23 home runs, I think, or something like that. Anyway, I was on my way right there. But I had a dismal World Series. I dreamed since I was so high that I was going to play in the World Series and play against the Yankees some day. And there I was in Yankee Stadium, first game of the World Series in 1949, and Allie Reynolds, a hard-throwing right-hander for the Yankees, was going to pitch.

And they introduced us and we got up and we went out and lined up along the third-base line; they introduced the batting order. I was hitting third. Well, when they called my name and I went out of the line and stood there, my knees were shaking, and I couldn't swallow. I looked around, there are sixtysome thousand people in Yankee Stadium, and I couldn't swallow. And I says, "Uh-oh. I haven't had this feeling before."

And when I came up to bat, Reynolds would throw me those high fastballs. And the harder he threw, the harder I swung, and I didn't make contact. He struck me out three times in that game. I tied a World Series record in 1949; I struck out eight times in five games and only got three hits in the World Series. So I was very disappointed in myself, because I was trying too hard in the World Series and I wasn't myself. I hadn't learned to relax in a real pressure situation like that.

We didn't get back in the World Series until 1952. But I came home after the '49 World Series. We got beat four games to one. We weren't ready to really compete and be as good as the Yankees, maybe not beat them but be as good as. I went home and my hometown gave me a big dinner, a welcome home dinner for being the first guy from the Compton area to get in the World Series. And I apologized to my friends that were there. I said, "I want to apologize to you all for the dismal World Series that I had because I tried to be somebody that I wasn't. I wasn't myself." And I said, "If I ever get in the World Series again, I'm going to make it up to you." They gave me a nice watch and a couple of presents and things like that and a nice dinner.

They were happy that I got in the World Series and made it to the big leagues. Well, in 1950, we got beat the last day of the season by the Phillies, and in '51 we lost to the Giants in the play-offs, and so in 1952 we got back in the World Series. I hit four home runs in that World Series.

So I was a major-league hitter then. That first home run I hit in that World Series was off Allie Reynolds. And I don't remember going around the bases and touching the bases. I had a very good World Series. Ewell Blackwell was one of their pitchers, and Johnny Sain. I hit those guys pretty good. We were very competitive in that World Series. In fact, I think the 1952 Brooklyn team was the best team I've played on.

Of course, in 1951, we had that three-game play-off against the hated New York Giants. We played the first game and got beat. Branca pitched it. And we got beat. I don't know the exact score, but we got beat. And we went to the Polo Grounds to play the next two games and Clem Labine shut them out 10–0 in the second game. And in the third game, we were ahead 4–1 going into the ninth inning, and you could almost count your money. But like Yogi said, "It's never over till it's over."

And it certainly wasn't over, because the Giants came back, a couple of seeing-eye base hits and pretty soon Don Newcombe, who was pitching, got tired. And so they took him out; they brought in Branca. Now, there's a cute story involved in that. We had three pitchers warming up in the bullpen. We had Preacher Roe, Carl Erskine, and Ralph Branca. Bobby Thomson hit a home run off Branca in the first game. But anyway, all three guys were throwing.

And our manager called down to the bullpen (they have a phone on our bench and a phone in the bullpen), and he said, "How are they throwing?" The coach said, "Well, Preacher Roe can't get loose and Carl Erskine just bounced a curve in the dirt and Branca's throwing okay." He said, "Well, bring in Branca." So Ralph came by me in center field and I wished him the best as he went in. He went in to pitch. Thomson was going to be the batter.

Ralph warmed up and first pitch, strike one. The next pitch, he threw up in here, and Thompson hit a line drive to left field. In the

Polo Grounds it was very short down the lines, 245 feet or so. That was the winning run. So I was running over to protect keeping the winning run as far away from home plate as I possibly could. And all of a sudden, the ball disappeared over the fence. And I didn't break stride. I just made a U-turn and went out to center field where the clubhouse was, where our dressing area was. I saw all the newspapermen, all the cameras, all the champagne being picked up and taken over to the Giant clubhouse.

It sort of hit me then, but it really didn't hit me until Branca came in. He came in, and he laid on the steps. It was a two-tiered clubhouse with about eight or ten steps. And he was laying on the steps, and he was saying, "Why me, why me?" And I transferred my hurt feelings about losing the ball game to feeling sorry for Ralph, the way he was taking it.

If I'd have gotten a base hit on September 6 to win a game instead of popping it up or something, we wouldn't have had to go to the play-offs. We would have won by one game. So it was all our faults that we didn't win a game here or a game there. It wasn't his fault because he gave up that particular home run. Because if one of us had come through in the right situation, that game would have never been played.

But, you know what, we finally got together one day and we were talking about it in spring training, the next spring in '52. We started talking about it and said, "Hey, look, that's going to make us better baseball players, to go through something like that. We'll get them next year." Well, we did. We won in '52, we won in '53, we won in '55, we won in '56. Next four out of five years, we were in the World Series. So it made better players out of us, but we didn't realize it at the time.

I think the media made the hype of Willie, Mickey, and the Duke. The three of us were center fielders and playing in the same city. But we were all having outstanding years. And so the newspapers in the afternoon would compare our averages and what we did the night before and everything else and made a big hype out of it because there were a lot of afternoon papers then.

I was quite concerned what the Giants were doing, but I didn't look to the box score and see how many hits Mays got or anything. It was no personal battle there. It was just a team battle, is what it was. The comparisons made things quite interesting because the three of us were in the top ten in the league in practically all the departments. And we were all having excellent years. But our teams were having good years, too, because the Yankees won the pennant. We won the pennant or came close, and the Giants either won the pennant or were in second place. So it was quite competitive as far as the teams were concerned—but not individuals. I don't think you can compare the three of us. We could all run, we could all throw, we could all hit, and we could hit with power. And we were all above-average center fielders. So I would say in a given year numbers wise, I might have had more numbers than one of the other two guys. In another year, they might have had them. We were very close during the course of maybe four or five years in that particular period. We were pretty close, but we were on very successful teams, and that was the important factor as far as all three of us were concerned.

You always hear about Brooklyn and the borough and the Dodgers and how they embraced each other. What made life in Brooklyn so special, I think, was just the success that the Brooklyn organization had on the field and the love affair that the fans had with the players and the closeness of the borough, as far as the team was concerned. Now, you hardly ever hear about the New York Giants any more unless it's football. But you do hear about the Brooklyn Dodgers still. And, of course, the Yankees just keep going on and on. They're baseball. They are the top franchise of baseball. And I don't know, it's just that the fans fell in love with us and it was a love affair because I could hardly wait to get back here to start the season because it was home. As far as baseball is concerned, Brooklyn was home. And when the team moved west, I didn't want to move to Los Angeles. I was born in Los Angeles, but I didn't want to move there. I wanted to stay in Brooklyn as far as baseball is concerned.

Roy Campanella, I don't need to say any more: three MVPs, outstanding catcher, great handler of pitchers. In fact, he told Erskine one time, he said, "Carl, you just listen to me and throw what I call for." He said, "You'll be all right. You'll win a lot of games." And so Erskine lost a close game, 2–1, one night, and he threw whatever Campy called for and he said, "Roy," he said, "I lost last night." He said, "In the paper, it said, 'LP-Erskine.' " He said, "If you are so good, so much in charge, why don't they put 'Losing catcher, Campanella'?" That got a laugh from everybody. But Campanella was the ultimate. He was a team player, a nice guy, and a super ballplayer. Just fun to be around.

Gil Hodges, the first baseman, as far as I am concerned, he should be in the Hall of Fame. He is a Hall of Famer in my book. Second base, we had Jackie. What can you say about Jackie that I haven't already said, because he was the best competitor I have ever seen—and he taught us an awful lot about how to play the game of baseball and how it should be played. The third baseman was Billy Cox. They

Roy Campanella

talk about Brooks Robinson and how great a third baseman Brooks Robinson was. Well, I think Billy Cox was just as good a third baseman as Brooks Robinson, but he was not the hitter that Brooks Robinson was. And Cox was outstanding. He was a shortstop. We got him from Pittsburgh. He was a shortstop, and they put him at third. Jackie was a shortstop in the Negro League. They put him at first and then at second. Pee Wee, our shortstop, was our leader. And he just helped everybody. You could talk to anybody that was on a Brooklyn Dodger team and say, "How did Pee Wee help you?" and they'll have a story for you. That's what an important man he was in the ball club—and a good friend and a great ballplayer. The outfield had Andy Pafko, who was a center fielder with the Cubs, and we got him and put him in left and he was a super ballplayer. He didn't have the years with us that we thought he would have, but a lot of times you don't have years that you think you should have or could have. But Andy was a super guy and a super ballplayer.

In center field, I was there; and in right field, Carl Furillo. And Furillo is a very underrated ballplayer. He was one of the best ballplayers we had on the team.

From the shoulders up, I was my own worst enemy. I thought too much, and I got down on myself if I didn't come through in a clutch situation and things like that. And Pee Wee would talk to me and get me to mellow out a little bit and shrug it off. And sometimes it'd be something written in a paper that I didn't like and Pee Wee would say, "There's nothing older than yesterday's newspaper. What do they do with it? They wrap fish in it, or they put garbage in it, or put it down for the dog." He would say, "Don't worry about it." And it was good advice. He gave me some real good advice.

In 1954, there was a batting race that went down to the end. There were three of us—Don Mueller, Willie Mays, and myself. I had the lead all year. We got down to the weekend before the end of the season, and I was leading by about 8 points. I got a hit my first time at bat in a doubleheader on a Sunday, then I went 0 for 8 the rest of the day. So I went 1 for 9 in the doubleheader, and I lost about 4 or 5 points. And that brought us pretty close together. Then, the rest of the week went on to the last day of the season. There were just percentage points between the three of us. The Giants were in Philadelphia, and we were playing Pittsburgh in Brooklyn. And whoever had a good day was going to win the batting title. That night, we were going to go on TV, *The Ed Sullivan Show*, for some all-star awards of some kind. I don't know what—some magazine or something. I forget exactly. *Look* magazine or something like that—All-Star team. And the first time up, I hit a line drive to the second baseman. The next time up, I hit a 400-foot fly ball to center field to Bob Skinner, I think it was, who jumped up and caught it. The next time up, I popped up. I went 0 for 3. Karl Spooner was pitching for us and he was knocking them down pretty good, just striking them out and everything. So I ended up only getting to bat three times. I was the next hitter up when, in the bottom of the ninth inning, we won the game 2–0, something like that. I was the next hitter up and Pee Wee made the last out and I didn't get up. But one more hit wouldn't have done it for me, because Mays went 3 for 5 and Mueller went 2 for 5. And I went 0 for 3. As a result, I finished third. It was the best year I had at bat; I hit .341. And I was hitting .350 the week before, or something like that.

Buzzie Bavasi was in charge of the contracts. He'd called Pee Wee up and he called me up and we really hadn't arrived at a figure for our yearly salary. Every year, you had to renew your contract, because there were no multiyear contracts then. But Buzzie had said, "Well, come on down." He told Pee Wee and me both, "Come on down to spring training, and we'll have you sign your contract down here." "Well, what am I going to make?" He said, "We'll talk about it when you get down here." So we went down, first day of spring training started. We went into the clubhouse and put our uniforms on. We still hadn't signed. And we came out of the clubhouse, out to the practice field, and here's Edna, who was Buzzie Bavasi's secretary. And Edna's got two contracts in her hand.

She said, "You can't work out until you sign these contracts." I looked, and I said, "Edna, there's no figure in here." And Buzzie said, "Well, we'll get that straightened out, but you've got to sign the contracts so you can go out and work out." And so Pee Wee said, "Well, there's no figure in mine, either." He said, "Same thing. Just sign it and we'll work it out. We'll work it out with you." So we signed. We didn't know what we were making until our first paycheck. Then we figured out how much we were making. And we never did sit down and talk about it. We weren't positive of the exact figure. It's just like Gil Hodges and Buzzie sat down one time and Gil wanted $27,500 for that year. He had had a good year the year before. And we're not talking about much money today, but that was a lot of money then. Anyway, Gil wanted $27,500. And Buzzie said, "Well, I can't give it to you, Gil. That's X amount of dollars raise and, if the ballplayers hear about it, they're going to come to me and want more money, and this and that." "I can't do it, but," he said, "I'll tell you what I'll do." He said, "I'll tear up five pieces here, and I'll write a figure on each piece of paper. And I'll put them all in this hat. And then, you draw one out and that's what you're going to make next year."

"Yes," Gil said, "sounds good to me." So what Buzzie did, he put $27,500 on all five pieces of paper. Gil didn't know this. And so Gil reached in, pulled it out. He said, "I got my $27,500." Buzzie said, "Well, you got me that time, Gil." And he took the hat with the other pieces of paper, put it under his desk. And Gil to this day doesn't know—well, he's dead now—he didn't know to his dying day that the other slips had $27,500 on them.

In 1955, we got into the World Series and lost two. We went to Ebbets Field and won three. Went back to Yankee Stadium and got beat. The Series was tied, 3–3. In Game 7, Tommy Byrne was pitching against Johnny Podres. Podres said, "Give me one run and that's all I'll need." Well, we gave him a bonus. We got him two runs. And that's all he needed. We won 2–0 and won our first world's championship. It was so heavenly, taking that bus back to Ebbets Field. For some reason, everybody in the city knew the route of our bus. There was confetti coming from all the buildings in Manhattan, going across the Brooklyn Bridge and into Brooklyn. People were playing baseball on the Brooklyn Bridge. We couldn't hardly get through the people standing on our route back down to Brooklyn. It was some kind of day.

Jim Gilliam was one of our guys in '55. And he was an outstanding player, switch-hitter, leadoff man. He told us one time in spring training, he said, "Man," he says, "I'm really happy to be on this team." He said, "I like to run." He said, "I want you guys to run me all the time. Just keep getting those extra-base hits. I'll score for you." But in July, he came up to us and he said, "You're overdoing it. I'm so tired, I can't hardly walk." He ended up having a good year. And that was a super guy to have on our club.

All I remember about Don Larsen's perfect game in the '56 World Series was that we had knocked him out of the box in the second game, in Brooklyn. We go over to Yankee Stadium. He's pitching against us. And we don't have any hits in about the fifth inning. And Jackie said on the bench, "Let's don't let this guy shut us out." He didn't say anything about a no-hitter then, but—we all knew he had a no-hitter. But "Don't let this guy shut us out." And it's only 2–0, I think, the score. Maglie pitched a whale of a game. But it got a little bit later and somebody says, "Somebody get a hit." You know, somebody hollered on the bench, "Somebody get a hit. This donkey's got a shutout and a no-hitter." And that was sort of the talk on the bench. And he pitched a perfect game. You've got to give him credit. He had good stuff that day, and every ball that was hit was right at somebody. The Yankees played good defense. Jackie hit a ball off the third baseman's ankle that went out to shortstop and they threw him out at first base. I mean, that's the luck of a bounce there. Otherwise, it's a base hit, because the ball was hit real hard. Gil hit a line drive to left center that Mantle made a good running catch on backhanded. I hit a sinking line drive to right field early in the game, and Hank Bauer came in and caught it about shin high or so. And Sandy Amoros hit a ball down the right-field line that curved foul by about four or five feet. There were a lot of chances for us, but none of them materialized. And he pitched a perfect game.

The last night of the 1957 season, we were playing Pittsburgh in Ebbets Field. We knew more than likely that would be the final game. I didn't want to play in the last game. My last at bat in Ebbets Field, I hit a home run, my 40th home run, on a Sunday. We played Pittsburgh two games, and then we went to Philadelphia for the final three games. I didn't want to play in that final game, and didn't. But it just looked like there was only about six thousand, seven thousand people in the stands. It looked darker. Didn't look like the lights were as bright as they usually were, that night, at Ebbets Field, to me. And I'm just sitting there on the bench, looking around—of course, I wasn't on the bench very much late in my career. Early in my career, I was. But I was just sitting there. "This is eerie. This is like a dream, a bad dream." It was the last game at Ebbets Field. Never took the field there again.

Nobody wanted to move, of the players. Nobody wanted to move, especially Gil, because Gil's wife and children were born in Brooklyn, and he stayed there year-round. The rest of us went to our respective homes and spent the winter. It was a very sad time. When the announcement came, my wife and I heard the official announcement over the radio. I think we were in a car. She had a tear or two, because of the friends and fans we had in Brooklyn. Most of my teammates said that they shed a few tears, too, when they heard about it, because we were born and raised, baseball-wise, in Brooklyn. It was like tearing something out of me, you know. I never thought of it as a National League town. I think the way we were received in Brooklyn, by people who lived in Brooklyn, it was home. It was home to us, and we were very comfortable.

The Coliseum was built for the Olympics in Los Angeles. It was not built to play baseball in. I used to go watch fireworks on the Fourth of July in the Coliseum when I was a kid growing up in Southern California. I used to go to football games there. USC versus UCLA, I'd go every year and see that game. I never thought I would ever see a baseball game there, let alone play four years of baseball in the Coliseum. I didn't play that much then because I had a bad knee, but still I was in uniform for a lot of games there in the Coliseum. The seats went up so high that every fly ball that went up in the air looked like it was going to be a home run, because you couldn't judge how well the ball was hit because it was going up in the air. They installed lights in the Coliseum for night baseball. They had a very short left-field fence, which Wally Moon learned how to reach pretty well, batting left-handed. He would inside-out the ball and slice it against or over the screen. It made him as a ballplayer, learning how to hit that way. I hit a few home runs over that screen, but most of mine were hit to the long part of the real estate in right-center field, which was 410, 420, 430, something like that. And I hit a lot of 400-foot outs the first year in the Coliseum. I had knee surgery that winter, so I think the knee surgery was more frustrating than hitting those balls, because I hit over .300 that season, but I couldn't play every day because of my knee. It was never the same after I had the surgery.

I never went on the disabled list with my knee, but Bob Gibson broke my right elbow after I sliced a home run over that screen we were talking about. The next time up after the homer, he threw a 95 mile an hour fastball right at my ribs. I put my right elbow down to protect my ribs and it hit me right on the bone and cracked a small crack in the bone in my right elbow. It's the only time I was ever on the disabled list. I know that Bob Gibson has told people he never threw at a player on purpose. Bob Gibson is a nice guy, but he stretches the truth a little bit once in a while.

Don Zimmer had a bet going. He bet these guys $500 or $600 that I could throw one out of the Coliseum. And he came over to me and he said, "Warm up." He said, "I've got a bet going." And he said, "You get two hundred if you can do it." I'm in the lineup, so I said, Oh, okay. So I warmed up.

And he said, "All right. Throw one out of here." I saw him out there throwing, all of them trying to see if they could throw one out. And nobody was getting near the top row of the Coliseum. I knew that I could probably throw one out of there. So the first one I threw, there was a concrete wall in back of the last row of seats, about that high, and I hit about the middle of that concrete wall. So the next one I threw hit right near the top of the concrete wall. And I said, "Okay, this is it." And he said, "Collect the money, because this one's going out." And just as I threw it, the ball slipped off my middle finger and my elbow popped. About twenty minutes later, I couldn't take batting practice because my elbow was so sore. I went up to Walter Alston and told him that I won't be able to play. I hurt my elbow. And he told; word got to Buzzy Bavasi, our general manager, and Buzzy came out into the clubhouse looking for Zimmer and myself.

He says, "It's going to cost you $200 for every game you can't play." And I said, "Well, I'll play tonight then." I said, "My arm is sore, but I'll play tonight if it's going to cost me $200," because $200 was an awful lot of money then. "No, you already said you can't play. It's going to cost you $200. You go home. You shower and go home." And so I showered and went home. The next day, I couldn't even shave right-handed, my elbow was so sore.

I finally got to the ballpark and stuck my arm in a whirlpool and they worked on it, diathermy treatments and all that kind of stuff. I went to Alston and I said, "For $200, I'm playing today." And he said, "Okay." So he said, "I'll put you in left field." Left field, you know, you didn't have to throw very far, with that screen. So I got two hits and threw two guys out trying to take an extra base because they knew my arm was sore and it really hurt, but I threw them out, and we won the game.

So then, the end of the season was about three weeks away. I told Zimmer, "Keep that bet open and I'll do it the last day of the season." So the last day of the season, I warmed up, threw it out. Threw the first throw out of the park. Got $200 from Zimmer, and so I got my $200 back that I'd been fined. And then I went in that winter to see Buzzy and he said, "Where are you going?" And I said, "I'm going to go out to Santa Anita and see a couple of races." He said, "Well." He took two $100 bills out and handed them to me and he said, "I fined you $200 for trying to throw the ball out of the Coliseum." He says, "I'm giving it back to you. Have fun at the track." So I got $400.

I think I pinch-hit against Sandy Koufax one time when I was a Giant with a count of three and two. And I knew the manager didn't like me very well when he sent me up to pinch-hit against Sandy with that count. Alvin Dark, the Giants manager, came back to the bench and he said, "Duke, get a bat." I said, "Alvin, I've got more strikeouts than Koufax has got and I don't pitch." And he says, "He might walk ya." And I said, "Well, I never thought of that." So I went up, pinch-hit against him.

Willie McCovey hurt his side on a three-one fastball, swung and missed it and hurt his side. So they needed a hitter. And so I went up to hit. I look over at the Dodger bench, and they're laughing. I looked back at Johnny Roseboro, and he's laughing. I looked out at Koufax, and he's laughing. He's laughing so hard he threw one eye-high for ball four. So Dark was smart. He said he might walk me and he did.

But I think Koufax was the best pitcher I ever saw, or ever faced, and Juan Marichal would be the other one. Marichal was some kind of pitcher. I would like to have hit against Marichal before I had knee surgery, just to see how I would have done against him, because with my knee the way it was, I was no match for him. He was tough.

He threw four pitches from over the top, threw four pitches from over here, four pitches from over here. That gave him twelve major-league pitches. He threw a fastball, a curve, a slider, and a changeup

Sandy Koufax

from here, here, and here. Give him twelve major-league pitches, and he wouldn't throw them in sequence. He wouldn't have one pitch that he counted on to get you out on. You might get the fourth pitch from the third angle and he'd get you out with it, because they were all tough. And then he came up with a screwball. To me, he was so deceptive with his delivery, with his kicking his left foot up real high, that I had trouble picking the ball up until kind of late on its way to the plate. And it didn't give you as much good time to relax and react.

You pick the ball up when it leaves the pitcher's hand. You see it in the pitcher's hand and you pick it up when it leaves his hand. And a lot of pitchers will show you. Koufax would show you when he was going to throw a curve. When he threw his curve, his thumb would be sticking straight up on the ball like that, above the ball. And you knew it was a curve and you still couldn't hit it, because it broke so big. A lot of guys did that. A lot of guys, their release points, they would release it this way if it was a breaking ball sometimes, and you could pick it up.

• • •

Casey Stengel is the most memorable manager I had. He was goofy. He was fun to be around. He called me "kid." I loved him. I was thirty-seven years old and he called me "kid." When he had good players, he was smart. But when he had the bad players we had on the Mets, he wasn't that smart.

Leo Durocher was a very astute baseball man. He loved baseball. He knew it inside and out. But he was an in-and-outer. Branch Rickey had a quote on Durocher. He said, "Leo Durocher is the only man that I have ever met that could take over an impossible situation and immediately make it worse."

To sum up my career would be like summing up the careers of a lot of my Brooklyn Dodger teammates and my L.A. Dodger teammates. I hope that today, whenever this might be, that baseball is still our national pastime, because it's a wonderful game. I love it.

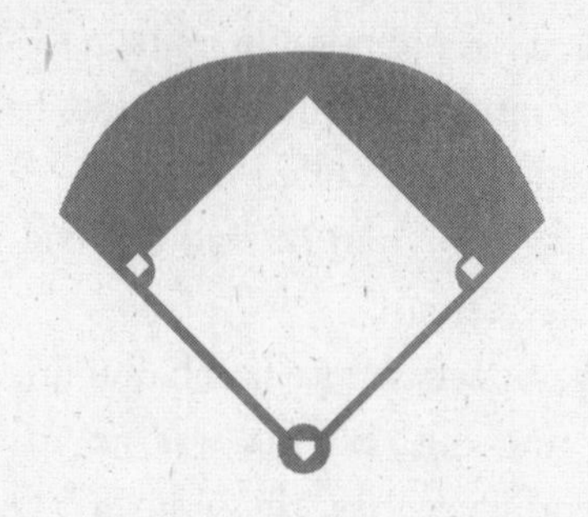

ROBIN ROBERTS

Robin Roberts had two attributes that combined to make him a dominating pitcher—speed and control. Hall of Fame batsman Stan Musial once said, "I've never seen a fastball pitcher who had such good control as Roberts. Or to put it another way, I've never seen a control pitcher who could throw so hard."

A mound mainstay for nineteen big-league seasons, Roberts made his name as a member of the Philadelphia Phillies starting staff for fourteen of those years. The right-handed workhorse compiled six consecutive twenty-win seasons in Philly, including a 20-11 mark in 1950 to help the Phils to their first pennant in thirty-five years.

Despite Roberts's track record, hitters were constantly surprised after facing him. "He looks like the kind of pitcher you can't wait to swing at," said Pirate Hall of Famer Willie Stargell, "but you swing and the ball isn't where you thought it was." Longtime coach Clyde Sukeforth concurred, adding, "Watching his stuff from the dugout, a lot of us used to say we'd like to take a whack at him. He doesn't show a hitter a lot of body motion, but he throws out of a smooth, easy style. It's deceptively smooth and easy."

According to Red Schoendienst, Roberts possessed an uncanny ability to get himself out of a tight jam. "I got a single, triple, and homer off him in one game. The next time, he gave me the treatment he usually reserves for a jam, the something extra he seems to be able to reach back and get when he's in trouble."

Former player and manager Ray Fisher attributed Roberts's success to confidence. "I've seen other young pitchers who showed as much physical ability as Roberts and they never got anywhere," Fisher said. "They lacked one thing that Roberts had. He had confidence in himself. That's what makes the difference in a ballplayer. If a man got a couple hits off him, Roberts was never satisfied that the man was going to get a hit the next time. He always thought he could beat the other fellow."

After ending his big-league career with 286 wins, 2,357 strikeouts, and a 3.41 ERA, Roberts was elected to the National Baseball Hall of Fame in 1976.

"To play behind him was a pleasure and a privilege," said longtime Phillies teammate and fellow Hall of Famer Richie Ashburn. "You always knew you would get everything he had that day and, more important, you always felt it would be enough to win. Robin, win or lose, never had to apologize for his effort."

Dad came from England. He was a coal miner. That's how he got to Springfield, Illinois. When he came over, he brought a cricket bat. And that was the first bat we had around the house. But we didn't have balls. We used to get a Bull Durham sack and fill it full of grass and play with that. It was a different world then. And the first thing we started doing, we started playing softball. I played a lot of softball. In those days, they didn't play Little League. They played softball until a guy was fourteen or fifteen and then you switched to hardball, which made a lot of sense then, and it probably makes sense now. But I remember going to the Three-I League games when I was about eleven or twelve, and that's when I first got a baseball. They used to

Robin Roberts

throw a ball up after the game. All the kids would get one. I was small. I stood way out in left field and the guy for some reason threw it out to me. That's the first baseball I ever had.

We were either Cardinal or Cub fans. Springfield, Illinois, is right in the middle. One day Dad came out when I was probably about twelve or thirteen and my brother was hitting fungoes to me. Dad came out to try to hit fungoes, and he swung and missed about five times. That was the only time my father ever made an appearance. He was on the disabled list for forty years, I guess.

I was a basketball player and a softball player as a kid in grade school and then I went into football as I got into high school. I played three sports in high school, but the baseball part of it didn't really start until I was fourteen or fifteen.

We were six kids. We didn't have much money. Dinner was at five. If you didn't show up at five, you were in trouble; you didn't eat, you know. And then I met a young teacher in grade school when I was in the fifth grade. He was about twenty-three, just out of college, and he was really gung ho about sports. He brought a softball and a basketball. We didn't have any organized leagues until he showed up. His name was C. B. Lindsay. And when I went into the Hall of Fame, he lived in Tampa, and drove all the way to Cooperstown. He was a big influence.

In those days, at Thanksgiving, you switched to basketball, and when the snows melted, why, you switched to baseball. And basketball was really the name sport, you know, like it is now, football and basketball. I was invited to Michigan State on a basketball scholarship. It was interesting, because the first year I went up I played and then I went in the Air Corps after basketball. Then the war ended, and I came back in November, ready for another basketball season. So I played two basketball seasons at Michigan State. They had no idea I played baseball. I had been a third baseman and a pitcher in high school. I was a good third baseman. I really enjoyed playing every day, and I could swing a bat. But when I went out for baseball at Michigan State, the coach knew me from basketball. He said, "What are you doing out here?" I said, "Coach, I can play your game." He said, "What do you play?" I said, "What do you need?" It sounds crazy, but that's a true story. He said, "Well, I need pitching." I said, "I can pitch." Two years later, I was in the big leagues. It's fantastic; that could not happen nowadays. You have to be trained, right? But I could throw strikes and I understood the game. I had a feel for it. Once I started, I spent a lot of hours playing baseball. We'd go five, six hours a day. There'd be five on a team in Glendon Park, where my high school was, and you'd hit eighty times, you know what I mean? We really had training for it just by playing it.

That first year I started with Michigan State, the big game every year was the Michigan game. By the time the game came around, the end of the season, I was the number one starter. I pitched against them and they beat me 2–0 in East Lansing. I had a friend on our team that was going to go to Vermont with Ray Fisher, the Michigan coach. He went over to see Ray after our game because this was the first week of June and Vermont started the fifteenth of June or so. He was getting instructions from Ray, when to get there and all that sort of thing. At the end of the conversation, Ray said, "Do you think that big boy would like to go with us?" And so this friend of mine, Pat Pepper, came running over, and he said, "Robin, you want to go to Vermont?" I said, "Yeah, I'd love to go to Vermont." So that's how I got to Vermont.

You couldn't believe how nice it was. We got $175 expenses. Well, you know, in 1946, the first summer I was there, that could last a long time. And they actually would give us $175. Michigan State wasn't in the Big Ten at that time. We were still an independent team, but some of the teams that were in conferences, a couple of guys were declared ineligible for going up there. It was a shame. We would start June 15 and we would play sixty games. The last game was Labor Day. My first year, we were a decent club and I pitched. I was 11-9 or something and we came in second. Bennington beat us out, but the next year, Ray didn't get beat very often. I won seventeen straight starts. That's when the scouts looked at me. After that season ended, I lived in Springfield, so the Phillies made arrangements for me to work out in Chicago. I was supposed to work out with six teams. There wasn't a draft then. They could just bid you up like they did the Cuban boys that came over, you know? I didn't have an agent or anything. You didn't have those then. I worked out with the Phillies. The first day—it was a three-day series against the Cubs—the first day the offer was $10,000. I still hadn't worked out with these other clubs. The next day, the offer was $15,000. And then the next day, the signing bonus was $25,000. I didn't work like my other brothers. I was kind of a goof-off because I was playing ball, and I had read where Lou Gehrig had built his mom a home. And I said to Mom, "Someday I'll build you a house. I'll build you a house." Well, when the signing bonus got to $25,000, I said, "Is that enough to build a house?" And the guy said, "Yeah, that'll build it." I said, "That's enough." I have no idea what I would have gotten if I'd have worked out with the Yankees and the rest of them, but I stopped right there with the Phillies. I got my $25,000 and built my mom her house, and I got up in the big leagues in a hurry.

I wasn't twenty-one yet, and you couldn't sign a contract then. So your parent, your father, had to be there. So Chuck Ward was the guy's name, an old ballplayer for Brooklyn, then a scout for the Phillies. So we took a train from Chicago to Springfield. And I remember—I could really eat then and he got me a steak dinner and I ate it. I used to eat fast. I was a terrible eater, but when I got through he said, "Did you like that?" And I said, "Oh yeah, it was delicious." He said, "Would you like another?" I said, "Yeah." He was only kidding me. But I had my first two real big steaks on the train.

My father used to work around the house. He worked nights his whole life, and then he'd work in his garden. He had an old sailor cap and no shirt and just a pair of shorts. It was in September, and he was sitting there and he'd have his beer there, and he was drinking, relaxing. I came in and I introduced him, and I said, "Dad, this guy wants to pay me $25,000 for signing with the Phillies." Well, he didn't bat an eye, you know. I could imagine what he was thinking. You know, here's a guy, he made—I don't know what Dad made as a coal miner, but he was thrilled, I'm sure. He didn't want me to build the house, though. He wanted to put it in the bank. He was happy with the house he had, but I talked him out of that.

Ray Fisher was a stand-up guy who pitched in the big leagues, by the way. He pitched in the Black Sox Series. He tried to get me to throw a curve, but every time I tried to throw one, I would stand up and it was a different delivery. I could throw one occasionally, but the only time I made an adjustment on my breaking ball was in '52. Sal Maglie beat us opening day. He had that little ping, you know, and he was so marvelous, the way he could do that. And he beat me opening day, and I thought, "By God, I'm going to come up with one of those." And I started shortening up and throwing it out of a good low delivery. Not a big one but nice. That's the year I won 28 games. And I think if Sal hadn't beaten me opening day, I wouldn't have made the adjustment.

I remember my first coach when I worked out with the Phillies was Cy Perkins. I heard him say, "Don't let that kid get out of here." Years later, when I went back, when I came up with the Phillies, he was still there. I said, "Cy, why did you say that?" He said, "You threw a ball harder and easier than anybody I ever saw." I had an easy motion and I had nice wrist action, and the ball would pick up speed. I was in Vermont when I really got organized. I would have good and bad games, but all of a sudden I had a feeling of getting my leg out of the way, and using my hip, and fitting it into a delivery. Once that happened, then I could throw a baseball. I never had much of a breaking ball, but I could throw a baseball with good action and with an easy delivery.

I never threw a changeup. I threw low. I would throw a low and away, high and tight. That's the way I threw, and then a breaking ball. I had a little bit of a slow curve as I got older, but I never did come up with a changeup. Cy Perkins, who was my guru when I got to the big leagues, he was the guy that really was wonderful to me. He said an interesting thing. He said, "You know, when you watch a guy, a hard thrower, throw a changeup, watch his next fastball. It won't be the same as a good fastball because his rhythm won't be the same for a couple of pitches." Well, I watched those things as I played. Everybody's changeup happy now and they've had success with it. Pedro Martinez throws a changeup. I don't know why he throws a changeup, but he does, and he's got a good one.

Somebody said my fastball was like skating on ice, that it moved. That was just a wrist pop at the end. When I was throwing like that, I could get most guys out. But some days, I would overthrow and wouldn't get the finish on it. It would be straight, but it wouldn't have that action on it. Those guys that hit .330, I knew why they hit .330.

Cy Perkins convinced me that I ought to win, that I had a gift, I could throw a baseball and I should win. But there's a few fundamentals. Stay ahead of batters, you know. If I got hit hard, he was there in a minute to tell me stories about when he saw Lefty Grove get hit hard. Well, that didn't make my getting hit hard so complicated. Those were the things he did for me, but more than anything he said, "I remember." He's the only guy I ever talked to about pitching for seven, eight years. And I didn't talk to him very much except when I lost. He'd come over and put his arm around me and tell me how they're big leaguers we're playing against and there were things that couldn't be done if you tried to do them. It was one of those things; we were just a perfect fit. But in 1950, I had won seven coming up in June and then I won fifteen. And I was warming up in spring training in 1950. He always called me Kid. He said, "Kid, you're feeling good, huh, now?" "Yeah, Cy." "Well," he said, "you're our next 300-game winner." Now, I had 22 wins and he's my coach, and I said, "Oh, come on, Cy." "No," he said, "Kid, I've seen—" Then he said, "The five best pitchers I ever saw were Walter Johnson, Alexander, Gomez—no, no, Herb Pennock, Grover Cleveland Alexander, and you." I said, "Come on." "No," he said, "you're right in here, you're going to win 300 games. Don't worry about it." I had 22 wins. He left me after the '54 season, and it was never the same from then on. I mean, baseball was never the same for me. I got hit around some days, but it never was an emergency with him because he'd seen other guys get hit around that were better pitchers than me probably.

I played basketball every winter when I pitched for the Phillies for ten years. I'd play basketball two or three times a week and play golf, I was just the kind of a guy that was active. I do think that today they're much better prepared than we were in those days. I think they do a little too much of it. We used to end the season in October, the first of October, and we wouldn't touch a baseball until the middle of January. We'd play golf or basketball. In the middle of January, Curt Simmons and I would go start working out in the gym in Philadelphia. We'd throw to each other and we'd play basketball, and by the time we got to spring training our arms were loose enough. We'd start batting practice the first day and boom, boom, boom. But I do think there is much better training now.

A lot of coaches now, I've heard them tell pitchers, "You stay out of the way. Let the fielders field the ball." Gosh, I'd jump on those babies, boy. I was fortunate I had a good delivery, and I ended up looking all right.

That really helps if you end up square because you're ready to field your position. But that has really been de-emphasized as far as pitching goes.

I reported at Clearwater, Florida. I got $25,000, and they wanted to see me throw there. I pitched and I got people out down there. I was pitching, and the first thing you know—Ben Chapman was the manager. And one day I was walking by him, he said, "Hey, Robin, come here." "Yes, sir." "You're the best pitcher I got," he said. He said, "You're going to Philadelphia with me." I said, "That's fine." I just came from college. But I figured he knew what he was talking about. He was the manager. So we're going north, playing the spring training games, and I got beat in Charlotte, North Carolina. Washington beat me, I think 5–2 or 5–3. After the game, I got dressed and went back to the hotel. Babe Alexander was the traveling secretary, and he said, "Robin, could I buy you a milk shake?" So we went in to have our milk shake, and he said, "Well, we're going to send you to Wilmington, Delaware." I said, "No, no, no, no, no. The manager said I'm going to Philadel—" He said, "Well, the owner says you're going to Wilmington, Delaware." So I went to Wilmington. And I was 9–1 there. That was a great club. I had 125 strikeouts in eleven games. I could throw hard. In my first game I struck out eighteen, I think. We won 18–3. That game must have taken forever. I don't remember. But I won nine games. I had one game was 1–1—or no, it was a 2–2 tie—and went fifteen innings. And this guy named Joe Muir pitched for Harrisburg. You know, he pitched the whole fifteen innings. So I'm 9–1 and we were in Hagerstown, Maryland. I was in bed, and the manager called me. He said, "Robin, come on down here." I said, "What the hell was that? I did nothing." So I went down and all the team was in the lobby. He said, "The Phillies have called you up." And that was kind of a nice thing for him to do. But I hadn't even thought of going to the Phillies. But he gave me a pen and pencil set engraved with "Robin Roberts" and the "Phillies."

So I go home back to Wilmington to get my stuff and I catch a train to Philadelphia. And I get in at 4:30 in the afternoon, checked into the Bellevue-Stratford Hotel, and now I'm going to the ballpark. So I get there about six o'clock and I walk into the manager's office—Ben Chapman. "How you doing, kid?" I said, "I'm fine." "Can you pitch tonight?" I said, "Yes, sir." I got there at 6:00 and at 8:05 I'm pitching. It was the Pittsburgh team. The first batter was a guy named Stan Rojek, and I threw four of the wildest pitches you ever saw. I was really nervous. The next guy was Frankie Gustine, and I got three and two on him. And he swung at the high fastball and struck out. I was all right from then on. I was never scared again—I mean, nervous—until I had a no-hitter in '55 on opening day. My damn knees started shaking just like they did that first time. I got beat 2–0. It was a good ball game. But I remember how beautiful the stadium was, kind of nice, though a lot of people didn't ever think it was beautiful. But I did. It was a gorgeous thing to see.

Chapman was one of those guys that there just was no way they could play with blacks, you know? They had never done that. They never thought that it would ever happen. Well, when it did happen, it was tough. So the first year, in '47, I wasn't there, but they said Ben would get up in the dugout and say to Jackie Robinson, "Jackie, here's my shoes. Shine them after the game," and all those silly things. And Jackie just wore him out. The next year didn't nobody get on him. He could play. And so they didn't get on him the next year. By the time I got up there, he was just established as one whale of a ballplayer.

Jackie could put on some show, you know what I mean? And

after the game, we'd go down the runway. We're on the same runway. And Curt Simmons and I were following Chapman down the steps to go to our clubhouse and, lo and behold, Jackie comes right by and they just meet right there. And that's when Chapman says to him, "Jackie, you're one hell of a ballplayer, but you're still a nigger." And I thought that's tough to have to live with that kind of thing inside you, you know what I mean? Jackie just looked and grinned and just walked right on by. You could visualize what would happen because they were both big, fiery guys. Ben Chapman was as big as Jackie. That was in '48, and Ben got fired. Nobody knew about that encounter because Curt and I didn't tell anybody. But Ben got fired probably a month later, maybe even less than that.

Roy Campanella was born and raised not three miles from the Phillies ballpark. Campy's father was an Italian man, used to come in our clubhouse. I mean, we'd have taken Campy, I'll tell you that, and all those guys, you know? We didn't take any. All of a sudden, I look up and the Dodgers had him, the Giants and the Braves were taking all those guys. And you think about who won all the pennants in the 1950s. We had good success against the Dodgers. We weren't as good as they were, but we didn't know it. I once had a stretch of seven straight wins against the Dodgers. I was right-handed and they were right-handed except for a couple of guys, and I would pitch well. We'd play them what, twenty-two games a year. That would be four series in each place, and I would pitch against them eight times. I never missed the Dodgers. There was no way I'd miss them. Well, they were an outstanding club. Ironically enough, they beat me more than I beat them in Philly, and I beat them more than they beat me in Ebbets Field.

The '50 season opened up with Don Newcombe and I against each other. We won 9–1, and then we ended up the season in a ten-inning game, Newk and I. In between, we must have pitched against each other three or four times. I had good luck against Newk, three to two. Then all of a sudden they quit pitching me against him, and

Don Newcombe

I'd pitch against Carl Erskine. Erskine beat me like a drum—2–1, 3–2. I couldn't beat Erskine. I always lucked out against Newk, but somehow they figured it out.

In August 1950, I think Curt Simmons didn't lose. We really were hot in August and were seven and a half games in front going into September. They had put Curt in the National Guard to keep him from being drafted, figuring they would never activate the National Guard and, by God, they activated it. They took him September 10, and we were seven and a half games in front. And about two days later, Bubba Church got hit in the eye with a line drive, which knocked him out for the season, and Bob Miller hurt his back terribly. So we went from a five-man rotation to—I was the only guy left other than Ken Heintzelman and Russ Meyer, who had had big years the year before but hadn't done well in '50. So that's how we ended up over the barrel at the end. We didn't have anybody. And I pitched Saturday night against the Dodgers and Newk beat me. Pee Wee hit a three-run homer in the ninth to beat us 3–2. A few days later, we played a doubleheader at the Giants on a Wednesday. I start the

Wednesday game. I had pitched Saturday. I started the Wednesday game, and in the fifth inning Hank Thompson hits a three-run homer. Puts them ahead 5–1. Eddie Sawyer took me out right away, and I didn't know why, but we lost that game, and we lost the twi-night, the second game. Come Thursday, another doubleheader. Sawyer says to me before the game, "You're starting." So I pitched Saturday, I pitched five innings Wednesday, I pitched the whole game Thursday, and I got beat 3–1. Whitey Lockman got a hit off me. Now we lose the second game. So now we got a day off and the Dodgers are playing the Braves in a doubleheader. All they have to do is lose one. Dodgers beat them. If they'd have lost one game, we would win the pennant. So now Saturday we go out and that's when they tried to pitch Miller. He had a bad back, so Konstanty came in, and the Dodgers beat us 7–3. Now Sunday, I don't know who is pitching. Nobody had said anything to anybody, so I'm sitting by my locker before the game, and I have a hunch I know who might be pitching.

So Eddie Sawyer walks over, and he taps me on the shoulder, and he had a new ball. He never did this the whole time he was there. He had a new ball, he gave it to me and said, "Good luck, Robin," and that's when I knew I was pitching. So I pitched that ball game and I went ten innings, and of course, when the ninth inning started, we were tied. Cal Abrams led off the inning and Larry Goetz—the things you remember. Larry was such an outstanding umpire. He was behind the plate on Saturday. So Sunday still has to determine the pennant, that final game. Ford Frick was the president and he calls the umpires. Augie Donatelli, who was in that crew, told me the story. He said, "Larry, get back there again today." So Larry was there Saturday and Sunday. He was a wonderful umpire. So anyhow, the count is three and one, and Abrams is up in the bottom of the ninth. I threw one in there, and I can still see it. And Larry goes, "Ball four." I'm telling you, I couldn't believe that was a ball. But he did. Pee Wee Reese came up and I threw two fastballs, and Pee Wee fouled them both off, and then I tried to crowd him, because you'd figure he could go the other way with two, you know? By God, he ripped one to left for a base hit. Now Duke Snider comes up. You talk about thinking bad. I was wrong on Pee Wee and now Snider—I figured Stoop's got to bunt. I laid one and I broke off the mound and covered third and he hit one. It's interesting, Abrams was on second and I turned right away to watch, and the ball was to the second-base side of the bag, you know, and it was a low line drive. And Abrams turned. They always tell you heads-up on the line drive. I think he thought the second baseman might be in a position to catch it. He didn't run right away, and I remember seeing that. He just turned. Now, he starts running. Well, Richie Ashburn didn't throw very well. He had an accurate arm but not strong, and they all ran on him, you know. Well, Milt Stock sends him in. And he didn't realize that Abrams hadn't broken. Milt Stock sent him in. And he was out by ten feet. By then, Stan Lopata was catching because Andy Seminick was injured. So now Pee Wee's on third, Snider's on second. Sawyer came out. Jackie was the hitter. Sawyer said, "Let's put him on, and keep the ball down on Furillo." Well, we put him on, and the first pitch to Carl Furillo was high, and he pops up. And then Gil Hodges hit a ball to Del Ennis, and Del went back, and evidently he had gotten right in the sun, and he kind of caught it off his chest.

So, our turn at bat, and I'm sitting there. Sawyer says, "Go ahead and hit, Robin," after all that. And don't you know, I bang one up the middle for a base hit, right? That started the tenth inning, and then Eddie Waitkus hits a little quail to right center, drops in, so I move up. Now Richie bunts, and I bust my can, and Newk can make a good play on that ball. He threw me out at third. Just got me, but I was out. And then Dick Sisler came up. Now, he had three other hits that day. He fouls one off, and then he hits a low line drive. In Ebbets Field, it was about 345 to left center, and you didn't know whether it was high enough or not, and it just turned out it was enough. So now we're up 4–1, and after all this struggling, all we need is three outs to win this thing that has just about escaped us.

And there was nobody warming up. And I got to say, I threw better that inning. I think I was just so relieved. The first hitter was Campy. Sisler wasn't much of an outfielder. And we had Jack Mayo, who was a good outfielder, a young guy. And right as soon as we went out in the field, Sawyer put Mayo in for Sisler. It's the only time he did it all year. Now, that's managing.

And Campy hit a ball pretty good. I think Sisler would have caught it, but Jack caught it easy. And then the next guy was Jim Russell. He struck out, and then Tommy Brown pinch-hit and popped up. Sawyer didn't use Jim Konstanty. I don't know why. We can't ask him. He left us. I never, never in my life inquired of a manager or talked to him one way or the other on the mound. You know, you see the conversations going on, and I often think, "I wish I had said something." That's interesting. Never said a word to anybody. They said to me, "How do you feel?" "I'm fine." I was always fine. And if they want to take me out, it was their choice.

I had four starts in ten days. The last day, I wasn't feeling so hot when I went out to warm up. The thing that saved me as I looked over, Newk was warming up and he had pitched just as much as me. I can't tell you how that relaxed me. I thought, "He's the same thing. Let's go, Newk." He's tired and I'm tired. We're two tired guys, right? And neither one of us had got hit around much, you know? It was a pretty good ball game when you think about it.

I had pitched ten innings on Sunday, and I was going to start the first game of the '50 World Series on Wednesday. That would have been two days' rest. Sawyer had to come up with something different, so he started Jim Konstanty the first time ever.

For some reason, when you're in Philadelphia—if he'd have pitched that game for a New York team, they'd have never forgotten it. I think the Yankees got five hits. Bobby Brown doubled and he scored on two fly outs. He moved up to third on one and then he came in on the other and the game ended up 1–0.

Vic Raschi pitched the first game. Then I started against Allie

Reynolds. The first two or three innings, they had a couple of men on, they scored a run in the second inning or something. And then we scored one. But then from about the fifth inning on, I had my pop-up deal. Joe DiMaggio popped up four times in that ball game. And now it's the tenth inning. Joe led off in the tenth and he hit one so hard, line drive into the seats. I got the next three guys out, but Joe, like Feller said, he had a special knack. He had popped up four times, and I just popped it in there and he hit a shot. We lost, 2–1.

That's one of the problems we had. I only saw Joe DiMaggio in spring training, couple of times. In spring training in those days, he and Ted Williams would hit twice, wave to the crowd—but they played every day, you know what I mean? It wasn't because they didn't go on trips. If you paid to see the Yankees, spring training, you saw Joe hit twice. But he'd hit twice, tip his hat, and I guess he had a limousine taking him back. I don't know. But I never saw him full-time. He made a couple of plays in that series. In my game, Granny Hamner hit a shot over second. And if it gets by Joe, it's a triple. And by God, he ran it down and it was only a double. Ham would have been on third with no out or one out in the bottom of the ninth. But I remember Joe said he never dove for a ball.

Eddie Sawyer became the manager in July 1948. It was one year before I had a conversation with that man other than "Hello." You know, "How are you?" "Fine." I hadn't quite pitched a year. It was just before the All-Star Game. And I was walking to the ballpark or to the movie or something, and he and Frank Powell, who was his driver, were out having lunch, and he said, "Hey, Robin, come here a minute." "Yeah, Skip, what do you want?" He said, "You think you can pitch in the big leagues, don't you?" And I said, "Yes, sir, I think." He said, "So do I." That was the first conversation in one year, which wasn't a bad conversation. But he never had a meeting, never bugged anybody. Typical of Sawyer, here's what happened when we lost the last game to the Dodgers in 1951. Newk had beaten me Saturday night, beat me 5–0. So Sunday was the final game, right? So I was sitting in the bullpen, it's the eighth inning, and he said, "Roberts, warm up." I'd pitched the night before that, so I warmed up and I could get it up there a little bit. So then the game got involved in one of these long jobs. I was out there, and it was the fourteenth inning before it was over. Jackie finished it. But in the eleventh inning, they got a man on second with two out and Jackie was the hitter and Campy was next. And Sawyer never came to the mound unless he's going to take you out. All of a sudden, I looked up and there he comes. He came jogging out to the mound. I thought, "I wonder what he wants?" He said, "Would you rather pitch to Jackie or Campy?" I said, "Doesn't matter to me, Skip." He said, "Doesn't matter to me either," and he turned and ran away. Here's a conference we're having on the mound, right? And by the time he got to the dugout, I had fired one and Jackie popped it right straight up for the third out. So then in the bottom of that inning—now, if we win this game, there's no Bobby Thomson home run. Sawyer always left me to hit late in the game. In the bottom of that inning, I singled off Newk. Newk had come in for them by now. So I single off Newk and Eddie Pellagrini bunts, and I bust my butt and slide and I'm safe. They tried to throw me out at second. So now Richie Ashburn gets us over to second and third and they walk Puddin' Head Jones because Puddin' Head hit Newk like he owned him, you know? So now Del Ennis comes up, and if he gets me in, it's all over. So the count is two and two, and Newk smokes him and he just takes that right there. So now Eddie Waitkus comes up and he hits a low line drive right through the box. And I'm on third and I see Jackie dive for it, and I know he trapped the ball. I could see it because I'm looking like this as I'm running. And Jackie rolls over and he throws the ball over his head to try to get the force at second and he throws it behind Pee Wee. So I run home. Game's over. Touch home and I'm headed for the clubhouse. I look up and my team is running out on the field. Lon Warneke was the umpire. He said, "Jackie caught it." So we had to go out and play again. So twelfth inning, thirteenth inning, and fourteenth inning. Jackie, he didn't pop this one up. He popped it out. He hit a home run. That's how they won—that's how it ended up a play-off between the Dodgers and the Giants.

If I'd throw 115 pitches, I'd throw 90 fastballs. Now people can't believe that, but I'm not lying. And one time somebody asked Andy Seminick, our catcher, about it. Well, he said I had good control, I had a good movement, and he said, "And Cy Perkins said never call anything he can't throw." Now you think about that, you know? It'd be wonderful if everybody threw a three-and-one changeup perfect, but what if you can't throw it? So you don't call it, right? And Andy said, "That really made sense to me. Don't call something he can't throw."

Jim Konstanty was a big guy. He was six-one and he looked like he ought to throw it through a barn, but he'd come up there, he had a palm ball and a slider, and he could hit right on the black with it, you know? He came in relief once against Cincinnati, ninth inning,

Jim Konstanty

tie game. Game went eighteen innings. He pitched the whole extra innings, and I even think he came in the next day. He didn't throw hard. He didn't really exert himself as far as power stuff. He had a great slider and a palm ball. In '53, he won 14 games as a starter. And then he went to the Yankees. One of Yogi's favorite stories is "Casey came out in Cleveland. They got the bases loaded with Indians. Casey comes out and motions to the bullpen and Yogi says, 'Here comes Jim Konstanty walking in.' He said, 'I could catch him without a glove.' Here's three guys coming up, and Yogi said, 'The one guy popped up, the next guy struck out, next guy popped up,' and he said, 'He walked off like he was Walter Johnson.' " Jim had great confidence. His palm ball was very deceptive. It was a changeup is what it was, what those guys today call the three-finger circle change.

It was Willie, Mickey, and the Duke in center field then. They could hit it a mile and they ran and they threw. Richie Ashburn—Whitey, we called him—hit singles, walked a lot, couldn't throw very well,

Richie Ashburn

although he made the biggest throw in the history of the Phillies, right? But he showed up every day and he played. You can't believe how hard he would play every day. He couldn't believe it if he made an out. He would get so mad when he made an out.

The authority of the umpires has been confused. I mean, their arguing with ballplayers to me is terrible. They don't have to argue with anybody. They're in charge. Once an umpire starts arguing and acting like a ballplayer, now he's not in charge anymore. Now they're just part of the act. Larry Goetz, first time I ever pitched to him, we're starting a game, first pitch is a nice low fastball right down the pike. He calls it a ball. And I look. Next pitch, same play. He rips his mask off. Steps out in front of home plate and says, "Ball two, you SOB." And I thought, "What have I done?" So out comes Seminick and he said, "Oh, Robin, I forgot to tell you about him. He takes charge. He's in charge, and he's the best umpire in the league." I never said another word in eighteen years to Larry Goetz. I knew he was in charge, and he was a marvelous umpire.

First time I got thrown out of a game, it was crazy. I had beaten the Giants the night before, a tough ten-inning, 3–2 job, beautiful ball game to win. And now we're out there Saturday afternoon, a beautiful day, and I'm in the dugout. I can hardly stay awake and I'm watching the game. And for some reason Andy Seminick and Artie Gore, the umpire, are mad at each other all day long. And they're at each other, and Andy comes and sits by me in the dugout. So he's still going on, "Oh, Artie—da-da-da." And Artie rips his mask off and comes over to the dugout. He says, "Roberts, get out of here." And I look at Sawyer, and then I start to say something to Andy. Andy says, "Go ahead. He knows Sawyer ain't going to use you." So I had to go from the dugout to the clubhouse in the Polo Grounds, which was out in dead center field. I think, "I wonder what my mother's going to say?" I got thrown out a couple of times for reasons I should have been thrown out, but that wasn't one of them.

• • •

The guys with good deliveries could complete their games. I remember Spahnie and Juan Marichal went sixteen innings once, and I think Marichal beat him 1–0. I think Mays hit a home run and the score was 1–0. But I remember when I was thirty-eight years old I pitched for Baltimore. I pitched against Jim Kaat, who was a marvelous pitcher, and we went thirteen innings. And I think it's deliveries. Some guys that are pitching now are muscle guys. They don't have good deliveries and they actually get tired. Their arms get tired. Not that Greg Maddux and Tom Glavine are those guys. They use their whole deal. Roger Clemens has got the most perfect delivery, you know what I mean? He doesn't have to pitch six innings. He could pitch twelve innings, but it makes sense to take him out. They're making money. They got more guys on the team that are participating. I think the way they do it now, with the exception of trying to pitch some guys without good deliveries, I think that detracts a little bit from pitching. You got some teams that have guys pitching, no way they could pitch nine innings.

I had 25 saves in the big leagues. Now, there's no way Roger Clemens or Pedro Martinez or anybody will have any saves. I had 25 saves, and I guarantee you half of them were in the years I won the 20 games. I remember one day I beat the Dodgers on a Friday, so I got off days Saturday and Sunday. It's my day to throw, so I'm down in the bullpen. And I used to throw right in the game. They'd call me in, in case they needed me. Well, I'm throwing in the bullpen, we're winning 2–1. They've got a runner on and one out. I look up and Mayo Smith's out motioning me in. No, I think it was Steve O'Neill. I come in and I don't have it, and I wasn't smart enough to say I don't have it, right? Jackie's the hitter, too. I think, "There ain't no way I can throw across him because I don't have it." I've got to try to dip it. So I went out, and the first pitch to Jackie—he was so observant, you know—it goes out of the strike zone. He said, "What the hell was that?" So I throw another one. He's done swinging. Now I'm two and nothing. And I thought, "Well, I've got to keep it up."

Same thing, only he couldn't really resist. He had to swing at one. It wasn't very fast, but it moved down enough for him to hit into a double play.

I think the way they do it now is good. I find it amazing when they take out Glavine or Maddux after eight innings and it's 1–0. I'm thinking, "Wait a minute," but that's the way they do it, you know? I remember they took out Glavine one year when the Braves beat Cleveland. The final game, Glavine pitched eight innings, two hits, and it was 1–0. And he didn't pitch in the ninth. They brought in Mark Wohlers. And I thought, "God, that takes guts to take him out." Of course, if they got a score off of him and left him in, they'd all have been second-guessed for leaving him in too long. Those guys that can really pitch, Martinez and Clemens, they're not going to win 27 games, but they're going to give you 22 wins that are beautiful.

I saw Willie Mays, and to this day, there's nobody who could play baseball like him. When they used to compare Mickey Mantle and Willie Mays, I used to think, every time I saw Mickey, he's limping. Willie never limped in his life. I couldn't believe they'd compared them. And then I'm with the Yankees for a short span. I was released. I was with them a week.

Opening day, we're playing Baltimore, and Baltimore has got us beat in the seventh inning. Jack Reed was a reserve outfielder, and I was sitting next to him, and I said, "Come on, Jack. Let's go. What's going on?" He said, "Oh, don't worry. Mickey hits this inning." And I thought, "What the hell does that mean?" And then, somebody got a walk. Mickey hit one to the bullpen and the Yanks won. I looked at Jack Reed and I said, "How about that?" He said, "Oh, he does that all the time." And then I realized with all this limping and everything, the people, the Yankees, and the American League, they thought Mickey was unbelievable. But I don't see him that way. Willie Mays never limped in his life that I saw him.

• • •

I never got that fan feeling like they get now. I see a basketball game and they say, "Well, that home-crowd advantage." I could have played in a barn, you know what I mean? I never had any feeling for the home-crowd advantage. The only thing I knew was they hit last when we played in their park, and I thought there was a little advantage there. But I felt bad that I didn't react more to those things and notice some more. A lot of people said how they rooted so hard and cheered and all that, and I thought, "God, I wish I'd have known." I didn't give any thought to it, you know.

I don't remember crowds in Philly except when the Dodgers came in with Jackie and Newk and we played those games against them. Then they started getting thirty thousand. It was interesting then. The ballpark is now a Baptist church. So my wife and I were in town one day and the Phillies gave us a car when we were there. So we asked the guy to take us out there. I went out there and there's this church and I said to Mary, "Let's go inside." So we went inside, and there's a black gentleman that came in. I said, "I just want to see where your church is." So he came in, and there's a beautiful pulpit where the guy gives his speeches, right, and I swear it's right on the mound. I swear it's right on the mound. So I said to the guy, I said, "Don Newcombe and I, we used to preach here years ago before thirty-four thousand." And he didn't even laugh. It's a bit humbling, but at least Mary laughed.

Del Crandall, when I first saw him, he threw BBs. He could throw, and then he went in the Army and hurt his arm. He never threw the same when he came back, but he was always a great catcher. Randy Hundley was as fine a receiver as I ever saw. I pitched to him. My last three months in baseball, Randy was my catcher. Boog Powell was a good fielder and great enthusiasm on the field at first. He was a good player. Second base is Red and Maz—Red Schoendienst and Bill Mazeroski. Jackie? I wouldn't pick him at a position. I just want him on my team. He could play wherever he wants. He's just one of those guys that can set any place he wants.

He played second and third and left field, and he was an outstanding fielder. Mays was an outstanding fielder. Jackie never missed the ball. He didn't look good. At bat, he looked kind of stiff, you know? Football would have been a better sport for him, the way he was built, but baseball fit under his program, too. His weakness as a batter was that you could crowd him with a fastball. So I could get him out in there, but that was all. I mean, that was all. My repertoire was the fastball. I didn't throw him many curves, because anything off-speed, he could murder it. Shortstops, Luis Aparicio was fun to watch. I was with Baltimore with him. A guy named Roy McMillan was as good as I ever saw. Larry Bowa was fantastic for the Phillies for all those years. And I guess Ozzie Smith was probably the best I ever saw at shortstop. He was unbelievable. But Larry was good, McMillan, Aparicio.

At third, Brooks Robinson was fantastic. You can't believe what he did. One of my early games with Baltimore, I was pitching against the White Sox. I got two quick outs in the first inning. Joe Cunningham was a left-handed hitter, was hitting third, and I got behind him two and nothing. I popped one in there and he laid a perfect bunt down the third-base line. Well, I had no idea the guy would bunt, you know, third hitter, two and nothing, and two out. And I just was going to pick it up and I heard, "Look out." And I fell on the ground, and Robinson threw him out by two steps. And as he ran around, it was a third out, he patted me on the butt, and he said, "Stay out of my way, old man. I'm good on that play." And I never—for three years, I never worried about any ball over there.

Eddie Mathews—what a ballplayer. He and Smitty—Mike Schmidt—were a lot alike. They both ran well. They both had good power. Eddie Mathews at the start was erratic in the field, but he became very good. Musial was marvelous. I guess Al Kaline was good. I didn't get to see him much, but I did see Willie Mays, Henry Aaron.

Spahnie—Warren Spahn—was such a pain to most people. He's always getting on everybody. I'm the only friend he's got, but I still think he's the best pitcher I ever saw. He was like Maddux and Glavine. He came up with little screwball pitches. And he never pitched against the Dodgers for about five, six years, you know. They had Gene Conley and Bob Buhl and all those right-handers, so Spahnie would pitch against Pittsburgh or the Giants. And he was a great hitter, great hitter, good base runner.

I didn't come up with anything as a way to loosen up before games. So a lot of games I'd start, I'd be out of kilter. I remember one game against the Cardinals, I was overthrowing. I felt good and I'd throw too hard, but I wouldn't let my wrist work. And then the ball would be straight, you know? We were playing at the Cardinals and the first hitter was a guy named Don Blasingame. He singles and Red Schoendienst doubles and Stan Musial triples, first three hitters. It was 2–0, a man on third. All of a sudden, it started raining like mad, so they put the tarp on and I went inside for about forty-five minutes and came back out. Musial didn't score, and I beat them, 3–2. If it hadn't started raining, they'd have gotten six runs.

I left the Phillies and went to the Yankees in 1962. Ralph Houk called me after a week with the Yankees. I hadn't started. I hadn't pitched. I'd been with them all spring, hadn't pitched well. And they had Al Downing and they had Jim Bouton and they had Rollie Sheldon and they had Whitey Ford and they had Ralph Terry. Who's the other kid, a right-hander—Bill Stafford. And they had Luis Arroyo pitching. They had a solid pitching staff. And I didn't pitch well in the spring. A week after the season starts, Ralph calls me. And he says, "This is the toughest thing I ever had to do in baseball." And I knew what it was. "We're going to release you." I said, "Fine." I got up and walked out. He said, "Well, wait, wait." And I said, "What do you mean, Ralph?" And he said, "I'd like to shake your hand." I said, "All right. You can shake my hand if you want." So we shook. I said, "I'll tell you something. Whitey might be better than me, but none of those other guys are." And I walked out. I called him the next day.

I said, "Ralph, I apologize." He said, "Well, I understand." I said, "I shouldn't have done that." But then I'm home. The team that calls me is the Tokyo Giants.

They called me, a guy from New York. "We would like to talk to you." I said, "No, I don't plan on going over to Japan." Nowadays, Mary would probably make me go. Cincinnati was in town playing against the Phillies. I was in Philadelphia, and I called Freddie Hutchinson. I said, "Freddie, I'd like to throw for you. I got released but I—" "Well," he said, "come on out to the ballpark. I'll meet you at four o'clock." I said, "Fine." So I went out early and, you know, got out there and got loose before four o'clock. He came out of the dugout. He said, "Are you ready to throw?" I said, "Yeah, Freddie." I threw five pitches. He said, "I'll give you ten straight starts. Is that fair enough?" I said, "Oh, that's more than fair, Freddie." He said, "Well, meet me in Pittsburgh now." He said, "Get squared away with DeWitt." He said, "He handles the contract. But ten straight starts, Robin, looking forward to it." I said, "Freddie, I appreciate it." So I called Bill DeWitt. DeWitt says, "Freddie wants you to join us." I said, "Yeah." DeWitt says, "Well, what do you want?" And I said, "Well, I'm making $33,500, Bill." "Oh, you're kidding me." He said nobody makes $30,000 on our team. I said, "Well, I got four kids in school. I need money to pay. That's what I make." And he said, "No, I'll give you fifteen." I said, "What?" He said, "Fifteen, take it or leave it." Then I said, "Well, I can't take that, Bill." "Well, sorry." So I didn't get my ten straight starts with the '62 Cincinnati Reds. I'd have liked to, though. So I went down to Balitmore and worked out. They signed me for $33,500. I stayed there three years.

I said to Lee MacPhail when I signed, "Lee, if ever you decide you don't want me to pitch, just send me home. I got four kids. I'm not trying to pick up a check." I said, "I just want to pitch or go home." "Fine. That's fair enough." So I pitched for him for three years.

I started six times against the Yankees and beat them four. I had one 1–1 game I left. Boog Powell had hit two home runs on a Friday night to beat the Yankees at home. Saturday, I'm pitching, and Boog comes up the first time and Bud Daley hits him. In the National League, that's just cut-and-dried. No big deal. The first guy up for them gets knocked out. I didn't like to get involved in it, but I'd get it over with quick. So I go out to pitch and look up and Roger Maris is the first batter. All right, Roger, and wham. He picks the bat up and he's coming at the mound with the bat in his hand. And I was always scared I was going to break my hand. I always said that was my summer job and I like it. If I break my hand, I'm in trouble. But I know I was going to take a poke at him. But Hobie Landrith jumped on his back and they wrestled and that kind of stuff and I didn't have to fight anybody. I always thank Hobie for that. But I looked up and Billy Hitchcock and Ralph Houk are going at each other. Luckily, they got them apart. That would have been a scrap. We won that game by the way. The next day, I'm out there, and they're out in back. Roger says, "Why me?" I said, "Roger, you're the first guy that showed up." I said, "If it had been Mickey, he'd have gone down. You can't knock our guys in the head and not expect to get thrown at." I didn't do that five times in my career, but every time it was when one of our guys got drilled.

In Baltimore, I had told Lee MacPhail, "Lee, if you're not going to pitch me, send me home." Well, Hank Bauer was our manager. All of a sudden, I started and won four straight complete games in 1965. I'm thirty-nine years old. I beat Washington, nine innings; Red Sox, nine innings; Yankees, nine innings; and Minnesota, nine innings. I lost in Detroit 4–3 when Al Kaline had a three-run homer. I went to Cleveland and got beat by one run by Sam McDowell, a nine-inning game. I pitched five complete games, and then I got hit hard. And then I got hit around a couple times. First thing you know, I'm in the bullpen. And so I sat out there, and I said to Harry Brecheen, just before the All-Star Game, "Harry, let me know what my story is because, you know, I got four kids at home. I'm sitting in the bullpen. Harry, check with Hank Bauer." So he came back after the All-Star

Game and said, "Well, you have the same spot you're in." I said, "All right. Thank you." So I called Lee. I said, "Lee, remember when—" So he said, "Well, come in and see me." So I went in to see him, and he had the release made out. He said, "I promised you, didn't I?" I said, "Yeah, and I thank you." So I got home and Paul Richards was in Houston, and he said, "I just saw you were released." I said, "Well, they're going to younger people, Paul." "Why don't you come pitch for me?" I said, "All righty." So I went down there and I pitched. I shut out the Phillies, I shut out the Pirates, I beat the Cubs. I'm 4-0 with Houston right out of the chute. And then I'm pitching against the Mets. I throw a curveball and feel something going on. I had bone chips. They took them out after that season. Well, I signed an interesting deal with Paul Richards. He asked, "What do you want?" And I said, "Well, I'm getting $33,500, Paul. Pay me the rest of the way, and if you want me back, give me a $10,000 bonus." "Well, that's fair enough," he said. So at the end of the year, he said, "Well, I want you back." And I said, "Well, that's good." He said, "I owe you $10,000." "Yeah." "Well, get those chips taken out." I said, "I'm thirty-nine, Paul. I don't think I ought to be having my arm cut on." And he said, "Well, if you have them cut out, you'll get a check for $10,000." So I went and had them cut out, and it never was quite the same. It never hurt, but it didn't ever have that pop to it.

I couldn't manage, because I didn't sleep at night after tough games. If I had to do that every day, I'd die. But I could have been a good general manager. I could be an outstanding person in the front office and work with young people and judge. I like baseball; I had great training with Sawyer and Perkins and watched guys, but I never even got a smell. I didn't have enough moxie to know how you do these things, to worm your way in there.

I wasn't very good at pushing myself onto people, you know? But the athletic director at the University of South Florida called me. He said, "My coach just left me." So I wasn't taking anybody's job. This was perfect for me. So I went down. I coached for eight years. I had one outstanding club. They were perfect. And then I told the boys, "If you can't play when you join me, you're not going to be able to play when you leave." And they go, "That's not a way to sell. That's not a recruiting tool." I'm not a teacher. I wasn't a teacher. I hear all these guys say they're teachers. I'm no teacher. I'm a collector. If you could play, buddy, I'll treat you nice and you will just handle it correctly. You got to really want to be out there. And if you're not, I don't know how I can threaten you to get you out there. But I did enjoy it. I enjoyed it because I had one good club. And it doesn't take much to satisfy me. Those kids could play.

I wish I could have been a part of baseball after I quit playing. I do regret that. I regret that, but I'm not blaming anybody but myself, because I wasn't a compromising person. And like I said, I wasn't a teacher. I was a collector. And most of your managers—most of your good people are collectors, you know what I mean? They get the best players, just like George Steinbrenner with the Yankees. But I don't have any regrets. I love to watch it. I watch it all the time. I manage all the teams. Nobody pays me.

I've seen people work hard all their lives, like my dad, and to be able to do what I was able to do and make a good living out of it, I'm so blessed. And I knew it at that time. I didn't wake up yesterday and find this out. I knew it all the time. I think most people realized that I could play, and I gave it everything I had. I have more respect for the guys I played against, and I think vice versa. That's something that you can't describe and you can't explain, but Henry Aaron can walk in here, there's a good feeling, you know what I mean? Stan Musial and the rest of them. You know, it's both ways. There is no bullshit. We teed it up and afterward, that was the end of it.

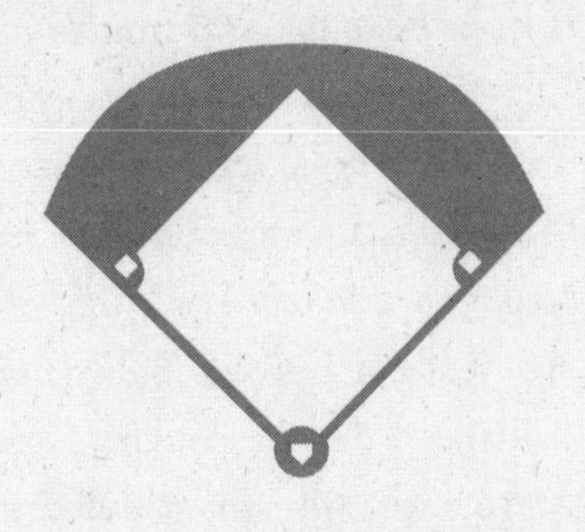

CARL ERSKINE

Carl Erskine was one of those rawboned, corn-fed kids from the Midwest who longed to compete. A scholastic star in a number of sports, the Anderson, Indiana, native chose to pursue baseball. After signing with the Brooklyn Dodgers in 1946, the right-handed hurler, nicknamed "Oisk" by his legions of fans, made his big-league debut two years later and was soon a star for the famed "Boys of Summer" team that would win six pennants in ten years.

Erskine's twelve-year big-league career, all spent with the Dodgers, included a 122-78 record, two no-hitters, a record-setting strikeout game in the World Series, and finally a World Championship with "Dem Bums" against the hated New York Yankees in 1955.

It was Game 3 of the 1953 Fall Classic in which Erskine established a new postseason record with his 14 strikeouts against the Yankees. Afterward, the Bronx Bombers were impressed. "Carl followed one pattern," Yankees shortstop Phil Rizzuto said. "He threw two good curves and then a bad one and he had us chasing that bad curve all day." Yankees outfielder Hank Bauer said Erskine had overpowered his team, adding, "Erskine showed me more stuff today than any pitcher had shown me throughout the season."

Erskine suffered from an injured right shoulder for most of his big-league career. When it looked like the arm trouble was catching up to the "Hoosier Hotshot" in 1957, longtime Dodgers captain Pee Wee Reese called him one of the best pitchers he had ever played behind, then said, "He told me he'd quit rather than hang around with his arm the way it is and I think he's the type of guy who would do it."

When the thirty-two-year-old Erskine finally retired midway through the 1959 campaign, convinced that he couldn't "give 100 percent anymore," Los Angeles Dodgers general manager Buzzie Bavasi said, "I feel badly about this; Carl is a fine boy. He needed only twenty-eight days to become eligible for the players' ten-year pension. But he said he'd just be fooling himself by staying with the club."

Early in Erskine's big-league career, a writer pinned the name "the Gentleman from Indiana" on him. After he retired, a columnist for the Los Angeles Times, *referring to the nickname, perfectly summed up the former pitching star's life up to that point: "Erskine's work with youth, his Sunday school teaching, his exemplary conduct on and off the field give him full right to a baseball copyright of that title."*

I was born in 1926, and baseball was king. There was no other sport. That was the sport. And the major-league level was so far away from me in Anderson, Indiana. It was all fantasy for me to think about players like Babe Ruth and Lou Gehrig. But my dad had a good arm, and he liked to throw. And my two older brothers—we would play catch in the summertime by the side of the house. People often ask me, "How did you ever become an overhand pitcher?" I used to throw straight over the top. I wasn't a big fellow, you know. My pitching weight was around 165, 168. I had a good live arm. But my brothers and my dad would play this game with me called Burnout.

You start nice and easy. Then each pitch gets a little faster and little harder. And so, when I'm nine or ten years old, they backed me

Carl Erskine

up against the barn. And I'm throwing back, and I'm throwing back. And I'm getting higher, and I'm getting higher. And the best velocity I could get was right over the top. So that was it. And my dad—even at the county fair—my dad loved to throw. He never got past the dunk tank. He always stopped to throw at the guy and knock him in the water. He must have spent his paycheck there, because we'd go back the second night, and the guy in the cage would say, "Oh, no. You're not back again tonight." *Ka-chew!* He'd take him down again.

I started my first game in a park league—no Little League in those days. And because I could throw, I pitched then. And as I recall, we didn't have a shortened distance even. We played the ninety-foot bases. So I started pitching actually at the regulation distance. I always could throw pretty good. Later, as I got into high school as a freshman, the coach—a very famous coach in my town known as Archie Chad—he sent for me. It scared me, because why would Mr. Chad, this famous coach, want to talk to me. I think I was fourteen. And he said, "Son, I want you out for baseball." He had seen me playing in this park league. And so right from the early years when my dad started throwing with me, somehow I had this magic feeling that I had something special and that I could—you know, other kids tried to throw as hard as I did. They didn't quite throw that hard. And so during my high school days I was beginning to feel like, "Well, I did have something special." So I had gone four years in high school. I think it was about my sophomore year, I played American Legion baseball. We played there in Chicago, and it was a tournament. I pitched against this big team from Hammond. They had a lot of big Polish boys, big swingers. I struck out a bunch of guys. I lost the game in the tenth inning, 1–0. But after the game, two men stopped me. They said, "Son, can we talk to you?" I didn't know who they were. They gave me a business card, and it had a Chicago Cubs logo on it. Oh, my golly. My heart was coming through my shirt. They said, "Well, son, we'd like to talk to you. Could we come down to your hometown and talk there with you and your father?" You have to remember, in those days, you had to be twenty-one to sign a contract. I was sixteen. That was my first contact with pro baseball, and what a thrill. Of course, my mother kept a scrapbook of the items along the way. And in the scrapbook is that letter. And it's dog-eared and dirty where I carried it in my pocket to show all my buddies. But that was my first real thrill of thinking about pro baseball. And, yet, I had a couple of years left in high school. But the Cubs offered me a contract to go to Hartford, Connecticut, which was Class A in those days. The system is different. Class A was like four notches up from the bottom. I couldn't do it. I couldn't quit school. In Indiana, I also played basketball. I was a little guard on the Anderson Indians. We played in a famous gym in Anderson, Indiana, called the Wigwam. Still there. I mean, a second version of it is there. But I stayed in high school and pitched. Then the Dodgers and those scouts began to come around. Well, I had a coach. His name was Charlie Cummings. And Mr. Cummings said to me one day—I probably was in my sophomore or junior year—he said, "Son, you're always going to pitch with a National League ball," even though it's during the war—World War II—and items were hard to get, baseballs were hard to get. Now, I didn't know what that meant. That didn't mean anything to me. But even he had a sense that this kid might do something. And so my last two years in high school, every game at home, I pitched with a National League baseball. Now, it took me a lot of years and looking back—and I became a coach myself eventually—to think how much a coach influences, or can, by just having the insights to encourage or to assist a young talent. So I was very fortunate to have those kinds of people around me.

My dad could throw this big roundhouse curve, and that just amazed me—just this big old sweeping curveball. But it's wintertime, and we're in the house—we're in the living room. My dad has this book that he's using to tell me about the rotation of a curveball. So I'm doing this, and he's showing me with this hand, and he's looking at the book illustration. And he said, "And, son, you grip the ball this way, and you get your arm like this." And he is so intent on what he's doing that he actually made an arm motion forward, and he released the ball. Well, the ball bounced once. It went through an open doorway into the dining room. And then, this crash. Then glass was falling for five minutes, it sounded like. And my mother yells, "Matt Erskine! What have you done?" It was her china cabinet. And my dad—he was always a lot of fun. He was a jokester anyway. He looks at me straight-faced—a little smirk on his face. He said, "Son, that's the best break I ever got on a curveball."

We were in the middle, sort of, in the middle of Indiana. We were closest to Cincinnati, so that's where we went if we went to games at all. The Cubs were, of course, a popular team as well. And, you know, it's interesting. I didn't have, like, a hero, one or two. Babe Ruth, of course, was a big name to everybody. He was the Paul Bunyan of the world in those days. But here was my take on baseball. I lived next door to a family who took the Chicago paper—*Chicago Tribune*. At first, we didn't take that paper. I don't believe we took any paper. But I cut their grass and did errands for them and so on. And I would ask them to save the paper for me. Not necessarily the whole paper, but the sports page and the . . . they had the comics in those days in color—the first ones I'd ever seen. And so they would sell me the color comics and the sports page. Now, in the summertime, the *Chicago Tribune* almost always had a baseball picture. I didn't care who it was. I didn't care which league it was from. It was baseball. I cut it out and put it in a scrapbook. And I'd read the caption under it, and I'd just be awestruck by seeing this major-league player. When we were in Cincinnati, we were by the parking lot of old Crosley Field, where the players used to come in. It was an iron gate, and the players would drive their fancy cars or come in taxis. And my dad got everyplace early. We were always early. We were there before the players got there. And we sat and watched the players arrive. And I'd stand at the little gate and just had my mouth open. Bucky Walters was a star pitcher in the late '30s, early '40s in Cincinnati. Paul Derringer. These guys were magic. I mean, and they were big. Paul Derringer was a huge man. And I could just never imagine me ever being in a major-league uniform when a guy like Paul Derringer was a big leaguer. But they were the magic names in those days. I didn't know many Cubs. My mother's favorite Cub was Stan Hack, who was a third baseman. She just thought he was fantastic. But I never got to see a lot of major-league games except in Cincinnati. And I'd stand at that iron gate when I was ten, twelve, fourteen years old. It was only about eight years later I was walking through that iron gate as a member of the Brooklyn Dodgers.

When I graduated, I had turned eigthteen, and so I was eligible for the draft and got drafted immediately. Just before I went into the service, the Dodgers, who had found me in high school, invited me and my catcher buddy, Jack Rector, who was a good prospect, to New York as a graduation present. Stan Feezle was the scout who followed me from Indianapolis. But he was a Dodger scout. And he came over and gave us first-class tickets to New York, which meant the Pullman on a train. We were going to stay in a New York hotel and work out with the Dodgers for a week. Wow! That was something. That was 1945. I graduated in 1945. Anyway, I worked out with the Dodgers for a week, and then I was called in for service right after that.

I was in the Navy. I went to boot camp. And when I was in boot camp, the bombs were dropped in Japan—in Hiroshima and Nagasaki—and the war, then, took a fast turn. I went to the Boston Navy Yard. While I was in the Navy yard, I was asked to play on the Navy team. Lou Sorge happened to be a bird dog for a scout for the Braves, who at that time were in Boston. He saw me and said, "Son, I want you to come back." Mr. Sorge took me in one day and they sat me in an office. And Mr. Sorge said to the owners of the Braves, "Carl would like to play pro baseball." We hadn't had any discussion about this. He said, "Carl would like to play pro baseball." And then the discussion went along, and he said, "You know, there's a bonus." I didn't know anything about a bonus. I'd never discussed that. So they said, "How much is he thinking about?" "Twenty-five hundred dollars." Well, in those years, there were no cash bonuses. Players didn't get signed with bonuses. It was unheard of. If you were a good player and got signed, you'd get a set of Grand Slam golf clubs made by Louisville Slugger, the bat manufacturer. If you were a real prospect—today, you'd say a top draft choice—you get a car. You get a Chevrolet or a Ford. Seven, eight hundred dollars, they cost. That was the best you could get as a bonus.

Well, they agreed to the $2,500. But I didn't want to sign with the Braves. The Dodgers had already got the hook in me. I wanted to play for the Dodgers. So I called Branch Rickey. And I said, "Mr. Rickey, I'm getting pushed real hard." He said, "Don't do anything." Mr. Rickey intervened, and he brought my parents to Boston, and I signed the night before the 1946 All-Star Game. I signed in the Kenmore Hotel in Mr. Rickey's suite. And that's how I signed into pro baseball.

• • •

Coaches in majors have a huge influence. The intimacy you had with a coach you're involved with is how your character is being developed. Are you putting values in the right place? I think a coach has the most influence there. And some of my coaches—good lifestyles, what you drank, what you ate, what you avoided was important. I behaved, and to this day I know that that's the right way to go to take care of yourself. You've been given a healthy body, a gift of athletic ability.

I was with Robin Roberts one time years later for the Fellowship of Christian Athletes. We were supposed to speak at a high school. And I didn't know what to say. You talk about your spiritual life, and I didn't know how to go about that. And Robin was first. And he said something very profound. I thought it was amazing. It helped me. It still does. Robin said to these kids—he said, "You know I could throw hard when I was a kid. I had a good arm, and I didn't know why. I'd just throw it, and they would go. And as I kept doing it, I kept thinking, 'Gee, I've got something these other kids don't have.' Now, I really think that if God gave me the ability to throw a baseball, God should have something to say about how I use it." Just a strong statement of simple faith and simple belief. And that helped me to this day—although I fought Roberts in some head-on battles there.

There were no agents speaking for me in those days. My dad couldn't help me negotiate. He was a factory worker out in little Anderson, Indiana, and a farm boy. Mr. Rickey was also a farm boy. And he had this eloquence about him. He always had this homespun feeling and could relate. And so he was a charmer. But he turned to me, and he said, "Son, I know the Braves have offered you some money. I don't know how much. But how much do you want?" And so very bravely, I said to Mr. Rickey, "Mr. Rickey, how would $3,000 be?" Sounds funny, doesn't it? But you know what? My dad didn't make $3,000 working his whole year. That was a lot of money. Now, Mr. Rickey knew, I think, that the Braves had offered me $2,500. So Mr. Rickey, who was very tight with the money, Mr. Rickey said, "Well, son, why

Branch Rickey

don't we just make it $3,500?" After I fell through the chair, I couldn't believe it. So I got the bonus of $3,500.

I got discharged from the Navy a few weeks later and reported to Danville, Illinois, in the Three-I League—Indiana, Iowa, and Illinois. And at the end of the season, Happy Chandler, who was the commissioner of baseball, was in Cincinnati—his office—and called me. He said, "I want you and your dad in my office next Monday at ten o'clock." Well, we didn't know what for or anything. So my dad had to lay off work. Now, that was not an easy thing. So we go to Cincinnati, and Commissioner Chandler says to me and my dad, "I'm going to declare you a free agent because the Dodgers violated my directive. They could not sign a player who was still under contract to the United States military. They signed you before you discharged. And the Braves have blown the whistle." So now, Mr. Rickey is on the phone. What happens to my $3,500? And Commissioner Chandler says, "Because there was some ambiguities in my memo, normally the violating club is banned from re-signing you. But in this case, I'm going to allow you to sign back with the Dodgers or anybody else you want to sign with." Well, I did not want to sign with anybody else, although I had offers from the Red Sox, the Phillies, the Cubs—I didn't even look at those offers. But I did say to Mr. Rickey later when we got out of the office and I'm now a free agent—I did say to Mr. Rickey when he asked me, I said, "If you'll give me another $5,000, I'll re-sign with the Dodgers." He gave me $5,000.

Years later, I was interviewed by Dizzy Dean after a no-hitter. I pitched two no-hitters, and Dean was the broadcaster for me. Dizzy Dean, who had pitched earlier in the Cardinal organization for Mr. Rickey, asked me who signed me. And I said, "Branch Rickey." "Oh, cheapest man in the world," he said. "I bet he starved you probably, like he starved me." And I said, "Actually, Mr. Rickey gave me two bonuses." When I told him that, he turned to the TV camera and he said, "Folks, this young man deserves to be in the Hall of Fame. Not because he pitched two no-hitters. He got two bonuses from Branch Rickey."

In the minor leagues, I was pitching against Waterloo, Iowa, which was a White Sox farm team. Their manager was Jack Onslow. At the end of the season, Jack Onslow, the opposing manager—he had no interest in me. I was in the Dodger organization; he was in the American League. But he was a good man. Saw this kid; he was doing something wrong. And he called me to the side, and he said, "Son, we hit some good pitches off you this year, and I'm sure you didn't know why. But we were calling your pitches. We could see every pitch you threw—if it was going to be a fastball or a curve. We knew that. You're telegraphing your curveball. And in doing so, if you go to a higher level, which you obviously will—you've won 20 ball games in this league. You're obviously going to go up to a higher level. You're going to be pitching against better hitters. That's going to be a real problem for you. Now, here's what you're doing wrong."

A curveball has to be rotated, and you have to get your hand in a little different position for the curveball than the fastball. And in my case, I was not covering it. I had my glove on top of the ball, and I was gripping the ball with my thumb underneath. My curve was more like a slider, really. It was more of a quick snap than it was a bigger break. My dad had attempted to teach me this bigger rotating break. That winter, after I had pitched that season and after this incident with Onslow, Mr. Rickey sent me to Havana, Cuba, along with a few other minor leaguers who played in this league in Havana. They were mostly Cuban players, but there were a few Americans there. My manager was Lefty Gomez, who was a former great Yankee pitcher. Lefty, for all of his charm and for all of his ability, was not much of a teacher. He didn't have the ability to impart all the good stuff he could do. So I didn't get a lot of help from Lefty on my curveball. So I kind of had to be self-taught to change what I was doing. It was difficult, because I had to change what I was doing on the job—it wasn't like I had half a season to work on it. I'm now pitching against some really good players. I would say that Cuban League was at least Double A—maybe Triple A. And some of the Latin players that came out of that league went to the big leagues. So I pitched against some good hitters down there. But I'm trying to learn this new grip for my curveball. And I worked on it all winter. And when I got through that season—I think I won nine games in that league that winter and pitched a lot of innings—I came back to spring training. And I was pitching in a spring training game. And the pitching coaches saw this new curveball of mine, and they all jumped right straight up and ran out and said, "Where did you get that? You didn't have that last year." Well, I had worked on it. And during the winter of that season, I had developed this good hard overhand curveball, which was what my dad was trying to teach me back there in that living room.

Mr. Rickey was excellent at having sessions—it was like a baseball college. You'd work out in the daytime. You do your drills. You'd play inter-squad games at night. And you would hear lectures about some phase of baseball. And it was in one of those lectures, it was taught how you really rotate the curveball off of the second finger.

You get more full rotation if you get it off the second finger. Now, some pitchers throw balls in all kinds of ways to make it work. But if you're starting with a youngster or even a young player prospect and he doesn't have a good curveball, then the right way to teach it is off the second finger for good full rotation. Well, that's what I did. I kind of self-taught myself after I learned the Dodger system thoroughly—the four seam. There's four seams to a baseball. And when you rotate four, you get more bite. You get more, umph—you get more break. So that pitch and that cue by Jack Onslow—that thoughtful man who helped this kid he didn't even know on the other team—made the difference in me being a struggling minor-league pitcher. By the half of the season that year, '48, I had gone to Forth Worth, Double A, won fifteen games by July, and was called to the Dodgers. Now, the lesson in my life from that is one of disappointment. I never thanked Jack Onslow.

In the spring of '48, I was selected to pitch one day against the real Dodgers, who came to play against us, their minor-league team at Forth Worth, Texas. I pitched about half the game and pitched well. The game was over, and I was in the dugout—the Fort Worth dugout. And a voice said, "Where's Erskine?" And a guy said, "Hey, Carl." And I said, "Yeah?" And I saw it was Jackie Robinson, who was in his second year of professional major-league baseball. Jackie Robinson had come across from the Dodger dugout. I didn't know anybody on the big club. I knew their names: Pee Wee Reese, Gil Hodges, Duke Snider, Roy Campanella—I mean, these were the names, but I didn't know anybody. It was Jackie Robinson. And he came and he shook my hand. And he said, "Son, I hit against you twice today. You're not going to be in this league very long. You're going to be with the Dodgers soon." Well, by mid-July, I had won fifteen games at Fort Worth. I was called to the Dodgers. And when I went in the locker room early to get a locker, I was there by myself. When the regular Dodger bus came and the guys were coming in,

Jackie was the first guy to my locker. He shook my hand, again, and he says, "I told you, you couldn't miss."

I grew up in a mixed neighborhood with a lot of black families, respected a lot of black families. But Indiana—not a southern state—was still segregated. Our train station still had separate restrooms, separate drinking fountains. My buddy Johnny Wilson was black, a poor kid. We grew up together from elementary school all the way through high school—played sports together. But when I wanted to go to the Y, because I wanted to swim or something, Johnny couldn't go, because the YMCA didn't have any black memberships or black services at all. So it was a time—it's hard to go back and really help people understand what it was like, that black people were just not accepted in the same way. They just didn't have the same open privileges. The Navy was segregated.

I had a son who was born in 1960. In those days, the term was mongoloid. I have three children. They're healthy kids. Jimmy was born my first year out of baseball. And the hospital—boy, I'm telling you the whispers just went through there like wildfire. The Erskine baby was mongoloid. Down syndrome is the term now that we use—a softer medical term. But that was a fearful term. And that really reflected society's acceptance of people who were different like my son, Jimmy. And so Jimmy was born into a society that wasn't any more prepared to accept him than it had been to accept Jackie.

That's what parents of handicapped children and handicapped family members say. Don't shut us out. Accept us. We want to be a part. And that's what's happened. In Jimmy's case, he went to school. He went to the Special Olympics. And when he wins a medal in the Special Olympics—a gold medal—it's interesting. I think Jackie had something to do with that. There's a momentum in life and in sports. And I think Jackie kicked off a momentum of change that had a sweeping effect. When Jimmy came along, and I look back at the linkage of that, I feel strongly that these two experiences were two of the greatest social changes in that century, that people know when I take Jimmy on the airplane, to spring training camp, a baseball camp, Jimmy is accepted. Jimmy is loved. He loves you right back. That's a beautiful change in how—now, people say to my wife, Betty and me, "Oh, you've done a wonderful job with Jimmy." He does great. He's very limited even to this day. I turn it around, and I say, "Look. We would have helped him in any way. Society changed. That was the change. That was the significance of what happened." Jimmy now works at a restaurant. He's been there several years. He gets a paycheck. His whole life has been lifted by being accepted. And so in simple terms, we went from a society—in Jackie's case—from rejection to inclusion. In Jimmy's case, from a spectator to a participant.

I was called to the Dodgers the middle of the '48 season. I joined them in Pittsburgh. Their stadium at that time was Forbes Field. I went there. Found my locker early before the rest of the guys came. And as I had mentioned earlier, Jackie was the first one to my locker to shake my hand. I was in the bullpen that day, and the Dodgers used a couple or three different pitchers. Late in the game, they called the bullpen to get me up and get ready. I came in the game two runs behind, and I pitched a couple of innings. Nothing sensational. I walked the first guy faced. George Shuba, a left fielder who was a very fine hitter, but he was a little shaky with the glove, was playing for us. Ralph Kiner, the big home-run hitter in those days for the Pirates—he hits a sinking line drive off me to left field. And Shuba makes a shoestring catch, then he doubled Johnny Hopp off first base. I get out of the inning. And then, we get some runs, and I get the win. The first day in the big leagues, I got my first win. Well, years pass, I saw Shuba at some function, and I thanked him for making that great catch in left field off Kiner to get me my first win. And Shuba, he was quite a jokester anyway, he says, "Yeah. I remember that catch. I trapped the ball." I don't know if he did or not. Well, my mom and dad drove from Anderson, Indiana—it must be four hundred miles—they drove breakneck to get to Pittsburgh to see their son wear his uniform for the first day. Burt Shotton, who had replaced Leo Durocher as manager, came to my locker after the game and says, "Well, son, I don't how you could have broke in the big leagues any better than that."

I've said that standing on the mound for that team was just in itself the thrill of my life. Roy Campanella, my catcher; Gil Hodges at first base; Jackie Robinson at second; Pee Wee at short; Billy Cox at third. Duke Snider was my roommate for eleven seasons. Shuba was in left and Carl Furillo was at the other outfield position. You know, it was such a fantastic feeling. How lucky I was to be pitching for this team. That team had a whole infield full of managers. I mean, Campy would have been the first black manager—no question—if he hadn't had the auto accident.

The first year I was there, we had Joe Hatten, who was a left-hander. Ralph Branca had already been a 21-game winner in '47, I guess, at age twenty-one. There was Jack Banta, a hard-throwing right-hander. Rex Barney was a hard thrower. Rex was dominant when he could get the ball over. He just absolutely was totally a dominant pitcher. But that pitching staff was always overshadowed by the great offensive team the Dodgers were. And mostly overlooked, too, is the fact that that team was a very good defensive team. We led the league almost every year in double plays. The pitching staff led the league almost every year in strikeouts. I bet you the average age of that pitching staff was probably twenty-two years old or something. We were very young. You got to remember it was after the war—World War II—and Mr. Rickey was rebuilding the organization, as all teams were. And so youth was accelerated. And that's why I bounced to the big leagues as fast as I did.

Baseball in those years had what was called a reserve clause. That was a clause that basically said that if you signed with an organization, then that organization had your rights forever. No time limit. You didn't sign a contract with an organization for a term. It was lifelong. And that was contested in the courts and so on. Maybe it was necessary in those early years to get baseball established. But the reserve clause prevented you from going to any other team unless the club itself traded you or sold you. Or, of course, they could release you.

What was interesting about the contract—nobody ever read it. No player ever read it. There was one line that was blank in it, and that's where your salary was typed. But all the details and the various clauses, you didn't look at it. You signed it.

The individual player really negotiated his own contract. And if you didn't agree, you became what was known in those days as a holdout. That meant that you didn't want to sign, and so the club said, "Well, we can't use you." So what do you do? You couldn't sign with another team, so you went home. So most players were never holdouts, because you negotiate for something to play for, but the club owns you. And then, the other thing was you played one year at a time. Your contract had to be renewed annually. And so you didn't have any security. Let's say you signed a contract for $10,000 for the year. The contract read that the club was only obligated to pay you 30 days and your transportation home if they released you. You really didn't have any rights.

In those days, if you could wear a major-league uniform, you almost didn't care what you got paid. And I think the clubs used that. I think an obvious thing to say was "You mean you were paid and you get to play in the big leagues?" It was such an honor. It was such a unique experience to be called a major leaguer. But the pay was somewhat incidental. And yet, people said to me when the money got real big back in the '90s and TV started pumping in huge amounts of money and players' salaries went high—they said, "Don't you wish you were playing in these days? Because if you had good years like you had, you'd be making big, big, big money." And I said, "Well, that's true. However, I look the other way. We were better off by far than the early players in the early 1900s—the '20s and '30s. They set the stage for the era that we played in. And they didn't make anything. They didn't have pensions. They had no security.

I'm not at all bothered by the big salaries that came later. I feel like we kind of set the stage for that era."

The owners had finally agreed to a minimum salary for all players in the big leagues. Five thousand dollars was the minimum. Now, how do you relate to that. Well, compared to my dad's salary, it's probably double what he could have made working in a factory. But when I got to Brooklyn, I didn't have a lot of money and I couldn't afford to stay in a hotel. So I asked, "Where's the YMCA in Brooklyn?" So I took my little bag and I hiked over to the YMCA in Brooklyn, and I got me a room. It was a corner room on the seventh floor. It had a cot and a bare desk and a wastebasket. And the shower was down the hall, and the pay telephone was down the hall. Well, I won my first game. And after I won in Pittsburgh, we came back to Brooklyn. And I won another game against the Cardinals. So I'm 2-0, and I called home on the phone down the hall to tell my mother and dad. Then I got my first start against the Cubs. Pitched a complete game. Now, I'm 3-0. I called home. I won four. I called home. I was 5-0, and all that time I stayed at the Y. I always said later when I got established and lived in Bay Ridge and I was in a slump, I was tempted to go back and check in at the Y again. But we didn't have a lot of money, and we didn't make a lot of money. But, you know, I didn't miss any meals and raised my family. And I felt the richness of experience. The team I played for—the era I played New York with three teams, and played in the biggest city in the world, the brightest stage in the world. Everybody's career was enhanced, I think, in those days if you could do it in New York.

But I want to make a point here about Mr. Rickey. Something he did was brilliant and was necessary. He could have signed Larry Doby, the second black player in the big leagues. He could have signed him, and he would have been our third outfielder. Think of that. In those years, you know, we had trouble beating the Yankees. If we had had Doby in the outfield, oh, boy. But what did Mr. Rickey do? He did the wisest thing. He said, "The American League is not integrated. Now, it would be a very bad scene to have only one of the two major leagues integrated."

Dan Bankhead was the first black pitcher. And ironically, Mr. Rickey told me, "I've got one spot left on the roster for a right-hand pitcher. And I've got two people, and only one of them very good at it. And that's either you or Bankhead." So I had to earn my spot by beating out Bankhead, which I eventually did.

Campanella? If you shook off Campanella, buddy, you better have had a good reason. Because Roy was older, more experienced. He'd been in the Negro League. He'd been in Mexico, South America. He played a lot of winter ball. And so he was very experienced. And he was in the game. He had a great savvy about baseball and calling pitches. And so he was a great help to a young staff.

People miss the fact that Campy was just an all-around baseball man. You wouldn't expect him to be a base stealer or a good base runner. He was very good on the bases. Of course, you didn't watch him close, because nobody expected him to run. But he'd catch a catcher that was careless or just kind of lackadaisical throwing the ball back or whatever. Campy would steal. He'd pick his time. And he always scored from second on a base hit. He just had good instincts. I think the guys that played with Campanella would all agree he would have been the first black manager in baseball had he not had that tragic car accident late in his career. Baseball history doesn't show this maybe, but he always contended that he was, in fact, the first black manager. Because in Nashua, New Hampshire, Walter Alston was the manager. And after he had Campy on the team a while, he said, "Look, if I get thrown out in a ball game, you take over." And Roy says, "I did that twice. So I was the first black manager in professional ball."

When you play in a league that has eight teams, you're facing the other seven teams each 22 times in a 154-game schedule. So we faced every team 22 times—11 at home, 11 on the road. What that meant was you faced the same batters, the same opposition, many, many, many times. So the catcher and the pitcher—yes—you had the fastball, curveball, off speed, maybe a slider, and you had no surprises for the hitters. The hitters had no surprises. You've seen them hit many times. So what happens, it becomes a mind game.

The Cardinals had a fine pitcher named Howie Pollet. A class act. I beat the Cardinals my second win in the big leagues. And I beat Howie Pollet, a left-hander. And he waited for me at Ebbets Field after the game. I was a rookie. This was only my second win. He waited for me after the game in the runway as the clubhouses came out. He was the losing pitcher. He waited to congratulate me. He said, "I like the way you throw. I think you're going to be here a long time." He was a class act. And I think he identified with me because he had a unique pitch—a straight change. It was very deceptive. Looked like a fastball, but it wasn't. And I could throw that pitch. They taught it to me in the Dodger system, and I picked it up quick. So if you throw that fastball a little more, then you throw the same pitch, the same motion, the same rotation, and it's about 86 miles per hour or something, you got him. Well, I threw that pitch in that game, and I think Pollet identified with that. Very few pitchers could throw that pitch. I think that's why he said, "I think you're going to win some games." I threw that pitch in Japan. We played a tour in Japan one time. And Pee Wee Reese came over to me and wanted to rap after I pitched a couple of games. And he said, "Carl, why don't you throw your straight change over here? I don't see you throwing that." And I said, "Well, these guys are kind of slack and hit off their front foot, and, you know, they're not free swingers." He said, "You could throw your pitch to anybody." Well, I threw that pitch to the Tokyo Giants one day, and they were mystified. And so they had me make a film showing how I threw my change. But now the pitching techniques have changed a lot, and a lot of people throw off-speed pitches. But in our era, it was really power—power pitching and big curveballs. It has changed over the years to now, the split finger—this and that—is a new pitch. The velocity cut fastballs. You don't see very many pitchers with real finesse like Howie Pollet.

Three New York teams, but the Yankees were in the American League. So the Giants in the National League and the Dodgers in the National League faced each other twenty-two times a season, but it was all in the city. It was all in the same city. Well, I never met a family in New York that wasn't split at least two ways, but many times, three ways. So the rivalry with the Giants was just fierce. And your manhood was on the line the day you played the Giants. It didn't matter what the standings were. It was just head-to-head with those rivals across town. And people on the street in Brooklyn, I'm sure, and I'm sure up in Manhattan, Giant fans, were the same way. That day, the world almost stopped when the Giants and the Dodgers were going to face each other. Before my time even; this rivalry had been there when I joined them. Well, of course, they had a respectable team.

By the time I got to the big leagues, Durocher had just been acquired by the Giants as their manager. And that rivalry was notched up with Leo having been a Brooklyn manager, but now was with the Giants. Somehow, that put even more energy in this rivalry. Snider, who was my roommate—the Giants colors were orange and black—Duke made a comment that we hated the Giants and those colors so much that we didn't even like Halloween.

They had, of course, Sal Maglie. I always admired Maglie. As a kid pitcher—you had to learn as a pitcher—to kind of take charge. You had to kind of have a mentality that "I'm in charge of this ball game." If you're out there on the back of your heels, and you're just kind of like you're intimidated, it reaches your whole ball club—your defense and everything. The team picks up on your vibes out there or something. Well, Maglie—and Allie Reynolds was the same way with the Yankees—when he walked out on the mound, you knew who was in charge. No question. And I admired that in Maglie, al-

Sal Maglie

though we hated him for his ability to get us out. He was a one-pitch pitcher. But he had the sharpest, latest-breaking curveball I ever saw. It would come right up under your arm, almost, and "shoom" across the plate for a strike. Because he was a one-pitch pitcher, he threw at hitters a lot. He had to keep guys pushed back, because he's breaking that ball away all the time.

When Willie Mays came, it transformed that team. Mays was this refreshing talent. Another kid like Campy. He played like a little kid. He was having fun. I didn't see Babe Ruth play, but they always said Ruth had great instincts and never threw to a wrong base. He always did the right thing on the bases. Mays was that way. He was not experienced. You know, Leo was like his second father. Leo took him under his wing and tried to help him mature as a player. But Willie was so refreshing, because he played wide open all the time. He made catches and throws because of his just unbreakable talent. And the thing that I liked about Willie is that he was durable. He hardly ever missed a lineup. If you think about Willie, you can hardly find times when he got hurt. He was just always in the lineup. So that was the key—the pitching of the Giants and Mays—that was their strength.

In the '49 World Series, we walk into Yankee Stadium to play the first game. We're all awestruck, anyway. A bunch of kids going into Yankee Stadium, the house that Ruth built and the baseball shrine and all that. The Yankees changed clubhouses. The Yankee clubhouse used to be on the third-base side. And they remodeled, and in doing so, they built a very luxurious clubhouse for the Yankees over on the first-base side. And the visitors, then, went into the old Yankee clubhouse. So we go in the clubhouse, and they hadn't quite moved all the stuff out of the Yankee clubhouse and put it over in the new Yankee clubhouse. So still remaining in our clubhouse were two lockers with the uniforms hanging in them—Babe Ruth and Lou Gehrig. We got beat in five games.

I have to mention that Newcombe pitched an outstanding game the opening game. He was a rookie. And then, the bottom of the ninth, Tommy Henrich hit a pitch off of Newcombe you couldn't believe. The ball was low inside. Not in the strike zone. But Henrich—a very fine hitter—he hit a ball right off his shoe tops in the lower deck of Yankee Stadium to beat him 1–0. And Newcombe never won a World Series game. I don't know. He was snakebit in the Series. He won 20 games or more in the regular season. He had trouble in the Series. But the Yankees with DiMaggio—of course, Bobby Brown was there at that time. Phil Rizzuto, Johnny Mize.

The pitching staff was what was difficult for the Dodgers. We had a right-hand-hitting power club. The matchup with the Yankees in their favor was two of the best right-handed pitchers maybe of any era, Vic Raschi and Allie Reynolds. The Big Chief—Reynolds—he threw hard, and they were just . . . they were a perfect match for a right-hand-hitting lineup. And so we had trouble with them. Then they had the contrast pitcher, Eddie Lopat, who was a soft-toss left-hander. What a combination. In the second game of that Series, the only game we won, there was a matchup between

Preacher Roe, our left-hander—Preacher Roe, a country boy from Arkansas—and Eddie Lopat. And it was a 1–0 game. Back-to-back 1–0 World Series games.

I knew Joe DiMaggio better after our playing days, because he and I had some business interests that took us together in banking. He represented the Bowery Savings Bank in New York. And when I got back to Indiana, I found a career in banking. So he and I used to do some things together, then. So I got to know Joe as a friend. But as a player, it was my second year. And I don't remember which game—maybe the fifth game—I was called in to relieve. And I didn't realize who was at the plate when they called me in. It was Joe DiMaggio. Naturally, I was a little nervous coming into my first World Series. I threw Joe a fastball, kind of up in the strike zone. And he hit a towering fly ball to shortstop. And Reese or Robinson, I'm not sure which, stood there forever and forever and forever. He finally caught it. That's the only time I actually faced DiMaggio. But he was near the end of his career.

The Yankee mystique or whatever that is, it was probably present in the '49 Series. We faced them five times in the World Series during my career. And in the other Series, there was no intimidation. We had an outstanding team. Just take position for position. So we didn't have any feeling of being inferior playing the Yankees, but we just had trouble winning the seventh game. We'd go six or seven games.

In the '52 World Series, I was scheduled to pitch a fifth game in Yankee Stadium. Raschi had beat me in the second game. Joe Black opened the Series as a rookie. He had been a relief pitcher all year. Well, he won 15 games, but he saved about 25 games or something. But anyway, the second game, Raschi beat me. And then we go to Yankee Stadium, and I'm scheduled to pitch the fifth game. So I go to the ballpark, and there was a lot of telegrams on my stool at Yankee Stadium, so I read all these telegrams. And there was one from a guy in Texas. He said, "Good luck in the fifth game in the World Series on this fifth day of October. And congratulations on your fifth wedding anniversary." I said, "What? That's right." Five, five, five. So Red Barber was walking up and down the locker room talking to the guys and getting little tidbits for the booth as a broadcaster. And he said, "Yeah. That's an interesting wire. Can I take it up to the booth with me? That's an interesting thing." So I gave it to him and forgot about it. I went out and did my warm-ups, got ready, started the ball game, and was pitching very well. I had a 4–0 lead in the fifth inning. Now, the Yankees had ways to score that you couldn't believe; they were a great team. So they got two of the cheapest scores off of me in the fifth inning. But that brought Mize up with two men on. Johnny Mize. He was a good hitter. He hit a three-run home run. Five runs in the fifth. What was happening? Now, Charlie Dressen charged the mound, and I'm gone. I mean, I'm gone. He took the ball away from me, and he talked to me, but he left me in the game. I said, "Well, he's going to pinch-hit for me." So I got Berra out at the end of the inning, and then I was in the dugout, and Dressen said, "You hit. You're the hitter. Get up there." He left me in the game. So after the five runs in the fifth, we tied it in the seventh, and we won it in the eleventh. I stayed in the game all eleven innings. And from the time that Mize hit the home run, I got the next nineteen in a row through the bottom of the eleventh. Berra struck out to end the game, and we won 6–5. Well, Vin Scully, who was one of the young announcers working with Red Barber, was upstairs in the booth. And he told me later—he said, "Carl, I was watching for any fives. You had the fifth game, the fifth day, the fifth anniversary, five runs in the fifth." He said, "I was looking for any fives in this crazy ball game." And he said, "Carl, so help me, when you struck Berra out to end the game, I looked at the stadium clock. It was five minutes past 5:00."

But '55, interesting things happened in there. A young pitcher, Johnny Podres, won a game. A rookie pitcher, Roger Craig, won a game. Clem Labine finished the game I started and picked up the win in it. And then Podres won a second game. Johnny was a good young pitcher, but he was 9-10 during the regular season that year.

And we won the pennant by at least thirteen games. And so Johnny had had just a mediocre season. But that week, he was our bread and butter. And, of course, the prior years against Yankees, we were dealing with Reynolds, Raschi, Lopat, and Ford. Whitey Ford had come along.

In my era, there was no organized players organization—no union. But each club had a representative who could go to the winter meetings. And if there was some concerns on the players' side, we were given the privilege to go and have a meeting with the owners. Well, the discussion was normally about mundane things. It was travel and getaway days or something. We didn't have a lot of heavy issues. There was no real pension in baseball. There had been a token pension, kind of, structured, but it was just nothing. I mean, you had to play five years to get anything, and then you got $50 a month at age sixty-five. I mean, come on. So it was really nothing. And then, during that era, television began to make its entry. And I think 1950 was when the first contract was ever signed with a network to give the rights to air the World Series and the All-Star Game—there were no play-offs, except for ties.

We couldn't pay for a pension for players very well when the franchise was not making any money. The St. Louis Browns and some of those old clubs weren't making any money. Even the clubs that were making money in those days, the benchmark was to draw a million paid. Well, a million-paid club could make some money. But payrolls were significantly smaller, and the revenue streams weren't big. So clubs couldn't take money out of an operating budget and fund any kind of reasonable pension until the magic of television. And in 1950—this is my recall, now—1950 was the first year that the rights to a World Series and the All-Star Game were sold. The network paid $6 million for five years. A. B. "Happy" Chandler was the commissioner, and he negotiated that year. That was the first new money that was coming into baseball from TV. So he talked to the player representatives and said, "Look. Go to the owners and lay a plan on the owners to increase or to upgrade a reasonable pension plan with these newfound revenues. And we'll take it out of the budgets—the newfound money." Well, we had a strong representation of the clubs. Stan Musial was a rep. There was Ralph Kiner, in the National League, Ted Kluszewski, Robin Roberts. We had a formidable group of good players, but also guys that could think. In the American League, we had Allie Reynolds, who kind of led the pack, and Eddie Yost. Dominic DiMaggio. Those were all quality players. So there was a degree of respect around the table which hadn't existed earlier. The owners kind of looked down their noses—"You guys are ballplayers; we run the business." But this time, we were beginning to get some respect. The player reps were able to negotiate a 60-40 split of the newfound revenues. Now, a million-two a year was what that broke down to—$6 million in five years. So 60 percent was like $720,000 a year. So that much new money was used to restructure what in later years became one of the best pension plans—not only in sports, but in any industry.

We had hit on the notion that we'd go back a decade. We'd try to do it in decades. The thinking was to try to go back and pick up as many older players, who, by then, were out of baseball, but who had, again, set the stage for us. So the framework was to go back a decade to pick up. Well, that was established. And then, each five years, at the new contract, the bid went up and up, because TV got bigger and bigger and more sets and more exposure. That money got so big in time that the owners called a halt to the 60 percent and began to fund the pensions at a fixed amount from the All-Star Game and World Series. But in my era, and then in my retirement years, I benefited substantially by a pension plan which baseball did not have before. When the big money really hit baseball, and the players were making into the multimillion-dollar contracts, without having to do it contractually or by law or anything, they went back and picked up a lot of the older players, increased their pensions, and gave them a dignified amount of money to live on. And I credit the players in the

'90s and the early 2000s with being sensitive to the players of the past to give them a dignified amount to live on.

In 1951, we made a trade in Chicago—four for four—to pick up Andy Pafko, who was a key to our outfield. That gave us a significant advantage to have a strong outfield. We had had a lot of left fielders but never one at the caliber of a Duke Snider in center and Carl Furillo in right. So left field was always up from grabs. So we traded and got Pafko.

Now, we just took off. And we were twelve—thirteen—in fact, in August, we had a thirteen-and-a-half game lead. And we were just breezing with no problem. From the end of August through the next month, the Giants began to win, and they closed the gap to ten games. No problem. Down to nine, eight games. No problem. But we just kept feeling them coming and coming. And we weren't playing bad, but we were playing probably .500 baseball, and they were playing at some clip like you couldn't believe. Until finally on the final day—it was a Sunday—in Philadelphia, we look on the scoreboard, and the Giants have won. And if we lose, we're going to lose the pennant. But fortunately, Jackie Robinson makes an outstanding play. Jackie makes a diving catch behind second base to save the inning and keep us alive. And then, in the fourteenth inning, Jackie hits an upper-deck home run in what was called Shibe Field or Connie Mack Stadium at that time to win the game for us and tie the Giants. We struggled even to tie the Giants. But now, we're tied.

In those days, the rule for a tie in the National League was a two-out-of-three play-off. The American League was sudden death—one game. So we played the first game. Now, here's a controversial matter that has been discussed back and forth over many years. The flip of the coin gave Charlie Dressen, our manager, the choice of whether we opened at home and played one game there or opened in the Polo Grounds and played one game, and then, the next two games would be played back at Ebbets Field. Dressen won the flip, and he elected to play the first game at Ebbets Field, which meant the next two games were going to be played—if needed—in the Polo Grounds.

Some people think that was a bad mistake not to have two games at your own park. So we lost the first game, Ralph Branca against Jim Hearn. Jim Hearn pitched a strong game, and the Giants beat us 3–1. In that game, Bobby Thomson hit a home run off of Ralph. Ralph had pitched a quality game, and we didn't get that many runs. So we're down one game. We drive the bus to the Polo Grounds the second day, and Dressen comes to me. I'm on the bus, and next to me on the bus was Clem Labine. We're both young pitchers, but I had won sixteen games that year. And I've always been most effective when we're in a lot of trouble. But anyway, Dressen says, "I don't know which one of you two guys are going to pitch when we get to the Polo Grounds." So we rode to the Polo Grounds across New York. We didn't know which one it was going to be. So when we get to the Polo Grounds, whatever tipped his hand, I don't know. But he picked Labine. What a choice. Labine shut them out, and we won 10–0. Now, we're even. We've got Newcombe. Down the stretch, trying to stem the tide, the starting pitchers were Preacher Roe, Don Newcombe, and I, and Branca. Dressen pitched us with two days' rest, relieved in between.

We had pitched a lot of innings right down the stretch, so everybody was a little tired. Newcombe was a workhorse, but he started the ball game. And Newcombe pitched a strong game, and it looked like for all practical purposes we were going to win it, because we're leading 4–1 going into the ninth inning. I'm in the bullpen with Branca. Well, after a couple of infield hits get through—kind of seeing-eye hits—and Whitey Lockman doubled, now, one run is in and two men are on. And the bullpen is heating up, and I'm throwing alongside of Ralph Branca. And the bullpen phone rings, and I can't hear what they said on the other end. I can hear our coach, Clyde Sukeforth, answer. And the way I remember, I hear Suki say, "Yes. They're both ready." So Dressen must have said, "Are they ready?" And then, he must have asked who's got the best stuff or who's throwing the best or whatever. And Suki says, "They're both okay. They're both throwing okay. Erskine's bouncing his curve some." I had this hard overhand curveball. Well, at the Polo Grounds, you had a long distance to the backstop. And our catcher that day was not Campy. He was hurt. Rube Walker—one of the slowest guys in history—was our catcher. And I think Dressen must have said, "We don't want any wild pitches in this inning. Let me have Branca." So Ralph goes in. Clem Labine, who just pitched the day before, he gets up and starts loosening up with me. So we watch Ralph warm up. He throws the first pitch. And we all knew Thomson was a good low-fastball hitter. Ralph had a good fastball. He bores one in there. I mean, he throws a good fastball. Right down his wheelhouse. And we all went "No. Ralph, you can't go down there. Not down there." The Giants must have been doing the same thing. The next pitch Ralph threw was up and in, where it should have been. Thomson fights it off, hits a line drive in the lower deck of the Polo Grounds—a three-run homer. The shot heard, round the world.

Russ Hodges was screaming. I could hear this thing later on the radio. "The Giants win the pennant. The Giants win the pennant." And they did win the pennant. And that famous home run, if you're a Giants fan, or the infamous home run, if you are a Dodger fan—that was so bitter. It was such a bitter defeat to lose that. And I'll always remember Labine. He started alongside of me. And this ball goes not too far from us, because the bullpen is in left-center field of the Polo Grounds. And this was hit pretty well straightaway left field. Labine looks up at the wall, and we're looking over. And so we drop our heads, and Labine says, "I didn't see a ball go over the fence. I saw my wallet." The best pitch I ever threw in baseball was that bounce curve in the bullpen. Well, who knows? I could have come in and done the same thing. It was almost like destiny that the Giants just did these miracle things all the way down to the last one and a half of the season. And it just seemed like when that happened, Cy Young could have been brought in. I don't know if he would have got him out or not.

Walter O'Malley, the Dodgers' owner, was a very progressive man. He was a futuristic thinker. He was conceiving an idea of how to get a new ballpark built in the borough of Brooklyn. I don't think Mr. O'Malley had any notion at all in the beginning of moving the team out of the borough of Brooklyn. He's a New Yorker himself. But there was resistance to this grand plan that he had of building a new park where the Long Island railroads came into Brooklyn. He wanted to build a stadium in that area—and that was rejected by the hierarchy in the city of New York. Robert Moses, I understood, was the key man there. He wanted the team to move to Flushing Meadows in Queens. And O'Malley resisted that. So in order to try to stay in the New York area, O'Malley did a very unusual thing. He would have moved the team out of Brooklyn over to Jersey, to Roosevelt Stadium. We played ten major-league games in Roosevelt Stadium over in Jersey in order to try and find a place to keep the club in the New York area. But O'Malley refused to go to Queens. Now, right in that time period, two significant things took place that people seldom ever relate. The jet plane had finally been developed, so you could fly from the East Coast to the West Coast in five hours. Otherwise, there was no way to expand to the West Coast, because trains and buses had kept major-league baseball no farther west than St. Louis for one hundred years. And so now, the jet plane makes this possible. O'Malley, who is a very futuristic thinker, as I said, began to hear the call from the West Coast. And the West Coast, which had a strong league in the Pacific Coast League, had always thought they had the third major league anyway, had some great ballplayers—a Triple-A league. They began to romance Walter O'Malley to move the team there. Once it was moved along like it might happen, the owners said they would not agree to just one team going. It would be ridiculous to have one team clear on the West Coast. It had to be at least two. So Walter O'Malley, I think, told Horace Stoneham, owner of the Giants, to be the second team to go, and go to San Francisco. I think, technically, the Giants went first. I think, technically, they ended up getting their deal worked out first. But the history of baseball will forever show this unique thing of two franchises moving at the same time. And Robert Moses and the city of New York officials really forced that to happen. Unreal. You would have had an uproar today if you lost two major franchises. We were successful.

Finally, it was announced '57 would be our last season in Brooklyn. And, of course, two things were going on there. The fans just thumbed their nose at that, and they quit coming to the ballpark. We had very poor attendance in '57. I think it was six thousand at the last game in Brooklyn. And the tragedy and the unfairness is that Walter O'Malley is the focus of all their dissatisfaction and hatred. And it's not truly a fair thing to do, but then, that's history now. We came to the same spring training site in '58.

That was the year we were going to move to the West Coast. We came back to the same training site at Vero Beach, Florida—Dodgertown. And so nothing was moved, nothing was different. We played our spring game schedule here in Florida. And then, what was different was instead of playing our way north with one of the other major-league teams, usually, the Braves—we'd go play Jacksonville, Mobile, Atlanta, Nashville, on our way north—playing our way up to open the season in New York. That didn't happen. We bused over to the airport, got on the Dodger plane, and flew to San Francisco to open the season in a minor-league park, at Seals Stadium. And I've got to tell you this. There was a fan in the centerfield stands in New York that used to get on Snider big time. Oh, he got under Duke's skin real good. He wore a big coat in the summertime, an old hat, and he called Duke "Horseface." And Duke was fuming. After a ball game, Duke would say, "That so-and-so. He sat out there driving me nuts. How many seasons is this guy going to get on me? Horseface. Horseface." Well, Pee Wee would be riding in the front seat and he'd turn around to Duke and he'd say, "Let me see, Duke. Yeah. Yeah. I guess . . ." and put the needle in real good. Well, now, we get off the bus at Seals Stadium in San Francisco, and I'm with Duke, who is my roommate. And we step off the bus, and the barricades are holding the fans back while we get to the clubhouse. Here's this guy standing there. He says to Duke, "Hey, Horseface, you thought you got rid of me, didn't you?" Even Duke had to laugh.

We opened San Francisco, and then we went down and opened the season in Los Angeles. So our first games in L.A., then, were in the Coliseum, which held one hundred thousand people. And it was skewed. The diamond was skewed in there so that you had a 250-foot fence down the left-field line, a 300-foot fence in right field, and a 440-foot center field. You just had this shape. Well, they put a big screen in left field to make it a little more legitimate to hit a home run. But, yes, you'd hit guys on the fist, and they'd still pop the ball up enough to hit it on that screen for a single and maybe a double. I pitched opening day in Los Angeles. I'm not sure why Walter Alston had picked me. I think he wanted a veteran pitcher on this historic day. There was a lot of excitement. Almost eighty thousand people came to that game in the Coliseum. We played the Giants, again. That was very exciting. But the crowd at the game was more curious than they were enthused, because it was a new team. They had heard about us, but they couldn't know. We weren't identified yet with Los Angeles.

It was kind of a celebrity crowd, too. There were a lot of Hollywood people there. I remember standing on the mound second or third inning or something. I glanced over at our dugout, and about six guys gawking back over our dugout, because there were movie stars sitting up there: Danny Kaye, Bing Crosby, and two or three of the gals in the movies—Lana Turner—I don't know. And so this was the kind of crowd that was opening day. You know, World Series time was always a celebrity crowd. It wasn't a standard day-in-and-day-out crowd. It was kind of like that. It was a strange crowd, because the cheering wasn't the same. It just was unusual.

It was a transition time when Pee Wee, Furillo, Hodges, Duke—of course, Campy had already been hurt and was not even with us.

So we were all toward the latter part of our careers. So it was tough to go to L.A. and kind of re-prove who we were, because we were toward the end of our careers. By the middle of '59, we were in fifth place and not going anywhere. And that's when the Boys of Summer were replaced by Johnny Roseboro, Larry Sherry, Roger Craig, oh, Frank Howard—big right-handed hitter.

Drysdale and Koufax were transition players. They had been in Brooklyn with us. Sandy Koufax in '55 and Don Drysdale in '56. Koufax was improving. He was a .500 pitcher in Brooklyn. He was like 37-37. He had a huge disadvantage. All of us had been through the Dodger system. And we had been in the minor leagues. We had been taught. We had had time to be refined a little bit. Sandy came right off the sandlots of Brooklyn. And because he had been paid a bonus of—I don't know—$20,000 or whatever, there was an owner's restriction where you couldn't option him into the minors. He had to stay on the big-league roster. Well, Sandy was green as grass. He didn't know how to hold on a runner. He didn't have any finesse as a pitcher. He'd just go out there and try to learn on the job. So he'd win one and lose one. So after four years or five years in Brooklyn, he was a mediocre fifty-fifty pitcher. Hadn't been given the refinements yet. And he didn't really like baseball. I'm cautious when I say that. What I mean was some of us would play for nothing, you know, just to be there. Well, Sandy was a good basketball player. He had other interests, and baseball hadn't caught him the way it caught the rest of us. But Drysdale had some minor-league experience. He was a very polished pitcher as a rookie. He was a good take-charge pitcher early on. But we moved to California. And in '59, the old guard was beginning to change, and Sandy began to come into his own. And finally, that team that was in the minor leagues when the season started caught the Giants, caught the Braves, won the pennant, and beat the White Sox in the World Series. And the guys like Larry Sherry, Roger Craig, Maury Wills, Frank Howard, Chuck Essegian, whom we had acquired—they were all not with us when the season started. Most of them were in the minors. Won the pennant, won the World Series, and then, the new era was beginning to blossom in Los Angeles. And the L.A. Dodgers began to have their own history. We won that World Series in '59, and then Koufax began his fantastic six years of dominance in the National League along with Drysdale. And Vin Scully, who was the young announcer under Red Barber—he sold baseball in Southern California pure and simple. His great style, his warm deliveries, his knowledge—that I think, was truly responsible for selling the Dodgers to Southern California.

When their careers were over, a lot of guys went in the Dodgers' system. Campy was not able to fulfill what he would have done as a manager, because he was injured and stayed in a wheelchair for thirty-three years. Hodges did become a manager—a good one. Died young, unfortunately. Naturally, Jackie—if he had a chance—I think he felt like he was denied the chance to manage. And one of the reasons, probably, Jackie wouldn't have been given the chance to manage is when he finished his baseball career, he was so outspoken and he was so controversial. He was pushing civil rights so hard, and he was unhappy with the pace. He was knowledgeable about the game. There was no question he was intelligent. Jackie was a very smart guy. And, you know, I often said this—when Pee Wee Reese passed away at eighty-one years old, I went to his funeral in Louisville. All of the living players, mostly, were there. We were interviewed. They said, "What about Pee Wee?" I said, "Well, you know, when I think of that team, Campanella could have been a captain. He was a heady guy. Sparked. Loved the game. Hodges could have been a captain. Jackie could have been a captain. But Pee Wee was, kind of, a senior member." And I think Pee Wee was like the captain of the captains. He had the respect. He had a personality, and he was an extension—always an extension of who was managing.

He had many chances to manage. He just didn't want to manage. But during his years as a player, whoever Pee Wee played for—first Durocher, later Burt Shotton, later Charlie Dressen, and finally,

Walter Alston—he was an extension of his manager on the field. I mean, that's what a captain is—should be.

We all recognized Carl Furillo, as a teammate, as being a workman. He came to the ballpark—he might as well have been carrying a lunch bucket. I mean, he went to work. And he was intolerant of any player who was halfhearted, didn't give his all. He had no time for a player who had good ability, but just, you know, was kind of a goof-off. When his career was toward the end—and that was in Los Angeles—he had already had a brilliant career in Brooklyn. Very well respected. He had a lot of Italian followers in Brooklyn. Furillo had a tough exterior, but he was a tender guy inside. He was good with kids. He was good with his family, but he gave you this rugged outer appearance. Great arm—great throwing arm. But we went to L.A. toward the end of his career, and his legs began to go. I voluntarily retired, because I knew that the club had to make some changes. So in the middle of '59, with arm trouble, I voluntarily retired, and stayed on as a coach through the rest of the year. But when Furillo came to the end of the line, he balked at being released. He thought he had more time to play and he wanted some of the club. Finally, it got in the paper. A paper battle began to happen between Furillo and the front office, Buzzie Bavasi. A lot of words were exchanged, and finally, Furillo was released. He couldn't get a job with another club and Furillo contended that he was blackballed, that the Dodgers had blackballed him. I don't know why Carl hadn't seen all around him, all the years he played, that a lot of players got released when the club felt like they were not productive. He was suing baseball for blackballing him. So I wrote Carl a letter, and I encouraged him to understand how the Dodgers' system always took care of their own. They always did. They took care of Campy. They took care of players later who had drug problems or whatever. They always took care of their own. But Furillo was so strong in his comments about being released, and he just got a bitter battle going, and so he left baseball. Years passed, and they started having fantasy camps, where businessmen who love to play the game but never did, except maybe high school or college, could pay to come to a major-league facility and be coached by ex-major-league players, get a uniform and feel like they—you know, it was fantasy camp. I'm doing a fantasy camp at the moment, and Furillo is my coach. He surprisingly agreed to come and be a member of our staff at a fantasy camp. So I thought Furillo had mellowed. And I was happy for him. At the end of his career, when he finally had to get out of baseball, he had to go take a regular job, a construction job. We didn't get many endorsements, we didn't get many appearance fees. We had no agents and all that stuff. You just did it because the club asked you to do it. Well, to get a little payday late in your career life, like a fantasy camp, that attracted Carl. So he came, and he was my coach. And, you know, the guys loved him. The guys that paid to come to camp somehow had a strong identity with this rugged personality. And Carl made a great impact because he had a good career and everybody knew that. But he never really lost his bitterness, and I was sad about that. I used to talk to him, and he'd agree up to a point. But he never agreed that he got treated fairly when he left baseball. And it's too bad. I hated that. But I think part of that was Carl's fault; part of it was circumstance.

I always heard people say, "When you know the time is right, you'll take that uniform off." I said, "Not me. You can't get it off of me. It's hard to get to the big leagues, and I'm not taking it off." But you know I pitched fourteen years, counting a couple of years in the minors. And in Los Angeles in 1959, my arm was not good, and I was not able to be productive. I had been a starting pitcher. I had been a contributor. I wasn't doing it. The club was not doing well. I was not having fun. And I began to have these funny heart palpitations. And I went to a heart guy, and he said, "You know, your heart is sound. You're under some kind of stress." He didn't know anything about the rest of it. And he said, "When you get rid of the stress, you'll get rid of that flutter." Well, after I pitched my—ironically, I pitched my first inning in Pittsburgh, Forbes Field. Eleven years later, I pitched my last inning in Pittsburgh, Forbes Field. I won the first game; I lost the last one. And I went to Bavasi when the club got back to L.A., and I said, "Buzzie, I'm not productive. The club is going to make changes. Before I'm shoved, I'm going to jump. I think I need to do something. What can I do?" "Well," he said, "I won't release you. I'm not going to release you in the middle of the year." I said, "Well, what are my options?" "I'll send you to Spokane. There's a Triple-A team. Go up there and hang around Bobby Bragan and pitch away. And I'll bring you back when we can increase the roster, and you need twenty-eight days to get your full pension for ten years. And I'll give you—I'll get your last ten." I said, "Buzzie, if I could pitch, I'd pitch here. I'm not going to drag my family to Spokane." And he said, "Well, the only other option you got, Carl—I'm not going to release you—just a voluntary retire. That's the only other option. That's it." I said, "What do I have to sign?" And so I retired, and you know what? The flutter went away. I was under pressure. I knew the club had to make some changes. I stayed on until the end of the season, and then was a coach, of course. And we got in the World Series. We won the World Series against the White Sox. And my good-bye to baseball was a victory party in Chicago after we won the Series. Got the World Series ring. Got a share of the Series and bowed out of professional baseball.

I had 122 wins in the regular season. I had 78 losses. I won two World Series games and lost two. I pitched two no-hitters in my career. I had one All-Star appearance. I opted out of the second All-Star appearance, because my arm was having troubles. My overall stats—I pitched around 1,800 innings. I always wanted 1,000 strikeouts. I got almost 1,000, and 31 in the World Series play. So a few personal goals there. I roomed with Duke Snider for eleven seasons—and Duke is a Hall of Famer. That's as close as I got to the Hall of Fame.

• • •

Pick the best ballplayers I saw? I must have pitched three hundred ball games to Campanella. It's hard for me to visualize somebody greater than Roy Campanella as a catcher. I know he was MVP three times in the National League, so he's not going to be a bad choice for a catcher. Berra was a better catcher than he probably gets credit for, because he caught an outstanding pitching staff. What I remember most about Yogi was not so much his catching, but that he was a hitter. He was a bad-ball hitter. It was hard to walk Yogi. He came up there to hit. The joke goes around that he had the trademark on the wrong side of the bat. And somebody, some catcher says, "Hey, Yogi. You're holding the bat wrong. You're supposed to hold the trademark up so you can read it." And Yogi supposedly said, "I didn't come up here to read."

If I go around and talk about positions, it's going to be hard for me to replace Gil Hodges with another first baseman. How great his hands were and how many infield bad throws he saved and how many games he won by his defense. Of course, he hit a lot of home runs. I will say this about Johnny Mize. I didn't pitch a lot against Ted Williams, because we never met in postseason games. I pitched him in spring training some. But you can't really count that, because he'd take a couple of swings and a couple of times at bat. They often said how Ted Williams didn't swing at a bad pitch, and he had the strike zone that he just owned. Anything outside that, it was a ball. He never chased a bad pitch. He had power, and he had a huge average. Well, you know, Mize fits that description a lot. Mize was a power hitter. He hit the ball to all fields. He hit a good average and was a tough strikeout. Johnny Mize hit a three-run homer off of me in the '52 World Series. And then he hit another ball that should have been a home run that Pafko caught in the low stands at Yankee Stadium. So Mize hit me pretty well. In 1953, in the third game, I'm pitching. Got real good stuff, and I got a lot of strikeouts. At the end of the game, I got a 3–2 lead. Campy hit a home run in the bottom of the eighth and they send Mize up to pinch-hit in the top of the ninth inning. We're playing at home. I got one out, and Mize is up.

Johnny Mize

Now, Mize must have told the bench on the Yankees how to hit Erskine, because he did. He was tough on me. And he comes up, and I get two good called strikes on him, that he didn't even offer at. Two good curveballs. And then, a fastball up and in, that he had a real terrific cut at. But he didn't get it, fouled it off. And then, I struck him out on the next pitch. And to me, all of baseball was wrapped up in one pitch. Because he became the fourteenth strikeout, which was at that time a World Series record. And I didn't know it until the game was over and I was inside.

The first few times I pitched against Eddie Mathews, I'd throw him a good fastball, and I'd think he had taken it. It went past the point where most guys commit. I would already think he took the pitch, then *shoom*. It would go with that quick release. He had the quickest bat of anybody I had pitched against. He could wait the longest before he committed. And then, of course, he had good power. Now, the guy that hit in front of him, Henry Aaron. We didn't want to walk Aaron to get to Mathews. And then behind him was Joe Adcock. Joe Adcock was a power hitter. And then they had

Wes Covington and Del Crandall. A very quality ball club; that was the Braves.

They compared Billy Cox to Brooks Robinson, who was, of course, one of the most fantastic third basemen. The only difference I saw between Cox and Brooks Robinson was Robinson was bigger and had a little more range than Billy. Billy had a different glove. At one time, somebody—Rawlings, maybe—made a three-finger glove. It was small, and the middle finger was one instead of two. And so it had only three fingers. Well, Cox used that kind of glove, and he was real quick with it, because it was small. I had to credit that for being part of it. He had great hands and a good arm. He could throw good.

I saw Phil Rizzuto play quite a bit. What I remember about Rizzuto is he did not have a very good arm. That's why Jackie Robinson—you know, he was a shortstop in the Negro League. But he was considered not to be a major-league shortstop, because he couldn't throw well enough from the deep hole. Well, Rizzuto could overcome that by how fast he got rid of the ball. It was amazing how he could field the ball and throw it. And he overcame his shortcoming of not having a good arm, especially as he got older.

If there was one nemesis in my career, it was Ralph Kiner. It's hard to explain how some hitters hit some pitchers and vice versa. Musial was a .331 hitter, and he hit everybody. Clem Labine, on our team—our relief pitcher—got Musial out forty-six straight times. The rest of us—Clem had a broken finger, and it was crooked. Well, all of us on the staff, we at one time or another, we considered breaking that finger, because he could get Musial out.

I had good luck against the Cardinals. In spite of their outstanding lineup, my record against the Cardinals was something like 23-8 or so. But Musial, to me, was still the toughest out. He had led the league five times in batting while I was pitching. Kiner hit home runs off of me. In twelve seasons, I think Kiner hit ten, and two I remember were grand slams. One of them was in my early career when he was with the Pirates, and I was just a young kid pitcher. I remember going to Pittsburgh. They had a tail-end team. We got to Pitts-

Ralph Kiner

burgh after they had played a doubleheader on Sunday, and we were going to play them on Monday. The headline in the *Pittsburgh Press* said "Pirates Lose Two: Who Cares? Kiner Hits Three." They packed the place to see Kiner hit home runs, and he hit 50 a year for a couple years. And, of course, he's in the Hall of Fame. But Ralph hit a grand slam off of me my first year. And then, some time later, he was with the Cubs, and he hit a grand slam off of me in Ebbets Field.

The first one was a fastball. It took a long time for us to realize that Kiner was a very good curveball hitter. Now, if you throw a curveball in the right place, it's almost hard for anybody to hit it. If you hang it a little bit—Joe Adcock was another one. If you didn't get the curveball down—if you hung it up in the strike zone, I'm telling you, they're going to hit it. I used to say, when Kiner came to Brooklyn, he'd send a cab to make sure Erskine got to the ballpark.

Mays loved the ball up. He wanted to get his arms out, extend his arms to hit the ball. You couldn't pitch Willie high outside. He'd hit it to right-center field like a bullet and maybe in the stands. You've got to have courage to pitch a guy like Mays inside. He'll rip the ball foul in the upper deck inside, if he gets around on it. But before we learned to pitch Willie—or I did—naturally, you threw him curveballs and other pitches. But to get him out with fastballs, you had to keep it tight. Otherwise, Willie'd get his hands out. Roberto Clemente was a little bit like that. You heard about stepping in the bucket—when you pull the left foot out on the swing, and then your body comes away. But both of those hitters, Mays and Clemente—both Hall of Famers—they had the knack of stepping away and throwing the top of their body at the ball, and they had some leverage there. So they hit with power to right or right center. I had decent luck with Willie. In the '56 season, I pitched a no-hitter against the Giants, and Willie hit the ball—it should have been a base hit, and Jackie Robinson saved the day for me. He made a fantastic pickup of a shot that Mays hit. He was playing third base that day.

Hugh Casey was an older pitcher when I got to the Dodgers. He gave me two pieces of advice. He said, "Hey, kid. Welcome to the big leagues. Let me tell you. There's hitters in this league that hit .340 every year. Now, I've never seen you pitch. I don't know if you throw overhand, sidearm, underhand—I don't know what you pitch. They're going to hit you just like they hit the rest of us. So my advice—bear down on the .220 hitters and the weak guys ahead of the good hitters. They're going to get their hits, but keep these weak sisters off the base." Well, that was good advice. And the second thing he said was "The things in this league you can't change: the weather on the day you're pitching, the park you're pitching in, and who's umpiring." Well, you know, those are the three things you've always heard guys complain about. "I hate to pitch at Wrigley Field. God. The wind is always blowing," or whatever. Or "I like it hot." Or "I like a cool night." "Who's back of the plate today? Who's umpiring?" "Oh, my God. He's back there today." Casey said, "Look. Forget all that stuff. You have no control over it. Control what you have control of. Keep your fastball where you want it. Keep your curveball down. Kid, you'll win some games." Good advice.

• • •

Two things in my career. I always respected the writers. They didn't always write what I liked, because if you had a bad day—and I had a few—they're going to write it. Well, some guys got offended by that. They wanted to fight. But I always respected the writers. They had a tough job. And the umpires had a tough job.

The tag "major-league player" is so uniquely sought by young athletes and young players that to have obtained that for any length of time is just almost a fantasy for me. What I remember about being in the big leagues—it's not the scores, it's not the good games you pitched and certain strikeouts you got and World Series play and so on. But when it's all said and done, the greatest feeling I have is for the guys I played with and against to say, "Erskine, yeah, he was a good major-league pitcher." It doesn't say Hall of Fame. It doesn't say, you know, he had the strikeout record. Just to be recognized in the game of baseball as important; that is American history to me. What it will be in the future? Who knows? You got a lot of competition now. At this time in history, I see baseball becoming international. So a lot of things will change, and our eras will be deep in history. But if you ask me what is the most precious thing you feel you took from the game, that would be it—that my teammates and the opponents say, "Yeah. Yeah. I remember Erskine. He could do it all."

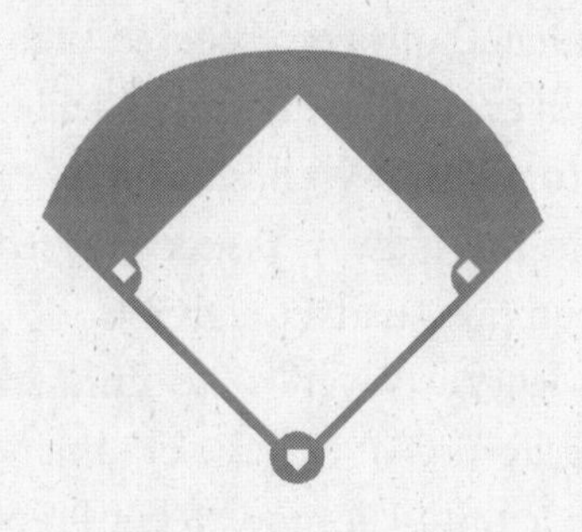

WHITEY FORD

At five foot ten and 180 pounds, Whitey Ford was far from an intimidating figure. But place him on a pitcher's mound with a baseball in his left hand and the sight could make even the most feared hitters shake in their spikes.

"Ford was the only pitcher who really could embarrass a hitter. Honestly, sometimes he almost made me want to cry," said first baseman Jim Gentile. "It was awful. It was the most frustrating experience I ever had in baseball, facing that guy."

Ford, who earned the nickname "Chairman of the Board" for his calm and cool demeanor on the mound, spent sixteen seasons (1950, 1953–67) pitching for the New York Yankees, one of the greatest teams of the era. "He'd get the ball over if lightning struck him during the windup," said longtime opponent Harvey Kuenn.

Using an assortment of pitches, Ford would finish with a career record of 236-106, his .690 winning percentage one of the best in baseball history. The eight-time All-Star and 1961 Cy Young Award winner would lead the league in wins and winning percentage three times and innings pitched and ERA twice.

"Nothing in this game gives me a greater thrill than to watch Whitey

Ford set up a hitter—then make that hitter look completely foolish on a third strike. That left-hander of ours is a real artist," said Yankees manager Ralph Houk. Ford's onetime catcher, Elston Howard, agreed, stating, "He gives it that extra something when in a jam. What an operator. I got to appreciate him more by catching him than watching him. Nothing bothers him, whether it's a lefty or righty batter. Knows what he's doing all the time."

During his tenure the team would win eleven American League pennants and six World Series crowns, with Ford setting Fall Classic marks for wins (10), games pitched and games started (22), innings pitched (146), and strikeouts (94).

Longtime teammate Mickey Mantle, who was inducted with Ford into the National Baseball Hall of Fame in 1974, once remarked, "I don't care what the situation was, how high the stakes were—the bases could be loaded and the pennant riding on every pitch—it never bothered Whitey. He pitched his game. Cool. Crafty. Nerves of steel."

I started off playing stickball here in New York City. I was born on East 66th Street in Manhattan. In my earliest recollection, I was about six, seven years old. Lived on East 66th Street, and across the street was where they parked the trolley cars at night. This building had no windows in it, and it was a great place to play stick, you know, pitching it in. We'd throw that "spaldeen" ball—that's what they called it. We had a broom handle or something. And that was my first recollection of a bat and a ball. And years later, we moved out to Astoria, Queens, and that's when I started playing baseball. They had fields out there and that was the start of it. And then I went to high school. Well, after I grew up—I was about fifteen—we had a team in Astoria and called it the "34th Avenue Boys."

I was the first baseman. Our pitcher got hurt, and they asked me to pitch. I didn't know how to pitch. I went to a tryout at Yankee

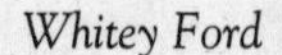

Whitey Ford

Stadium as a first baseman and they saw me hit and they said, "Did you ever try pitching?" I said, "No." But Paul Krichell, the scout that signed me later on, he went over on the side and showed me how to hold the ball and throw a curve. And lo and behold, I pitched that whole summer with this team, the 34th Avenue Boys.

We ended up winning the New York City sandlot championship at the Polo Grounds in 1946. And right after that game, the Yankees signed me for a big bonus of $7,000.

It wasn't much of a bidding contest. It started at $4,000 and got up to $7,000, and no matter what they offered me, I was going to sign with the Yankees, because I'd been a Yankee fan for—I think 1938 was my first game at Yankee Stadium. I was nine years old. And I would've signed with the Yankees regardless of whether they gave me any money or not. My uncle Rudy, Rudy Johnson, was the first one who took me to Yankee Stadium in, I think it was 1938. And I remember Lefty Gomez and Joe DiMaggio, Lou Gehrig, I got to see play. I think Tommy Henrich might've been there. But that was my first game. Sat in the bleachers. I think it cost about 25 cents.

When I got signed by the Yankees, I went to Class C, Butler,

Pennsylvania. And I was 5 feet 9 inches and weighed about 150, and I didn't throw hard. I had a good curveball and pretty good control. I was eighteen years old. I had a good year there. I won thirteen or fourteen games. They promoted me to Norfolk, Virginia, in 1948, and I had a good year there.

But the third year, I went to Binghamton, New York, in the Eastern League. Now, I was about 5 feet 10 inches and 170 pounds, and I was throwing a little harder. George Selkirk was my manager at Binghamton, the former Yankee outfielder. It was then that I really thought I had a chance. I got to throw the ball, as my speed picked up. I had pitched almost three full seasons in the minor leagues. That was the first time I thought I had any chance of pitching in the big leagues.

I really didn't get any help in the minor leagues. I hate to say it, but the three and a half years I played in the minor leagues, I had a first baseman and three outfielders as managers. We had no other coaches. In the minor leagues, one of the players would coach first base, and the manager would coach third. And I really never had any help there. I just pitched a lot. I got to pitch almost 200 innings every year in the minor leagues. That helped more than anything.

But when I finally got called up to the Yankees, July of 1950, from Kansas City, the first game, I went straight to Boston. In about the fourth inning, Tommy Byrne was losing about 8–0 and Casey brought me in. I'd just got off the plane from Kansas City. They just banged me around. I think I pitched three innings. They got about seven or eight runs. Tommy Henrich came over to me after the first inning.

He called me "Eddie." That's what the players called me when I first came up. He says, "Eddie, that first-base coach for the Red Sox is calling all your pitches." He said, "I guess when you're throwing a fastball, he hollers in, 'Be ready,' and when you're throwing a curve, they say, 'Make him bring it up,' you know." I had no answer for it, and they banged me around. So the next day, Jim Turner, our pitching coach, and Eddie Lopat—and I was really getting my first lesson in pitching—they watched in the bullpen what I was doing and they picked it up right away.

When I was going to throw a fastball, my wrists would be flat against my stomach. If I was going to throw a curve, I'd bend it. It was so easy to pick up. But it was a little thing that I never learned in the minor leagues, or, actually, they didn't pick it up in the minor leagues. But Jim Turner and Eddie Lopat, they were just great.

Eddie got me to make sure to try and find out the weaknesses of every batter in the league. He just talked baseball to me all the time. For instance, one of the games I was pitching, I had a little fastball that tailed off and sunk. I remember Paul Richards with the White Sox, the manager. Like I said, he must've told those players not to try and pull the ball off me. Go to right field. And Jim Turner always made sure that I watched the other team take batting practice. Well, this one night, I was pitching, and I saw all the guys on the White Sox trying to hit the ball to right field.

I told Eddie Lopat and he said, "Well, they were told they can't pull that sinker of yours, so go to right field." He said, "You know, change your pattern this time. Pitch them inside." And I did. That was the kind of thing that, you know, Eddie Lopat put in my mind.

At the beginning of the year, the first month I was there, Casey would only pitch me against the St. Louis Browns or the Washington Senators, the poorer teams in the league.

And then I won five or six games. Then he decided to let me pitch against Cleveland. And then, toward the end of the '50 season, we had a three-game series in Detroit, and we were tied. We lost the first game. So we went one game behind and then we won the next. And then he let me pitch the third game against Dizzy Trout. I was really surprised that he did, because we had three other good starters.

That was the first really big game I thought I pitched in the big leagues. Joe DiMaggio hit a home run off of Dizzy Trout and then, in the seventh inning, they hit back-to-back doubles off me to tie the score. So when we got up in the ninth inning, it was 1–1, and I thought for sure Casey was going to put a pinch hitter in for me. And he didn't. It really made me feel good. I got up. I was the leadoff hitter in the top of the ninth, and I got a walk. We went on to score seven runs in the top of the ninth and it put us back in first place.

I was twenty-one when I came up with the Yankees. But I think by the time I was twenty-five or twenty-six, I was throwing a little harder. Yogi Berra called me "sneaky fast." They had no machines in those days, so I'm kind of glad I didn't know how fast I was throwing. My speed picked up. I always had a good breaking ball. And then, I learned with Turner and Lopat. One thing that helped me more than anything, I could throw from three different angles, like El Duque—he throws sidearm, three-quarters, and overhand. And that helped me more than anything, because I could throw a fastball from three different angles. My curveball, I could throw three-quarters or overhand, and the changeup from two angles.

So it really helps you. If you keep throwing, like, straight overhand, you know, the batters are going to zero in on you, eventually. And I think that helped me more than anything. Plus, I had really good control.

In the 1950 World Series, everybody said we killed the Phillies, but look at the scores. Jim Konstanty lost 1–0 to Vic Raschi, and Allie Reynolds beat Robin Roberts 2–1. And then Lopat won the third game. I pitched the fourth game. I can't remember—I think it was against a fellow by the name of Miller. And what I remember about it is I had left sixty-seven tickets for the World Series for my family and friends from Astoria.

I still lived in Astoria then. I was twenty-one years old. And I got to the ninth inning and I think we were winning 5–0. And they've got a man on, or two men on, or something. I had two out, and if somebody hit a fly ball to left field, it would've, you know, ended the game and I would've had a shutout. It was late October. It was tough playing left field. But anyhow, Gene Woodling dropped the ball and because of that two runs scored and made it 5–2.

And Casey came out and took me out of the game. And he put in Allie Reynolds. Well, when I walked off the mound, Casey was, like, a little behind me. I didn't realize it, but I hear all this booing and I thought they were booing me. And then I realized they were booing Casey for taking me out. But Allie Reynolds came in and threw three pitches and struck out Stan Lopata, the catcher, and the World Series was over. So Casey was right, again.

We had Bobby Brown and Billy Johnson playing third base, one right-handed and one left-handed. And then Phil Rizzuto was at short. And Billy Martin was there, and Jerry Coleman. So Billy played a little bit. Actually, Billy played with me a little bit at Kansas City earlier in the year. He got sent down for a while. And at first base, we had Joe Collins, Tommy Henrich a little bit, and Johnny Mize. He was also our pinch hitter. And in the outfield, it was Hank Bauer and Woodling, who would share left field. DiMaggio was in center, and that was the only year I had to play with him. I was thrilled. Like I mentioned before, my first game was in Boston, where I got banged around. I couldn't believe when I went out on the mound and turned around. And there's Joe playing center field for me. And, you know, he'd been my idol since that very first game I went to back in 1938. But Joe was playing center, and they just had everybody playing in the outfield. Tommy Henrich would go out there sometimes.

Yogi did the catching. And Ralph Houk and Charlie Silvera were also our catchers. They didn't get much chance to catch, with Yogi around.

Pitching, we had Vic Raschi and Allie Reynolds, Eddie Lopat, Tommy Byrne, myself. Oh, Fred Sanford was also a starting pitcher. And in the bullpen, we had Joe Ostrowski and Tom Ferrich, and our stopper then was Joe Page. He was like Luis Arroyo or Mariano Rivera.

That first year when I went to spring training with the Yankees, I got sent out to Kansas City; now I'm a twenty-one-year-old rookie with the Yankees in spring training. And Joe Page—after a few weeks, I started throwing pretty good—he's trying to teach me how to throw a spitball. I'm saying to myself, "Why is he teaching me this?" I've got a good curveball and a fastball, and very controlled. But that's how Joe was, you know. I don't even think he could throw one himself.

Raschi, you know, his record was so great in the big leagues. He got a late start in the major leagues. I don't know why, but I think he was, like, twenty-seven when he got started with the Yankees. But you look at his record. He pitched almost .700. He'd win seven out of ten games for the Yankees, and he was such a competitor. I really learned a lot just watching how he concentrated out on the mound. He was a bulldog, and he didn't want Yogi coming out to the mound.

Yogi was actually afraid to go out to the mound and talk to him. Sometimes the coach, Turner, or Stengel would motion to Yogi to go out and talk to him. Yogi didn't want to go talk to Raschi, because he'd come out there, Raschi would say, "Get the hell back there and catch and leave me alone." He was such a great competitor.

Allie Reynolds was probably our fastest pitcher, and mean. I mean, a lot of players in the league were actually afraid to hit against Allie because he would think nothing of zipping one under your chin.

But what made him so great was he could also be a relief pitcher for us. He was great out of the bullpen, and he was a great starting pitcher. And he was another guy that was a bulldog out there. He had a great fastball and he had a very good curveball.

Eddie Lopat was just all control and different pitches. He didn't throw very hard. For his natural ability, he was just as good a pitcher as could be. People ask me, what are you the proudest of as far as your pitching? And I said, "I think I got everything out of my natural ability." I didn't throw real hard. It was average, but I said for my natural ability and my size and everything, I said I think I got everything out of it.

We went to Japan in 1955, after the World Series. The Dodgers beat us in the World Series. Between Hawaii, Japan, and the Philippines, we were gone seven weeks. And I thought this would be a good time to practice my pickoff play. I'm trying to think who the first baseman was. It had to be Moose Skowron. I practiced it a lot over in Japan because we won all the games we played there. I think we had one tied game, but it was a good time to do it. We were ahead most of the time, and it really worked because the Japanese weren't as good players as they are now. They didn't have the training then. And it worked pretty good, and then I had pickoff plays with Jerry Coleman and Billy Martin at second, and Rizzuto.

We even had a pickoff play at third base with Clete Boyer later on. He was the one we did it the best with. But that's where I learned. I came back in the '56 season after that trip to Japan, and I really picked a lot of guys off first base that first year. And it's like Andy Pettitte with the Yankees now. Nobody takes the lead on him because Andy has such a good move.

You just got to let that runner think you're going to home. It's a lot to do, your shoulders and kicking your leg up and then looking toward home and it's just fooling the runner, letting him think that you're going home with the ball. But the next year after that, it didn't help. I mean, it helped, but I didn't pick many off because, you know, the manager or the coach would say, "Hey, don't take a big lead." They were actually afraid that I'd pick them off. But it did help me that they would stay close to first, and not many guys could go first to third on a single; or if it was a bunt, you know, they didn't get a good lead off of first base. So having a good pickoff still helped me later on in my career.

When I joined the Yankees in July of '50, Joe DiMaggio was hitting about .230 and, you know, it wasn't like him. But he must have hit

.380 the rest of the year because he ended up hitting .301 for the season and ended up having a good season. But for those three months—July, August, September—when I was here, he really had to hit in the high .300s. I thought he was great. He lost a little bit of speed, but he got such a great jump in the outfield on balls and never threw to the wrong base. I don't think he ever—he was such a great base runner nobody realizes. I don't think Joe was ever thrown out going first to third or stretching a single into a double. He had that big long stride, and he was just the best ballplayer I ever saw.

He was a very, very quiet leader. Mantle was sort of the same later on. Mickey was our leader then, but I remember Joe. Yogi begged out of a game in Washington. It was a doubleheader. It was hot, and Yogi caught the first game. He said, "I'm tired," or something, and Joe sort of lit into him. Joe was thirty-five or something, he told Yogi. He was playing a doubleheader. That was the last time Yogi ever tried to get out of a game. And Yogi told us that one time he didn't run a ground ball out to second base, and DiMaggio said to him, "Kid, you can run harder than that." Yogi said, "I never loafed again." He said that "when DiMaggio spoke to me, that was it." He said very few words, but you caught on right away. He ran right until he quit baseball. He ran hard. He played hard. He couldn't tolerate teammates not doing the same thing.

Johnny Mize used to lead the league in fielding average. John didn't move that fast, but he was very sure-handed. If he could get to the baseball, he was a good fielder. And a really great hitter. The only funny thing I ever remember about John was in the '53 Series against the Dodgers in Ebbets Field. Carl Erskine was just really pitching good. He broke the record for strikeouts in the World Series that day. He had fourteen. Johnny Mize was sitting on the bench; he wasn't playing.

Carl Erskine had struck Mickey Mantle out four times and Joe Collins four times. And Johnny Mize kept saying in the dugout, "How can you guys swing at that low curve?" Erskine's curve was just dropping right off the table. He was almost unhittable. Well, with one out in the top of the ninth we were losing, and Johnny Mize went up to pinch-hit, and Erskine threw him three curveballs, one lower than the other. John swung at all three of them, and he was the fourteenth strikeout. He just headed right for the dressing room after the game. He didn't want to see any of the players because they really would have got on him.

Phil Rizzuto was the MVP in 1950 in the American League. I had followed the Yankees for years before that, but he had—the only thing Phil didn't have was a good arm, but he was so quick, charging the ball, getting rid of it quick. So it didn't bother his fielding not having a good arm, but he just hit so well that year. He stole bases. I think Ted Williams thought that Phil Rizzuto always was our most valuable player because I know Ted said, "If we had Phil Rizzuto in Boston, we might have won a couple of pennants."

When I went to spring training in my first year in 1950, I hooked up with Billy Martin. When I got back to the Yankees in July, I

Phil Rizzuto

roomed with Billy the rest of the season. Then I went into the Army. When I came back for the '53 season, Mickey had joined the club. So he and Billy had spent '51 and '52 together. Through Billy I got to be very friendly with Mickey, and the three of us palled around together.

I played with Henrich that one year in '50, but he was just great. He played first base, played the outfield. He was a very good hitter. You couldn't throw a fastball by him. That's one thing I remember about him. He was such a good guy to have around. He knew baseball and he was wonderful with the younger players.

When I got to meet Mickey in '53, we sort of raised hell once in a while, but we picked our spots. I read things about Mickey Mantle even now today, they say he did this and that. Mickey played more games with the Yankees than anybody in history, and I lived with him on the road eighty games a year and was with him except in the winter, when he'd go back to Oklahoma or Texas, wherever he was living. And it just wasn't so. If we had a doubleheader on a Sunday, and we weren't playing until Tuesday night, sure we would go out Sunday night and have fun if we were on the road. The media got it to look like Mickey was out every night. It just wasn't so. The more time goes by, the stories get more exaggerated. Billy, Mickey, and I had a lot of fun, but it really never interfered with our playing baseball. Sometimes I'd say, "Okay, Mick let's go to bed," and things like that, but he sort of realized how important he was to the team. He took good care of himself.

After he got through, Mickey wished that he had quit two years sooner. He quit in '68, but he said he shouldn't have played in '67 and '68. His knees, his shoulder, he couldn't throw and his bad shoulder also hurt his hitting so. And one of the things he really hated to see happen was his batting average dropped a little bit below .300 by playing those last two years.

He was a shortstop for Joplin. Still holds the record for most errors. We kidded him. We said that we heard in Joplin that people

Mickey Mantle

wouldn't sit behind first base in the stands because he kept hitting them with his throw from short. He knew he wasn't a good shortstop. With his speed, he became a good outfielder.

I actually saw him in '50, but he was only there two weeks, and he was so quiet nobody even knew he was around. But then, in '53, I finally got to play with him. First time I saw him, I saw the build on him; he looked like he was a weight lifter, but he never lifted a weight in his life. Worked hard as a kid in the mines. He did work hard, but he just had the build, big strong arms, and could run. I wasn't in spring training in Arizona in '51, but Casey couldn't believe the speed he had. They used to have races in the outfield. Casey would hook up two or three young players and they would race. Mantle was just pulling away from everybody, guys they thought could run hard. And his power.

We had a sportswriter following us then. He also did racing and he always had a stopwatch. Lou Miller, his name was. And Lou was the one that got Mickey timed in 3.1 from home plate to first base. On a bunt going to first base. If he could hit the ball on the ground left-handed fairly slowly, he'd beat it out probably all the time.

He had seven or eight operations. In those days, they didn't do that arthroscopic surgery where they just make a little hole. He had scars all over his knee from the operations. But I'll tell you one thing that I remember and a lot of players that played with him do. When he got dressed, he'd put these great big Ace bandages around his knees. You'd watch, and he was always in a little bit of pain. But those young players would look over at him putting those bandages on and getting his uniform on and going out running as fast as he did. Those guys just couldn't try and jake out of a game. There was no way they were going to say to the coach or the manager, "I don't feel good today." You watched Mickey playing every day and there was no way you could try and get out of a game.

Eddie Lopat told me this story about when he was pitching, probably in '51 or '52. A ball was hit to right center and it looked like Mickey jogged after, and the guy got a triple. Lopat got on him a little in the dugout when he came back after the inning. Mickey said he felt so bad because he really didn't think he was loafing after the ball.

But he felt so bad about that, he just never, ever did anything like that again. He ran hard. He was a very quiet leader, very similar to how Joe DiMaggio was. He didn't have to say much, and he more or less led by his example. Even now, you talk to Moose Skowron, or to Bauer. Hank was older than Mickey, but they admired him so much for his courage. He was very quiet. He was the leader on the Yankees.

I think we had good players, but I think we had a great farm system. We had eight or ten teams in our farm system. Like the '51 season, we'd come up with Gil McDougald, Tom Morgan, who was a real good pitcher out of the bullpen for us, and Mickey. You got three guys, all young, they were all nineteen, twenty, twenty-one years of age, made the Yankees in one year. Yogi coming up and Bobby Brown at the end of the '46 season from Newark; they just played for years. We were able to put good teams together, but I think our farm system was one of the tops.

• • •

In 1950, I got $5,000. That was the minimum. I was there half a year, so I really made $2,500 for pitching. For winning the World Series, we got about another $6,000. So that's how I was able to get married. I made that World Series money. I'm 9-1, I really think I helped the team win the pennant because we only won by three games. Now I go in the service for two years and I come out, and by this time now we've had a baby, our daughter Sally Ann was born. Now I'm ready to go for the '53 season and I'm living in Jackson Heights in an apartment with my wife and daughter.

I asked for $9,000. It was a $4,000 raise, and Roy Hamey says you got to be out of your mind. You've been in the service for two years. We don't even know if you can still pitch. I said I know, but I won nine games for you in '50. He said, no, we'll give you $6,000. I said, you're going to give me a thousand-dollar raise? I don't think I can live on that. So a week went by and he said, "Okay, we're going to give you $7,000. If you're not on the next plane to St. Petersburg, we're going to go back to $6,000." So I started packing and went to St. Petersburg.

I mean, I was tickled. I made $7,000 my second year, but that was okay. In those days, ballplayers worked in the wintertime. When the World Series was over, you went to work for four or five months. The next year, we went to talk to Roy Hamey about a raise again, and Roy Hamey said to Gene Woodling and me, "Do you know our payroll is going to be over $600,000 this year?" That was for the whole team, $600,000. And then later on they said, nobody's ever going to make more than Joe DiMaggio. You know, Mickey played for $100,000 his last five or six years. They would never let him go above $100,000 because they said nobody is going to make more than DiMaggio did.

In '56, Mickey won the Triple Crown, and he got a good raise, about $20,000 or something. The next year, he hit .365, hit 34 home runs, and knocked in 94. He called me from Dallas and he said they wanted to cut him $10,000. He wouldn't even go to spring training.

For a couple of days, he held out, but they finally gave him the same amount. A player now that had that kind of year would ask for a couple million more.

Yogi is a very unusual guy, as everybody knows. They try and play Yogi with these things he says but, I'll tell you, he's really sharp. And he was that way as a ballplayer. He was a great catcher, a smart catcher. He learned, through Bill Dickey, how to be a really good catcher.

I hardly ever shook Yogi off. After I pitched a few games and he saw how I pitched, we were both on the same wavelength. We just knew what was happening, you know. All he had to do to give me a fastball was just move his glove a little inside. I knew exactly what he wanted. I very seldom would shake him off. I just want to tell you a funny story. In the middle '50s, Mickey was on Yogi about calling the games. He said, "Why are you calling that pitch and that pitch?"

And Yogi got annoyed and he said, "Why don't you—" I didn't

Yogi Berra

know this was going on. Yogi said, "Why don't you call the pitches?" And Mickey said, "How am I going to do that?" And then Mickey thought, and he said, "You know, I could be in center field giving the signs." Well, I'm pitching in Cleveland one night, and I don't know this. But Mickey's in center field; and if he stands up straight, he wants a straight ball, fastball; if he bends over, a curveball; and if he wants a changeup, he waggles his glove.

And Yogi's looking out at center field every pitch. We get to the sixth—and I don't know this is going on, because Yogi's giving me the signs. We get to the seventh inning, and Mickey comes in. The score is 0–0. And Mickey's getting nervous. He says, "All right, Yogi"—I hear him say, "All right, Yogi, you can take over now." I don't pay any attention to it. Well, after—we end up winning the game like 2–0, 3–1, or something like that. And I say to Yogi, "What was that going on?" He says, "Mickey was calling all the pitches the first seven innings." I say, "Really?" And then he got nervous with the score nothing, nothing and he said, "All right, Yogi, you take over." In other words, "I did a good job."

Cleveland in '54 and in those years, I don't know how we beat them. They beat us in '54. They won, I think, 111 games. We'd go into Cleveland for a four-game series and get three Hall of Famers. We'd get Early Wynn and Bob Feller and Bob Lemon pitching against us. And Mike Garcia was their fourth pitcher. He didn't make the Hall of Fame, but our hitters would rather hit against the other three guys than Mike Garcia, that's how tough he was. They had a great bullpen with Ray Narleski and Don Mossi. They had Al Rosen at third. Bobby Avila led the league in hitting at second, Vic Wertz and Bill Glynn at first. Dale Mitchell out in left field used to get a lot of hits every year, and Larry Doby in center. And I forget who was in right field but, I mean, they were a powerhouse. And, you know, they were comparing the Yankee teams of the last few years with us back then. And I said that I would like to see this modern-day Yankee team go into Cleveland and play a four-game series and hit against those four guys four days in a row and pitch against those hitters. And Boston was the same way, except they had some outstanding pitchers, but nothing like Cleveland. You'd go into Boston my first year and they had Walt Dropo and Vern Stephens, the shortstop, tied for the lead in RBIs with about 144. They got Johnny Pesky and Bobby Doerr and Billy Goodman, and Ted Williams, in center Dominic DiMaggio. I used to kid Birdie Tebbetts. I said, "I was so happy to see you get up once in a while in this lineup, because you were the only guy that couldn't hit."

Ted Williams said to me after we were through, "I had worse luck," he said. "I hated to hit against you." I said, "Well, I hated to pitch against you, too." But I found out later, through him—I didn't look up any record—Ted said, "I didn't hit very good against you." I know he hit one home run in the ninth inning in a game we were winning 2–0 in the stadium. He hit a home run in the top of the ninth. It just made the score 2–1. We still won, but that was the one home run he hit off of me. But he was just the greatest hitter I've ever seen. I think Yogi had something to do with it; he used to talk

Ted Williams

to Ted when he was hitting all the time. And he'd throw a little dirt on his spikes when he was up hitting.

It was very hard the first few years, because I think the umpires thought that Ted Williams had a better eye than they did. So if Ted didn't swing at a ball, or if it was close, it was a ball. But later on, when I pitched a few years and the umpires knew I had good control, it turned around a little bit. Then I thought I was getting a fair shake. But he had such a great eye and he was so quick. I mean, if he had wanted to hit to left field, I think he would have hit .400 every year. He could hit anything. He just had such a great eye. He'd take pitches. You know, now you see left-handers chasing curveballs in the dirt. You never saw Ted do that. When he swung, he usually made contact. He hit left-handers like Herb Score really good. You know, hard throwers, he'd just wear them out.

The night we won the pennant—I'd never pitched in relief too much, but I relieved Don Larsen in, I don't know what year it was. But we won the pennant this night up in Boston. And I relieved Don Larsen in the eighth inning. There were men on second and third and Pete Runnels got up. Ted was the next hitter. Casey says, "Okay, let's get this guy out and we'll put Williams on." Well, I walked Pete Runnels to load the bases. And it was one out. And we only had, like, a 3–1 lead or something like that. And up comes Ted with the bases loaded. And I go three and nothing on him. And I throw a strike. And I said, "Well, I'm not going to walk him." I throw another fastball. He hits a little two-hopper to Billy Martin for a double play. I think he was so surprised that I threw him a fastball right down the middle that it just took him by surprise. But he hit into a double play and we won the pennant the next inning. But he was just such a great hitter. Best hitter I ever saw, lefty or righty. He was just great.

Cleveland and Boston were the two toughest lineups for a few years there to pitch against. Boston, I think if they had better pitching, would have won a lot of pennants and World Series. Detroit had Al Kaline and George Kell. They were both tough. They didn't try and pull the ball. They were smart hitters. I've been asked the question, who was the toughest batter you ever pitched against? And I said, my right-handed hitter, the toughest was Harvey Kuenn, and left-handed was Nellie Fox. They just didn't try and kill the ball, just hit it through, you know, singles and through the box. They were the two toughest hitters for me to get out—and Frank Howard. I just thought of another one: Jim Lemon, played with Washington. I pitched one night in Washington against him and he hit three home runs off of me in front of President Eisenhower. That was embarrassing. But the good part was we won, 5–3. Lemon was getting up in the ninth inning with a man on and Casey took me out of the game after he'd hit three homers. I'm trying to talk Casey into staying in the game, and he said something like, "You gotta be kidding." And he brought Tom Morgan in. Morgan got him out.

Casey Stengel was friendly, but he talked more to the writers, I think, than the players. I used to hear him talk to the writers, and he didn't make sense to me the way he was talking. But when he had a meeting with the players, we understood every word he said. He had very few meetings. But I really enjoyed playing for him. The first thing he did, he surrounded himself with three great coaches. He had Frank Crosetti, who coached third; Bill Dickey, who coached first; and Jim Turner, the pitching coach. And that was it, three coaches. You couldn't have three better guys. Jim Hegan came later on, but Bill Dickey was in charge of the hitting, Crosetti the fielding and the bunting, and Jim Turner ran the pitching staff. He'd say to Casey, "Okay, it's time to get him out." I think that was his biggest—Casey's biggest asset was the coaches that he surrounded himself with.

I considered myself a good bunter. But we practiced it. You know, the pitchers used to hit batting practice every day at home. And you didn't get any swings until you laid down five or six good bunts. Then you could take a few swings. But he emphasized it, and Bill Dickey made sure when we took batting practice that we got our bunts in. We just worked at it.

Mickey always teased Billy Martin, "Casey's little bo-bo." But, for some reason, after that last year or two Billy was with the Yankees, I always had a feeling that he wanted to be a coach or a manager, because he would sit next to Casey during the game and ask him questions. And he'd ask Bill Dickey questions and Frank Crosetti. And I just knew. And then he got traded to Kansas City. And then, before you knew it, he started managing. I thought he was a great manager, but he was a good guy.

Casey used to get annoyed at the guys who complained about platooning. Bobby Brown wanted to play all the time and Billy Johnson wanted to play all the time, but they both played third. But, you know, we were in the midst of winning five World Series in a row, so these guys really didn't have too much to say. Casey was winning the World Series every year. So, Bobby Brown and Billy Johnson got used to it. And it was the same with Woodling and Bauer. They were screaming but, you know, Woodling would play against right-handed pitchers and Hank against left-handers. And they screamed for a while, but then they all calmed down and said, "Hey, we're winning the World Series every year." And the way Casey used them, you know, their record at the end of the year didn't look great, but they knocked in, say, 60–65 runs and hit 15 home runs. But you put the two of them together, and you got, you know, 30 home runs and 130 RBIs from that one position. So I think Casey wouldn't explain to them, he just did it. And then they started realizing later, that's our best team when Woodling's playing against the right-handers and Hank against the left-handers.

The famous Copa incident? It was a Sunday night. It was Billy Martin's birthday. And we took him to dinner—we went to dinner at Danny's Hideaway. Danny Stradella was the owner of the restaurant. He had a table at the Copacabana reserved every night. So there was like ten of us. So it was Bauer and McDougald and Mickey and Billy and I and our wives. And we didn't have a game till Tuesday night and this was Sunday, Sunday evening.

So we all went over to the Copacabana and sat down. Sammy Davis was performing. We had ten at our table, and a few tables away was a bowling team with their wives. We found out later they were a bowling team. And they were getting on Sammy Davis a little bit, you know, racially, and it wasn't nice. We were getting annoyed, and Hank Bauer finally asked them to cool it. They said something bad, and a guy said to Hank Bauer, "I'll meet you in the back."

So the guy started walking in back. We realized he was serious. So Hank went to the back of the Copa, and when we got back there—now, Hank never left our sight. Billy was behind him, and Mickey and I and McDougald. And Hank never left our sight. When we got to the back of the room, this guy on the bowling team was stretched out on the floor. And I found out later the bouncer—it was a little guy, but they called him the bouncer. He was like the maître d'. He had done it. I went home. I lived in Glen Cove, Long Island, at the time. Billy and Mickey called me the next day and said, "We gotta be in Topping's office tomorrow morning. He's fined us a thousand dollars each." I said, "We didn't do nothing." Anyhow, we went before the grand jury a couple days later. And I said, "You know, this is getting crazy. Nothing happened." I remember we had to get up before a grand jury. The Yankees hired a lawyer for us.

We told the lawyer the story, just like I'm telling you. And he said, "Just tell that to the grand jury, just like you told me." So we went in there. Mickey was the first one, and he was chewing gum. And the guy at the grand jury said, "Can you take that gum out of your mouth?" Mickey took it out and didn't know what to do with it. He's standing in the middle of this room holding the gum. He told the story, then we all did. And the grand jury threw it out of court. Well, the Yankees fined us each $1,000. The lawyer was $7,000, so that was another $2,000 each. And in those days, you know, we were making like, you know, $23,000, $24,000. That was 10 percent of our salary. Just for walking to the back of the nightclub. Then we won the pennant. And Mickey and Billy said, "Topping's giving us our $1,000 back." I said, "Tell him to take it. I don't even want it." I was really mad at him.

Dan Topping [the Yankee president] gave each of us a check for $1,000. But we still had to pay that lawyer $1,000. So it was expensive for something we didn't do. The worst part of it was George Weiss [the general manager] was looking for an excuse to get rid of Billy Martin, because he thought he was a bad influence on Mickey and me, and he wasn't, believe me. He traded him to Kansas City about a month after the incident. That was—that was the worst day in Mickey's and my career with the Yankees, when they traded him. And, sure enough, they traded him and we went on a road trip, and the first team we were playing was Kansas City. And I had to pitch against Billy. I'll just tell this quick, but we got a big lead and Billy got up in about the eighth inning. And I saw Elston Howard calling a slow curve. I threw one, and he took it. Then Elston called for it again. I said, "The same thing?" And he hit a home run. Casey came out to the mound and he said, "Did you tell him what was coming?" I said, "No, no, no, no, no." But the Copacabana thing was really very innocent on our part.

No one liked a beer better than I did. Billy Martin, as a player, hardly drank at all. And Mickey didn't like beer, but he liked other things. We probably drank a little more than we should have, but I don't think it ever affected our playing. It never did in both our cases. Billy started drinking a little more when he got to manage. That probably drove him crazy. But we had some problems. Ryne Duren, whom I still speak to frequently, had a bad problem with the Yankees. Sam McDowell, big, left-handed pitcher, was another one that had a bad drinking problem. What's nice about it is, Ryne Duren is a counselor now and Sam McDowell is a counselor. They talk to the players, from BADD or major-league baseball alumni. And they send letters out. If anybody has a problem drinking, please call Sam or Ryne. They devote their life to it now, trying to get guys to straighten out. I'm sure there were guys on other teams that were the same way.

But the ones we knew even to this day, Bobby Richardson and Tony Kubek, talk to a few ex-Yankees, whom I don't want to mention. But they're talking to them right now, every day, about trying to go see somebody.

My father had a bar. He was a bartender. I think maybe he taught me a lot about it. I drank, but I would consider myself a good drinker. I don't mean I drank a lot, but I knew when to quit. And the day before a game, never. Mickey even used to tell people about that. And he was a lot the same way. If he drank as much as the writers in this town said he did, he never would have played 2,400 games with the Yankees.

Elston Howard gave me the nickname "the Chairman of the Board." I can't remember the year, but he said it once to a writer. Maybe in the middle, toward the late '50s, probably. I used to say to Yogi, "I'd rather pitch to Elston. You know why, Yogi? You got this big, old glove and I throw my fastest fastball, and when it hit the glove, it would just go 'poof.' " Elston, first of all, would stand closer to the batter. He'd be like two or three feet closer to me when I pitched, and it felt like I was right on top of the hitter. Yogi would be way back there. And Elston, when I threw my fastball to him, it'd go "pow." It really made that loud noise. I said "Yogi, Elston's a much better catcher. I'd rather have him." This was after Yogi caught about fifteen years for the Yankees. But they were both great. They were both good hitters. Elston had a better arm. Yogi was probably a little quicker around home plate, like on a bunt or a little slow roller or something.

Elston got accused of everything. Toward the end of my career, I would fool around. Elston would think, you know—this was the last two years—I wasn't pitching good. He'd take the ball and he'd hit his shin guard and try and scrape the ball up a little for me. And I said, "Elston, if I want to do that, I can handle it myself." I said, "You don't have to help me." I couldn't throw a spitter. I knew how to throw it, but I had no control of it. I really didn't. You want to grab

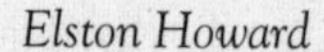
Elston Howard

the ball and not touch any of the seams, you know, just the white part of the ball, with your first two fingers and your thumb. So, you would just wet it, or some guys, I think—I won't mention names—maybe used Vaseline or something slippery. And the idea is when it comes from your hand it comes straight out. It's not revolving. The ball just goes in like a knuckleball and had a habit of going straight down, almost like the split-finger fastball nowadays. I tried it in practice. Joe Page tried to teach me as a twenty-one-year-old rookie. I could never throw it over the plate. Even warming up, so I didn't have much luck with it.

I guess Gaylord Perry would be the most famous pitcher who threw it. They never threw him out of the game or fined him or anything like that. They used to accuse Pedro Ramos, when he came to the Yankees, of doing it. But even playing with him, I never knew how he did it, or if he did it.

Mickey and I got picked for the All-Star Game in '61 in San Francisco. So we called from Chicago the night before and said, "Can we play golf at the Olympic Club?" And Horace Stoneham, who owned the Giants and was the host, said, "Oh, sure." So we went to the golf course and we spent about $500 or $600. We bought alpaca sweaters and shoes and we signed Horace's name to everything.

So that night, he and Toots Shor had a cocktail party at the St. Francis or some hotel in San Francisco. We were invited. It was Toots Shor and Horace and Cyd Charisse and Tony Martin. She was my favorite in those days. They were with us. And I went over there—I said to Mickey, "We got to pay Horace back the money." So he gave me $300 and I went over. I wanted to give him—I think it was $600. I said, "Horace, I think we spent this today. Will you take it?"

He thought about it and he said, "Well, if you get in the game tomorrow, in the All-Star Game, and get Willie Mays out, we'll call it even. If he gets a hit off you, you give me $1,200." I went over to Mickey. I said, "Horace wants to make this bet." And Mickey knew how well Willie Mays hit me. He said, "I ain't going for that." So we had another one or two drinks and Mickey said, "All right, let's do it."

Man, Mickey and I stayed out late that night. It was just an All-Star Game. We didn't pay much attention to All-Star Games in those days. And Mickey woke me up the next day, and he said, "You ain't gonna believe it, but you and Spahn are starting the game." And I said, "Oh, boy." So, I got the first inning. I got the first two batters out. Roberto Clemente hit a double and up came Willie. And old Mickey and I were thinking it's $1,200 or nothing. So I got two strikes on him. Willie hit two foul balls down the left field line about five hundred feet. And I had him two strikes and no balls. I said, "This would be a good time." This was one of the few times that I threw it. It almost started at Willie's hip, and it just broke down over the plate. Willie actually jumped back, thinking the ball was going to hit him. And the umpire said, "Strike three." And Willie's lying on the ground. And in Frisco, to go to the dugout, you went near home plate. And as I was coming in to the dugout, I looked down at Willie, and he looked up at me and he said, "What's that crazy SOB in center field clapping for?" Mickey was running in from center field clapping, figuring we had just saved $1,200. Commissioner never got on us about that.

I watch television now, and I see catchers holding the glove outside of the plate. I mean, they don't even have the glove over the plate, and if the pitcher hits that spot, a lot of times the umpire will say, "Strike three," or whatever. The strike zone just isn't the same for everybody.

Bill Summers was a good umpire, but he was too short. And the reason I say that was when Jackie Robinson stole home off me in the '55 Series, if you ever see a picture of that, Bill Summers was the umpire behind home plate. And he was about five feet six. Now, Yogi's got the ball and he's holding the glove in front of home plate and Jackie slides into it. You look at Bill Summers, he's three or four or five feet behind Yogi. He cannot even see where that ball is—he can't see it. Today, an umpire at least gets down there and he can see it. I mean, Jackie's gone now, but he was out, and he never would admit it. I never saw Yogi go crazy like that. But you look—Bill Summers never saw the plate.

It was a big thrill to be the starting pitcher for the Yankees in the World Series. I don't know if it was eight times or what, but the manager thought you were the top pitcher, in other words. But the one year I wish I'd started the first game, I didn't. That was in 1960 against Pittsburgh. Art Ditmar started. I was out half of the year with an injury that year. But I came back the last month and was pitching pretty good. And then we went into Pittsburgh and I didn't pitch until the third game back in Yankee Stadium. We outscored them 55 to 27, something like that, in that World Series. Ralph Houk still talks about it. He was the coach that year. He says, "I can't believe that." You know, I would have had a chance to pitch three games, see. We scored a lot of runs in every game, so I think we would have had a chance of winning the World Series. That was the only time I ever got mad at Casey. I didn't let him know I was mad, but I was really annoyed that he did that.

In the winter of '60 and '61, I was at Madison Square Garden at a basketball game. Casey had just gotten fired and Ralph Houk was the new manager, and he was at the game. We started talking. He said, "Now, when we go to spring training this year," he says, "how would you like to pitch every fourth day?" I said, "Great." He said, "I'm getting a new pitching coach, Johnny Sain."

Jim Turner was retiring, or whatever. I said, "I'd love to pitch every fourth day," because there was nothing worse than sitting in the dugout. I always wished I was the first baseman so I could've played every day. But I thought that was great when he let me pitch every fourth day. When we went to spring training, I said to John Sain, "You know, I've been in the big leagues ten or eleven years." I said, "I'm losing a little off my fastball and my curve isn't quite as fast or sharp as it was." So he got me to become a sinkerball, slider pitcher, and use a changeup. In '61, I was a completely different pitcher than I was the previous years.

In 1961 I was 25-4. But just pitching every fourth game, with the help of Luis Arroyo, I was 25-4.

The 1950 and 1961 teams I thought were the two best teams I ever played with on the Yankees. DiMaggio, Henrich, Rizzuto in '50. And then, I think the Yankees hit like 240 home runs in '61. If Mickey didn't have that injury—you know, he missed the last couple weeks of the season—I think that he and Roger Maris would have gone right down to the wire, you know, because they were very close at the time. Our three catchers—Yogi, Elston, and Johnny Blanchard—hit over 60 home runs together. Blanchard mostly was a pinch hitter. He caught a few games. But Elston would play left field once in a while and Yogi would catch and vice versa. Yogi would go to left field and Elston would catch. We had a good pitching staff. Bob Turley was there and Bill Stafford and Art Ditmar and Ryne Duren. Ralph Terry, too. We had a good pitching staff. Hector Lopez was a big part of the team. But the thing that is never mentioned was our infield. We had Clete Boyer and Tony Kubek and Bobby Richardson and Moose Skowron in the infield, and they were so good. I was a low-ball pitcher. I got a lot of grounders, and they just were great for me. And it was never mentioned. It was always the home runs and the pitching, but we had a great infield. Bobby you couldn't strike out. I think he got about 170 hits that year. And Moose was a great hitter, good fielder. Kubek and Clete, it was hard to get a ball hit in the hole off those two.

I liked the 1961 home-run race because the writers would all come in and talk to Roger and Mickey and they'd leave me alone. We would get writers from little towns that we never heard of. The clubhouse was just packed with TV—it was the worst I've ever seen in the Yankee dressing room. And they would ask Roger some of the craziest questions. Like, one guy asked him if he'd rather hit .300 or hit 60 home runs. And, you know, Roger would be good for a while, and then he'd get a little snappy with them. This was going on day after day, and he actually started losing some of his hair. The doctor thought it was from nerves. Roger was a really nice man and the players loved him. He and Mickey lived together out in Queens during that season. And guys would put in the paper there's a feud between Mantle and Maris. They were living together over by Kennedy Airport. Everybody loved Roger, but he just couldn't handle the press. He would tell the truth, really. He'd snap after a while, and when he got that reputation, the press made him look a little bad, but he really was a nice person.

Pitchers pitched to Roger because Mickey was up next. Somebody said Roger never got an intentional walk that year. And that was the reason; Mickey was the next hitter. So that was to Roger's benefit. They had to pitch to him. If Mickey wasn't hitting behind him, I'm sure he wouldn't have got as many pitches to hit as he did.

In spring training one year, I said to Johnny Sain, "You know, my curve is still breaking big, but I can't throw it as hard. And my fastball isn't quite as hard." So he said, "Let's work on a sinker, which you don't have to throw as fast." A sinker's something you want the batter to hit. You don't strike a batter out on a sinker. And he said, "Did you ever throw a slider?" And I said, "No." And he said, "A slider is like a little curveball, but it goes faster to the plate." And in, like, ten minutes, John had me out on the mound. I was able to throw a slider, like, in ten minutes. He said, "That's perfect." That whole year, I pitched sinking fastballs—two fastballs, the regular four-seamer, and the one that sunk—and then a slider. And I'd use my curveball for a changeup. I'd throw a big slow curve. And then I had a straight change. And it worked out great.

The sinker was just the way you held the ball. I put a lot of pressure on that thing and I'd just throw a fastball and it would sink. I threw it with the intention of having the batter hit it.

All these batters had been hitting against me for years in the American League. They'd never seen me pitch that slider. So that year, it was a little strange. I'd go into a town the first time and they were waiting for a big curve and changeup and that. And all of a sudden, a sinker, slider.

Johnny pitched with Warren Spahn. Warren, when he was younger, had great stuff. Fast, good curve. And John always had the big curveball, good control, with a little screwball. He was sort of like a right-handed Lopat. He had to really work on being a good pitcher. He had to be just precise. He had to spot his pitches perfect, where Spahn could throw a high hard one or a big curve. So John really had to work hard to be a pitcher. And I think those guys make the best pitching coaches, the guys that really had to learn themselves. So that's why John, I think, became such a good pitching coach.

I think one of the problems is a guy gets a five-year contract now, pitching. We had to pitch every year to get our salary for the following year. So I never wanted to get hurt, or go on a disabled list. And I should have a few times. But I said, "I've got to keep pitching or they're going to cut my salary." But when you get a five-year contract for pitching and your arm's got a little twinge in it, you'll say, "Hey, the more years I pitch, the more money I'm going to make."

So they watch themselves a little more closely. Some of them, I mean, there's some guys that just want to, you know, pitch all the time, but a lot of guys will be very careful that they're perfectly healthy before they'll pitch.

I don't call six innings of pitching a quality start. The day after I pitched, when I was pitching every fourth day, I would go out on the mound and throw about ten minutes. This was Johnny Sain's idea, to throw. And I'd get rid of all that stiffness. Let's say I pitched on a Sunday. Monday, I'd throw a little bit, seven or eight, ten minutes, off the mound. I'd rest Tuesday and Wednesday and, you know, I'd be ready to pitch Thursday again.

Johnny Sain didn't believe in running. He would hardly ever run, unless the pitching coach ordered him to. But during batting practice, he'd be in the outfield and he'd run after fly balls, and he got as much work in running that way as guys going out and doing twenty laps in the outfield. I didn't particularly care to run, and if

Johnny Sain

you pitch every fourth day, you're not going to get out of shape. You just don't. Your legs stay strong.

I wanted to pitch as long as I could. I joined the team in '50, but you know, I missed '51 and '52. So in '64, I was pitching the first game of the World Series in St. Louis, and in about the sixth inning, Elston threw a ball back to me. And I had no strength in my hand. It was the craziest thing ever happened. I'd just thrown a pitch, you know. I don't know what it was—a fastball, curve. He threw the ball back to me, and I didn't have enough strength to throw it back to him again. And the trainer came out on the field and I said, "I have no feeling. There's no strength in my hand." And I think the trainer thought I was having a heart attack. I had no pulse in my left hand.

I went in the dressing room. And I'll never forget. Richie Guerin used to play basketball for the Knicks. He was a good friend of mine. He was at the game. He came in the dressing room. I know he thought I was dying. And they've got me lying there and, you know, all these things on me. And what happened, the artery in my left shoulder at that instant got completely blocked off. There was no blood going down into my arm. I found this out a couple weeks later. I went to Dr. Denton Cooley in Houston and he operated on me. And he put a bypass, like they do with your heart, except he did it with my shoulder. He put in a new vein and it bypassed the blocked-off part. I came back in '65 and pitched pretty well. But then, in '66, my elbow kicked up. And I was, like, thirty-seven at the time, and so, in '67, I packed it in.

I pitched the first inning in Detroit, gave up one run, walked to the dugout, and I said to Ralph, "That's it. Get somebody else." He looked at me. And I said, "That's it." I went into the Detroit dressing room. I got a piece of paper, and I said, "Ralph, I've had it. I'll call you when I get to New York." I wasn't about to go through another operation, and so that's how I packed it in.

After all these problems with my shoulder and my circulation, then, all of a sudden, I come up with a bad elbow and I was going to be thirty-eight. And I said, "Man, no, I'm not going through with another operation." But I should've quit two years sooner.

I never thought about the Hall of Fame until Jack Lang called me to say, "Oh, you're on the list for next year, the voting," you know. And then, he called me the first year and said, "You just missed it, by ten or fifteen votes." So then I, you know, I felt bad. But then he said, "But you know what? Next year, you and Mickey are going to go in it." And he was right. That's what happened, which was great.

When they announced it—the day they announced it was in January—we were in New York City and we had to have lunch with the commissioner at the 21 Club. But first, we met at a hotel. And they had a press conference, a big press conference. And Mickey and I were up on the stage. And then, about twelve o'clock, we were supposed to walk to the 21 Club and have lunch with the commissioner—Bowie Kuhn, I think it was. But Mickey and I got mixed up with our directions. We stopped and my friend Buzzy Buzzalino had a restaurant next to Toots'. We went in there first. Met some people we knew. Then we went and stopped in Toots'. By the time we got to have lunch with the commissioner, we were—but he was very nice, and it was a long day. They had a party for us at Shea Stadium. Those were the years—'74 and '75—the Yankees were playing at Shea Stadium when they fixed up Yankee Stadium. Mickey and I got up about eight o'clock that morning to go to the press conference, and we got home at 3:00 the next morning from Shea Stadium. So we celebrated pretty good.

I was so nervous with that speech. The night before, Mickey's four boys were up there with him. And my two boys and my daughter. My two boys and Mickey's four boys were very close since they were babies. They found, in the other side of the hotel, there was a room with a pool table in it. But it was locked. And there was a transom up there. So I went up in the room to write my speech for the next day. Mickey took himself and boosted one of the kids through the transom. They opened the door and drank beer and shot pool all night.

They weren't that old, the kids. But they had a ball that night, and, you know, they loved Mickey. My boys got home a little late and I said, "Where were you?" And they said, "Well, we were shooting pool with Mickey." Mickey, you know, had about three hours' sleep. Never wrote a speech. And I got up and made my speech. I was terrible. I was nervous. Mickey got up, no notes, and he was just great. He was just wonderful. Made a great speech. That was the high point of my career.

Mickey and I had no money when we got out of baseball. I had a house that was paid for, and that was about it. I said, how are we going to make our living? And Mickey had no money. You know, even though he made $100,000 a year, he had a home in Dallas, he had to live at the St. Moritz Hotel here. You know, he didn't save anything. But when we got in the Hall of Fame, I'll tell you, that money started coming. These card shows. It sounds bad, selling your autograph, but it's really not that bad. A grown-up person runs the show, and most of the people that come to it are grown-ups, and they have a purpose. If they want a bat signed, Mickey might get $20 for signing it. That guy's going to sell the bat now for, like, $1,000 or something. So everybody did well on it. In Mickey's case, he then worked down in Atlantic City for a few years there, when he was barred from baseball. But getting in the Hall of Fame meant a lot to us financially, too. A cute story about Mickey and the restaurant that he opened years ago. His hamburgers in there were, like, $7.50. And Mickey and I were sitting in a booth there one day and looking down at this table and this lady came in with four children. And they ordered hamburgers and French fries and Cokes. And Mickey said, "Boy, this lady's going to be shocked when she gets the bill." And we were watching and she got the bill and she went "Oh, my God." You know, it was, like, $80 or something. Mickey went down, and I thought it was so cute. He went down and said to the lady, "I'm Mickey Mantle," and the kids got excited. And he smiled and said, "You're the ten thousandth customer we have, and it's on the house."

I'm sure there's a couple of ballplayers in the big leagues that, you know, might get a little fresh with the fans and not be nice to them, but maybe in a couple of years, they'll learn that the fan pays part of their salary—not as much as it used to be, because television is the big thing now. But it's so easy to be nice to them; it only takes a few minutes out of each day.

I was lucky enough to be born here, get in the Hall of Fame. A couple of things I'm proud of: I think I got the most out of my natural ability. You know, I didn't waste my ability. I pitched probably as well as I possibly could with my size and the way I threw a baseball. I think as far as a team, the Yankees, there's never one game I was more proud of than the other.

But the thing I remember most is that from 1950 to 1964—that's fifteen seasons—we were in the World Series thirteen of those fifteen, and that's the thing I'm the proudest of, the team doing something like that. I mean, that is a dynasty when you only miss being in the World Series twice in fifteen years.

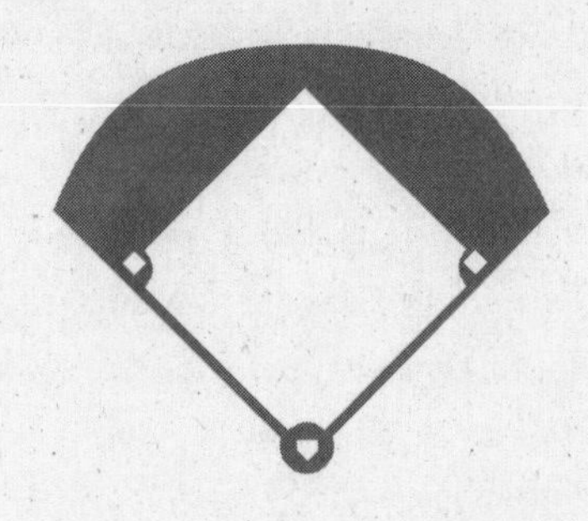

LEW BURDETTE

Selva Lewis Burdette Jr. was born and raised in tiny Nitro, West Virginia, and went to a high school without a baseball team. When he was attending college a scout told him, "I don't like the way you pitch. You may as well forget about baseball." But perseverance paid off for Burdette, as he would enjoy an eighteen-year big-league pitching career, finishing with 203 victories and one of the game's most incredible World Series performances.

A stalwart of the Milwaukee Braves pitching staffs of the 1950s, Burdette teamed with Warren Spahn to form one of the greatest dynamic mound duos. The repertoire for Burdette, a fidgety right-hander, included fastballs, curveballs, screwballs, changeups, and sinkers, all thrown from different angles, with different speeds, and with magnificent control.

After losing Game 2 of the 1957 World Series to Burdette, a former Yankee farmhand, New York Yankees pitcher Bobby Shantz, said, "We have no pitcher in our league with his assortment and crafty skill in cashing in on it. He threw sinkers and sliders, curves and fastballs, letups and just about anything else a hurler could show. Lew was splendid." Burdette would go on to tie a World Series record with three victories, including two shutouts, in the 1957 Fall Classic, winning Game 7 on two days' rest.

After thirteen seasons with the Braves, Burdette ended his career with short stints with the St. Louis Cardinals, Chicago Cubs, Philadelphia Phillies, and California Angels. Despite being dogged throughout his career with accusations of throwing a spitball, partly due to the fact that he would constantly fuss with his cap and jersey, or wipe his brow while standing on the mound, Burdette would just deny and continue with what he had been doing. Cincinnati Reds manager Birdie Tebbetts called him "a cheating spitballer," but National League president Warren Giles referred to him as a master psychologist, adding, "His fidgety actions on the mound are accomplishing exactly what he desires. I think he has the hitters (and managers and coaches) looking for something that isn't there."

Opinions varied, though, as longtime baseball man Clyde Sukeforth said of Burdette and the spitball, "He doesn't throw many, but he throws 'em. He throws just enough to keep the batters guessing. You can tell when it's coming as you can see him take a long look at the catcher. That's the tip-off." Longtime umpire Larry Goetz disagreed, stating, "I'd swear Burdette doesn't throw one but he's using this as a psychological weapon. Everybody is accusing him and he's going along with it. So they're looking for it every time the ball moves down on them. I've seen quite a few players swing at bad balls and then tell the manager it was a spitter because they're looking for an alibi."

Burdette, a small-town boy with big-league dreams, passed away at the age of eighty in 2007.

We lived down on the edge of town in Nitro, West Virginia. We more or less lived on what you call a "two-by-four" farm. We had cows and pigs and chickens and a big garden.

In my senior year of high school, I went to the chemical plant in town to get a job. They had a baseball team, too. My father said, "Why don't you tell them you're a pitcher?" He said, "You broke out every window around here for years." I told them I could pitch, and

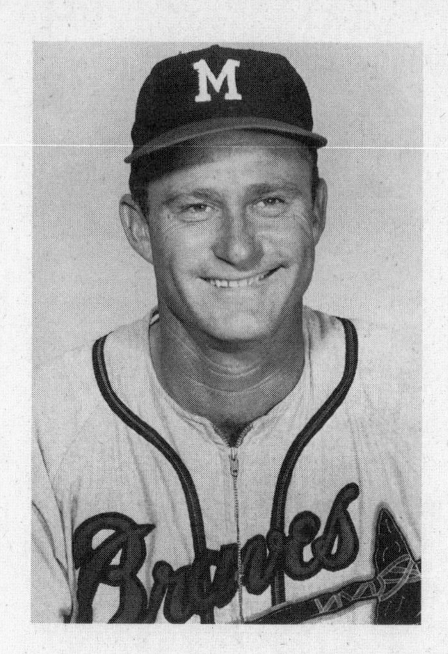

Lew Burdette

they let me pitch. I got to bat for two or three innings, and I got the job, riding a bicycle around in the plant, delivering mail.

I had played a lot of street ball where you throw one-hoppers and hit them way out, and stuff like that. I never played baseball until I was playing for a semipro team.

I was in the service, in the Air Force Cadet Program. I never played in the service. And I came out of the Air Force, and a Presbyterian minister there in Nitro asked if I would like to go to college. He said, "Coach Mac Pitt over at the University of Richmond is a very good coach." So I figured I might as well go over and see what it was like. So I went over and I got a scholarship, so to speak, at about $65 a month. It's funny. I won 12 and lost 2. And a scout came to Richmond, I'm not going to say from where, but I asked him to sign me. I said, "I don't want any bonus or anything. I just want to play baseball." He said, "Well, in my opinion—I've seen you pitch—and in my opinion, I'd say forget about baseball." Anyway, later on, after I was in the major leagues, I met him again. And I looked at this guy and I said, "You're the one who told me to forget about baseball." I said, "You don't remember me, do you? I'm the one who came to you at the University of Richmond and asked you to sign me up for nothing." His face fell and he said, "Oh, God. Do me a favor? Don't tell the front office." But anyway, I asked him to play and he turned me down.

While I was there, I learned to pitch every two days because I pitched for two local teams during the week and pitched on Friday for the university. So I'd had a little bit of experience, then.

I had little experience, because you get fifty bucks if you win and $25 if you lose. But, anyway, when I was back home working, I got a telegram from the Yankees wanting to know if I would like to come down and try out for Norfolk. I said, "Nah." I told my older brother, "I'm not going there." He sent the telegram back and said I would be there. Well, I thought I might as well go, you know, and see what was going on. So I went down and I pitched. The first game I pitched was a 2–0 shutout, and the second game I pitched, I came in after that game and the manager said, "Hey, I already had you on a train going to Amsterdam tomorrow morning; now you've got to stay and pitch again." I won the second one and I lost this third one, and the next morning I was on the train to Amsterdam, New York.

The Yankees offered me $150 a month and I said, "My dad won't let me sign for a penny less than $200." And they paid me $200.

I spent five years in the minors. The first year was with Amsterdam, New York. The second year, Quincy, Illinois. The third year was with Kansas City. It was AAA—and I stayed there two years, went up with the Yankees, and I got sent back down to San Francisco and Lefty O'Doul, one of my favorite people. Whitey Ford and I were roomies in Kansas City. We were good friends.

I pitched for O'Doul. Lefty was a great guy, and he was a good pitcher, and a good hitter. Lefty used to step up on the first step of the dugout in the game, you know, and say, "Hit him in the belly." Manager's word's law. And I read in the paper that Sunday morning—I'm pitching that afternoon—I read in the Sunday morn-

Lefty O'Doul

ing papers that I had tied Lefty's record that he set for most hit batters in the league. So he stepped up on the dugout and said, "Hit him in the belly." I shook my head no. And he said, "I said hit him in the belly." He came running out to the mound and said, "What are you shaking your head at me for?" He said, "I told you to hit him in the belly." I said, "I read in the paper this morning, Lefty, that I tied your record that you set way back, and I'm pretty proud of my company. I'm not going to go ahead of it." He said, "Oh, okay." Man, he was a great guy to play for. Then the Yankees traded me and $50,000 to the Braves for Johnny Sain.

I never really paid any attention to what level I was pitching at. But once I got in the big leagues, it was very good. Bucky Walters was catching me in the bullpen. He said, "Throw me a fastball." I said, "That's what I've been throwing you." He said, "Throw me another one." And actually, I threw a two-seam pitch all the time. I think Roger Clemens thinks he invented it or something because they talk about a two-seamer. We didn't call it anything. You got two seams working on one side of the ball and it just makes the ball do things, that's all. Bucky said, "You can't throw a fastball." He said, "You're going to be all right. You're going to do well." He said, "What's your goal?" I said, "I want to win as many games as you did, Bucky." Bucky won 198 and I won 203.

I always figured the best hitters in baseball got three hits out of ten times at bat. And that leaves 70 percent. I just thought it'd be nice if I can be in that 70 percent.

There was one time when Jackie Robinson and I got into it. Billy Cox of the Dodgers was on third base, two outs in the ninth. I had a 1–0 lead. Jackie Robinson was the hitter. He pulled a great play. He laid a perfect bunt. Eddie Mathews was just playing back, you know, with two outs, and he laid a perfect bunt down the third-base line, beat it out, tied the ball game up. Well, I turned around to first base and I said to him the same thing I would have said to my brother, you know: "You dirty bunting so-and-so." Well, he felt I called him a black guy. Well, he charged me. He charged me on the mound. Of course, I got out of the way and Eddie took care of it. That was a little rule: "Start something and get out of the way." You know, Jackie bunted on me twice a ball game every ball game that we played after that until he retired.

And he tried to run over me once when I was covering first. He went over the top of me once, but I raised up and threw him on his back. I mean, we had a lot of it for a lot of years, and I got all kinds of hate mail. Racial. "Dirty racial slurring degenerate" and all that stuff. And my son even got into a fight in school because of it. But when I found out that Jackie was not going to go to the West Coast, I asked Walter Alston, "Is Jackie not going to the coast?" He said, "No." I said, "Well, can I talk to him in that little room behind your dugout?" He said, "You promise me you won't fight?" I said, "I promise. But if he's not going up, I want to settle something with him." He said, "Promise me you won't fight." I said, "Yeah." He went back in the dugout in the clubhouse, and we were over in our clubhouse, and Walter came right in, came up to me, and he said, "Jackie says he'll meet you there in five minutes. Promise me you won't fight?" "Yeah, I promise, Walter." So I went up there and Jackie comes in in a little bit, and he said, "Hi, Lew." I said, "Hi, Jack." He said, "What do you want to see me for?" And I said, "I want to tell you something; that you pulled the best play that I've ever had against me. You laid a perfect bunt down, scored the tying run, and that's better than popping up or something like that, you know. But I thought it was a very brilliant play. But I turned around and called you what I would call my mother for bunting in that situation. I called you a 'dirty bunting so-and-so' and you charged me on the mound." I said, "I wouldn't change anything, because you and I had some great collisions down the first-base line." He said, "I don't think I got the best of that." I said, "Well, I wanted you to know that I understand you're not going to the Pacific Coast, and I wanted you to know what a great play you pulled on me, and you thought I said something about being black." I said, "But I didn't." He said, "Gee whiz." He said, "We went through all that stuff and you didn't even say it?" He said, "You hurt me several times." And I said, "Well, you tried to hurt me, but I had the

Jackie Robinson

advantage because I had the bulk." And he said, "Lew, I'm sorry." I said, "Don't be. I enjoyed it." He said, laughing, "I understand that." He said, "You make me feel a lot better." And I said, "Well, I wanted to settle it." I said, "I heard you weren't going up." And he said, "No. I'm a little bit older, and I got a good job with Chock full o'Nuts, and I don't want to have to move my family." And I said, "Well, it's been great playing against you, and I wish you the best of luck." He said, "Thank you." He said, "And I'm sorry that I bunted on you all the time." I said, "Now, don't worry about that. I'm not." But they asked him that year who did he think would be the best pitcher for the Braves against the Yankees in the World Series? Jackie said, "No doubt in my mind: Lew Burdette." I never carried any grudges or had anything against anybody in baseball. It's such a good game, and I didn't want to mess it up.

I threw a sinker, slider. We had a pitcher, Dave Madison, in AAA Yankees. He had one of the best change of paces that I ever saw. And he told me how he threw it. I watched. I tried it and tried it and tried it, and it became a very reliable pitch. Just try to keep your back foot on the rubber. Isn't that a tough thing? Lose your forward motion, lose your push-off, and still have control of the ball. I had good control over this change slider, change sinker. Just kept the back foot on the rubber.

You know, Burleigh Grimes was the pitching instructor for the Yankee organization. And when they outlawed the spitter, some people were grandfathered in so they could keep throwing it. Burleigh Grimes was one of those. Burleigh Grimes was allowed to throw the spitball. And I was in AAA in Lake Wales, Florida, and Burleigh came in there. He stayed there for two weeks or more. And I said, "Burleigh, teach me how to throw the spitball, will you?" And he said, "No." He said, "If I teach you, you'll get caught and you'll get thrown out of the game." He said, "But I'll tell you one thing, you can go through gyrations and all," he said. "I threw a lot less spitballs than they thought I did." He said, "If you can get hitters—who are egotistical so-and-sos, you know—if you can get one of the first three guys in the first inning to go back and complain," he said, "by the fifth inning, the batboy will be yelling, 'Look at the ball.' " And Burleigh called me up after he had seen me pitch on TV. He said, "You got it down good." He said, "You got them good."

I would talk to hitters. Sing to them. If I saw a guy in a country-music place the night before, I'd sing a song that he liked real well, anything to get his attention on something else. It worked most of the time. But pitching is a mental thing as well as a physical thing. I had an uncanny ability of throwing strikes. If you don't throw many pitches, you can pitch a lot of innings. I think I threw—in one game, I threw sixtysome pitches.

Pitching is not as tough as people make it. I just watched the College World Series and base on balls, base on balls, home run. I had Lou Chapman [a writer for the *Milwaukee Sentinel*] keep track of my base on balls. The guys that I walked, 70 percent of them scored. It taught me one thing. Don't walk anybody, absolutely.

Warren and I decided that if you get the reputation that you don't walk anybody, like Greg Maddux had, you don't have to throw strikes. They swing at anything.

I pitched a couple of games without any signs. Just gave me some target. Shortstop and the second baseman called a meeting at the mound. "What signs are you using?" Del Crandall said, "We decided not to use any." He said, "You know that Lew doesn't miss much when he misses. And they're all going to hit the ball on the ground, 90 percent of them." He said, "We just thought we'd try it without them." And then I would pitch the ball game without.

Orlando Cepeda hit me like he owned me. Sammy White came over from Boston and he's catching me in the second game of a doubleheader. He said, "Crandall says the Baby Bull hits you like he owns you."

And I said, "Yeah. He does. Try to keep people off base in front of him."

And Sammy said, "Could he hit you any better if he called the pitches?"

And I said, "No. I don't think so."

He said, "I'll present it to him."

And so Baby came up to bat and Sammy said, "Lew wants you to call the pitches." He said, "You can't hit him any better if you call the pitches."

"No, man. No, man. Can't do that. No, he can't do that." And that went on and on. He got back in the box and Sammy said, "He won't call them, Lew. You call them."

I said, "Slider on the outside corner." Strike one. I said the same thing; strike two. I said, "Now, fastball right down the middle. See how far he can hit it."

"No, man, you can't do that." And he didn't want to get back in the box. The umpire said, "If Lew wants to tell you what's coming, it's his business. Now, get in there."

I threw him a fastball right down the middle. He popped it up to me on the mound. And I was saying, "Should I catch it behind me?" But I didn't. I called every pitch to him for four or five years after that. He never hit the ball out of the infield. He did not want to know what was coming.

I threw at batters only when I had to or thought it would be a good idea. For example, Tony Gonzales. Hit me three times in spring training with a line drive on my arms. And it's funny; he's up to bat, and I never paid any attention to it. It's about the third, fourth inning. And I said, "I think I'm going to drill you. You drilled me three times in spring training." I put it under his armpit with the first and he tried to hit the ball. He hit it to Johnny Logan. Logan threw the ball wild to first base, and then Gonzales tried to go to third, and Joe Adcock threw a perfect strike. Very unusual. And he was out. And I pitched a no-hitter. That play kept it from being a perfect game, but I got even with him anyway.

• • •

I had a sore arm all the time. Del Crandall talked about one time when I had six straight wins and I could not straighten my elbow out. But it was my turn to pitch. I couldn't shake hands with people. I always figured if it's going to hurt just sitting on the bench, I might as well be out there.

I was the second-highest-paid pitcher in baseball. My roommate, Spahn, was the highest. And John Quinn [the Braves general manager] always said, "Your roommate is the highest-paid pitcher in baseball, and you're not going to make more money than him." I said, "Well, he won the same number I did. Give him a $10,000 raise and give me ten." He picked up the phone and called Warren. He said, "Warren, your roommate is here." And he said, "You both had good years. I'll give you a $10,000 raise and give him one." Warren said, "I'll take it, but my roommate won't." But I did.

Warren said to me, "Where have you been all these years?" He said, "That's the easiest that I ever saw and the most raise I ever got." We didn't have agents back then. There was only one agent, and that was Frank Scott with the Yankees. He used to be the Yankees' traveling secretary, and he became the only agent that I ever knew in baseball.

Pitching is a very sensible thing. First strikes: the best hitters in baseball only hit three for ten. And those strikes were something I-Maddux got the reputation. He never had the first strikes in. They swing at bad balls. Do you know that hitters aren't good enough? They aren't as good as they think they are. They may not remember one time at bat from the other time. But I threw every pitch that I threw to almost every hitter, except for a couple of guys that I wouldn't throw anything up high. I found out from Eddie Mathews—Eddie and Bob Buhl and Spahn and I ran around together, the four of us. I got Eddie to admit one night, "What bothers you more than any other pitch?" He said, "The flat slider from a right-hander bearing in on me." That was nice to know. I'll never forget Whitey Ford

Warren Spahn

and I were pitching against each other in the fifth game of the 1957 World Series, and I got a 1–0 lead. And I shook Crandall off a sinker, and he gave me the slider sign, and I threw a flat slider, and it broke in on Yogi, and he yelled, "No. No." He was going downtown, he yelled, "No. No." And he popped it up, right up in the air. You have to think. The guy stepped up there, I didn't know his name or anything, but if I'd faced him before, I knew what he hit and where he hit it.

In 1957, I was 17-9. And then came the World Series. Spahn lost the first game. I pitched the second game. Gave up a home run to Hank Bauer. He had two home runs in that series.

Then, in Game 5, I beat Whitey Ford, 1–0. The Yankees' second baseman backed up to catch the ball on a big hop. They didn't realize that Mathews was the second-fastest guy on the team, and Eddie beat it out. Then we manufactured the run, moving him over. I remembered Whitey in Kansas City, and I knew his philosophy: "Don't let him get ahead of you." He was a great pitcher, so I figured that if you get a run, you better nurse it. Things worked out really well. In that series, I pitched twenty-seven innings in three games. I pitched two shutouts, the last one on two days' rest. Now, they don't do that anymore. Two days' rest is only good for two innings nowadays. In Game 7, I won 5–0, and Del Crandall hit a home run. I can't remember where in the game that was. I like what Casey said, at the end of the seventh game, I think. He said, "That pitcher, that damn pitcher made us look sick."

I've never had a closer friend in my life than Warren Spahn. We both liked identically the same things. Warren and I'd go into a restaurant, "It's your day to order. You're pitching; it's your day to order." We did that all the time. We ate the same things every day.

You know, Spahn and I were at an old-timers game at San Diego, and we decided to go in the hotel bar to have a nightcap before the exhibition game the next day. We opened the door to the bar, and there's only one person in there: Casey Stengel. He says, "Hey, fellows, come over and join." He said, "One of you sit down on each side of me." He said, "I've been wanting to get you two guys together for a long time, and I wanted to tell you, you two are the worst darn trades I ever made in my life." Casey was managing the Braves. Warren wouldn't knock a guy down like Casey said. "Zip him," you know. He said, "You're gutless," and sent Warren back down to the minors. Then Warren went in the service and all that. But he said, "I just want you two guys to know that you're the worst trades I ever made in my life. Now we'll have a beer."

Stan Musial, I never threw him the pitch that I got him out on the last time up. I never threw it the next time up. Maybe not for two or three times, because he's laying back, camping for it. Roberto Clemente—if you crowded Clemente, you had better luck with him than if you'd pitch him away, because he hit up the alley in right-center field. If you forced him to get the bat out in front, he'd pop a lot of balls up. Richie Ashburn was always complaining. He was always complaining. "It's a crapping spitter. It's a crapping spitter." He's a very religious guy, never cursed, but, "It's a crapping spitter, it's a crapping spitter." I touched the ball on my arm and put it on the dirt and got down and tied my shoe. Put the ball in my glove.

Crandall was laughing. I saw him laughing. He knew what I was going to throw. And I threw the mud ball, which Whitey threw, too. I showed it to Whitey once up in Cooperstown. And he'd go down and tie his shoe once in a while. But I threw one—Crandall was laughing like the dickens back then. The ball broke about that much before—and Richie swung and missed. He took his helmet off, his batting gloves, everything. Laid his bat down on the plate, and I was up there, I walked up there and I said, "Now, that's a crapping spitter." He said, "I'll never complain again, Lew. I'll never complain again."

We won the pennant again in '58. I won 20 games, had 36 starts, 19 complete games. I had 8 complete games in the month of August. The World Series that year was a terrible disappointment. We were up three games to one. I was part of two errors, covering first base. Both times I dropped the ball because the ball was behind me. On two consecutive plays in the second inning of the seventh game. The Yankees scored twice. If we had made both plays they would've ended the inning. They wouldn't have gotten any more runs.

Someone asked me, after the '57 Series, did you feel like, "Well, we'll get back there next year," that it was sort of our destiny that we would always win the pennant and always play in the World Series? But the Yankees are the only ones who do that.

Even though it was a do-or-die situation in the World Series, I didn't put pressure on myself. If I won, I'd done my part, and if Spahn won, then he'd done his. And if the other team won? Well, they were trying to do the same thing we were trying to do. It was whoever lucked out or made the right play at the right time or something. It's a game of inches.

I was traded to St. Louis. I never got to start on a regular schedule. I went to the Cubs, and I started there on a regular term. The last half of the season I won nine ball games. Then I went over with the Phillies, and I won the first game or two. After a while Gene Mauch put me in the bullpen. About the last week of the season, they advertised that Spahn and I were going to pitch against each other. We were pitching the second game of a doubleheader. And Spahn came up by the dugout and he had two guys on each arm, holding him, and he was growling, "Ahh. Ahh." And I said, "Turn that boy loose." We were agitating each other, and it turned out it was a 0–0 ball game in the eighth inning. Alex Johnson hit a home run off of Warren. And then Bobby Wine hit a home run. It was a 2–0 game, and I pitched the ninth inning. Got them out one, two, three. And that was the last game I ever started. The first game I started, I pitched a 2–0 shutout, and the last game, I pitched a 2–0 shutout.

If I could have taken Del Crandall with me when I was traded, I would. Joe Torre was another good catcher. Tim McCarver was pretty good. He was a lot of fun and a good guy.

When I became eligible for the Hall of Fame, I don't think I missed by more than seven votes or so. And then Whitey Ford, Mickey Mantle, and all the guys started retiring. I just kind of slid out. I won over 200 ball games, was 60 games over .500. A lot of people in there don't have that good a record.

I am very proud of my career. I never dreamed of being a major leaguer. If my older brother hadn't sent the telegram back saying that I would be down to spring training for Norfolk, I may not have been in baseball.

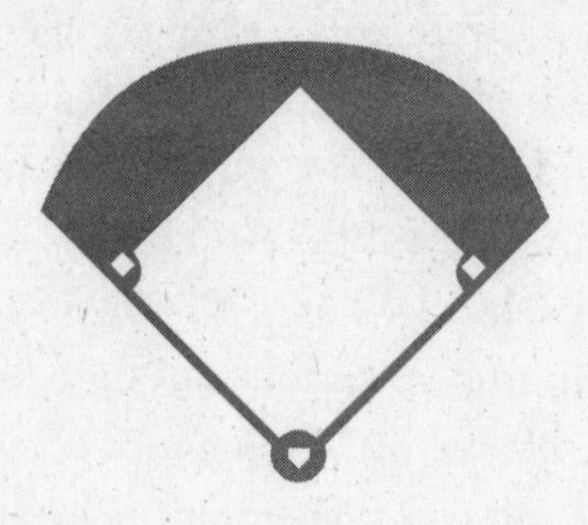

HARMON KILLEBREW

Though quiet off the field, Harmon Killebrew was a killer on it. In fact, the barrel-chested "Killer," as he was known, epitomized raw power at the plate. "I didn't have evil intentions," he famously said, "but I guess I did have power."

During a twenty-two-year big-league career, spent mainly with the Washington Senators/Minnesota Twins, the righty-swinging slugger from Payette, Idaho, finished with 573 home runs, many of them of the tape-measure variety, which places him second only to Babe Ruth among American League batters. An eleven-time All-Star who split his playing time between third base, first base, and the outfield, he tied or led the league in home runs six times, belting 40 or more on eight occasions.

"He hit line drives that put the opposition in jeopardy," said Ossie Bluege, the Washington scout who signed Killebrew. "And I don't mean infielders, I mean outfielders."

Killebrew won the 1969 American League MVP Award, leading the league with 49 home runs and 140 RBIs. According to his manager Bill Rigney, Killebrew "is one man who can beat you, if you give him a chance. Opposing teams plan around him because they know he is the one man who can do it to them. Even if he isn't hitting well, he gives others on the team a lift just by being in the lineup. As long as you have a man like that in a game, it gives security to others. Without him, we wouldn't be the same club."

It was in 1959 when Senators owner Calvin Griffith directed his manager, Cookie Lavagetto, to start playing Killebrew. "Lavagetto told me he thought Harmon would play his way out of the lineup," Griffith recalled years later. "But I liked the way he swung the bat. Power . . . that was what I was looking for."

Once he was in the lineup it was impossible to take him out. Longtime baseball man Paul Richards once said of Killebrew's awe-inspiring presence at the plate, "Harmon Killebrew could hit the ball out of Yellowstone Park." Similar sentiments were shared by manager Charlie Dressen: "Harmon hit home runs like Babe Ruth. They hit fly balls so high they didn't look like they would go out of the park, but the ball just carried and carried and carried over the fence."

A Killebrew contemporary and fellow Hall of Famer, Reggie Jackson, who himself finished with 563 homers, once said, "They definitely were right when they named him Killer. Man, I love to watch that guy work, even if he is beating our brains out. It's a pleasure to watch someone in the same business do things so well."

Teammate Dave Boswell may have captured Killebrew best: "If I had to size him up, I'd call him 'The Quiet Killer.' "

Those were great years for me growing up in Payette, Idaho. People say, "How'd you ever learn to play baseball?" But I started playing when I was very young, about eight years old, and I played through grade school and then on into junior high school and high school and some years of semipro.

I played four years of American Legion baseball. I think I probably got more experience playing American Legion baseball than anything else. We were on a state championship team there and

Harmon Killebrew

then turned semipro; we won the state championship in semipro baseball and some championships in high school. We had some very good teams.

It seemed like I always played with older players—older boys, and then older men as I got a little bit older. And I think that was a thing that really helped me get the experience, playing with older guys.

My father helped me—not only with baseball but football, basketball, and some track. And he used to teach my brother and I how to punch a punching bag and skip rope and do lots of things. And it was my father that really got me started in not just baseball, but all sports. My father was from Illinois. He played football in college and was a track star there.

I don't know if I ever really reached that point where I felt like I had what it took, but I always had the desire to be a professional baseball player. I wanted to play baseball for a career. I'm not sure that I knew, even when I signed a major-league contract, that I knew that I had what it took to be a major leaguer, but things seemed to fall into place and I got lucky somewhere along the line.

I had accepted a scholarship to play football and baseball at the University of Oregon after I graduated from high school. I was a high school All-American quarterback and I had several colleges recruiting me to play football. But in those days, they weren't giving scholarships much for baseball. So I was going to have to play football and baseball to get my college education. My brother had graduated from the University of Oregon, also my brother-in-law. I had been pretty familiar with that program over there. They had a great football and baseball program. We had a United States senator from my hometown by the name of Herman Welker, who used to go out to Griffith Stadium in Washington a lot and became friends with Clark Griffith, who owned the Washington ball club at that time. And Senator Welker kept telling Mr. Griffith about a young boy in Idaho that he thought could help the Senators win some ball games. In those days, the Washington club wasn't winning many games. They used to call them first in war, first in peace, and last in the American League. And I think more than anything else just to keep Senator Welker quiet, Mr. Griffith sent Ossie Bluege out to see me, who was the former director of the Washington club. And I really think that he just intended to invite me to come to Washington for a workout with the club, not thinking about signing me at that time. When Mr. Bluege arrived in Idaho, it was rainy. He rented a car in Boise and drove to my hometown, which was about sixty miles from Boise. And when he got there, we sat in his car. I was supposed to play a game that night, but it didn't look like we were going to play because it had rained. He said that the Washington Senators would like me to come to Washington and work out with the club. And I said, "Well, I appreciate that, Mr. Bluege, but I'm going to go play football and baseball at the University of Oregon." I really hadn't intended to sign a contract at that time. In that small town, everybody knew everything, of course, and they knew that there was a major-league scout there. They got the field in order after it stopped raining. They even burned gasoline on the infield to dry it up, and we played that night. I'd been going to that park since I was a little kid, and they had some pretty good teams that came through there over the years. And I've never seen anyone hit one over the left-field fence at that ballpark. It was over 400 feet down the left-field line. And that night I happened to hit one over the left-field fence. Mr. Bluege went out, stepped it off, said it was 435 feet, and he thought that was a pretty good hit for a seventeen-year-old kid. He called Mr. Griffith and said, "Hey, maybe we should try to sign this guy." So Mr. Griffith authorized Mr. Bluege to leave a contract in Senator Welker's law office, and then he went back to Washington. At that time, my father had passed away, and it was just my mother and me at home. I talked it over with my mother, and I said, "Well, that's really what I wanted to do—play baseball. I can always go to college, and if I go to college now, it's four years. I'd be twenty-two or twenty-three before I'm through college." And in those days, guys were apt to go to the service for a couple of years. And then, if I did sign, I might be twenty-eight, twenty-nine years old before I had the chance to get to the major leagues. But the contract that Mr. Bluege left was a bonus contract. In those days, anything over a $6,000 salary was considered a bonus. It's kind of laughable now when we look back at those times, but that's the way it was. It was three years, $6,000 a year for three years, plus $4,000 a year bonus. So I decided that's what I wanted to do. My mother had to sign the contract because I wasn't of age yet.

I went to the big leagues, and the rule was you had to stay there for two years before you go to the minor leagues, and so I was there for two years, and then finally went to the minor leagues.

In those days, there weren't any jets, but I took a prop plane from Boise to Chicago, where the Senators were playing the Chicago White Sox, and joined them there. Mr. Bluege's brother met me at the airplane, took me to the hotel, and there I met the manager of the ball club, Bucky Harris at that time, and several other players. That night, we played the White Sox. I just sat on the bench that night. But the next day, I was put in, of all things, as a pinch runner. That was my first exposure to major-league baseball, as a pinch runner. I got on first base. Somehow I made it down to second base, and there was Chico Carrasquel at short and Nellie Fox at second, guys that I'd read about all my life. I was wondering what I was doing there with those guys. Somehow, I got through that.

My first roommate in the major leagues was a veteran ballplayer by the name of Johnny Pesky. Old Needle Nose. Johnny was a great guy. He was from the Northwest, from Oregon. I think they thought Johnny being a veteran player and being from the Northwest, that it could help me learn the ropes. He was a great guy. That was a great experience, being John Pesky's roommate. The road trip was over—I think we actually went from Chicago back to Washington, and I'll never forget when I got to Washington. The next day, they wanted to throw me some batting practice and see if I could hit the ball at all. So there was a veteran left-hander on the mound out there. I didn't really know who he was, and they had him throw to me. In those days, the Griffith Stadium left-field fence was 405 feet down the left-field line—long, long, biggest park in baseball. This pitcher threw me everything up there: curveballs, sliders, fastballs. I don't know if he threw any knuckleballs or not. But I hit quite a few up in the seats, and they seemed to be impressed with that. I really didn't think much about it, because I thought all the ballparks were like that in the big leagues. I found out later that was Johnny Schmitz, a real veteran pitcher. So that kind of impressed them, but I was a little bit too naive to know what was going on at that time.

In those days, we didn't have the luxury of not working or training like they do today. We had to have different kinds of jobs. I did many different things in the off-season. I worked in a clothing store, a men's clothing store. I fed cattle one winter. Several winters, I worked for a natural-gas company selling connections to homes for natural gas and just different odd jobs.

The first year I didn't get into too many games. I got into very little. I hit .308 my first year: four for thirteen. And I'll never forget the first ball game I played in. I played at second base. Well, I wasn't really a second baseman, but somebody got hurt that day and they put me in at second against the Philadelphia A's, at Connie Mack

Stadium in Philadelphia. I went three for four in my first game, two singles and a double, drove in two runs, and we won 9–2 against the A's. And I thought at that point, "Gosh, this is going to be easy." I found out very quickly it wasn't going to be easy. It took a long time before I became a regular player. I think I learned a lot by just observing and watching, and, of course, I worked out before every ball game at home for hours: taking batting practice, fielding practice, and trying to learn a lot of the things that I needed to learn. But it took my going to the minor leagues before I really learned those things that I needed to learn to become a player.

The players on that ball club were very helpful to me. And I never forgot that, and I always tried to help some of the younger players as I became a veteran player myself. They treated me very, very well, and it's interesting, because I was the first bonus player of the Washington ball club, and the attitude could have been different toward me, but they accepted me very well.

We didn't win a lot of the games, but they had some great players. Mickey Vernon was certainly one of my favorite players, Roy Sievers, Pete Runnels, Eddie Yost—all great players and great people.

My first spring training was in 1955. The guys on the ball club told me that Mr. Griffith didn't like the players to fly. So I took a train from Payette, Idaho, to Orlando, Florida, for spring training. It wasn't too bad from Payette to Chicago, but it seemed like it took forever to get to Orlando. And when I got there, the joke was on me, because the players were flying in from all over the country. And that was the last time I ever took a train to Florida for spring training.

I guess the number one thing I'll always remember is that first home run I hit in the major leagues. That was a home run against the Detroit Tigers. I hit it off of Billy Hoeft, who was a veteran left-hander of the Tigers. When I went up to home plate, they had a guy named Frank House who was catching. And he said—I was only eighteen—and he said, "Kid," he called me Kid—and he said, "Kid, we're going to throw you a fastball." And I didn't know whether he was telling me the truth or he was lying to me. And sure enough, there came a fastball, and I hit it 476 feet. I rounded the bases, and when I touched home plate, he said, "Kid, that's the last time we're ever going to tell you what's coming." And it was. I never heard a catcher ever tell me what was coming after that.

I joined the club in June of 1954. And then in 1956, in June, my two years were up. And they sent me to Charlotte in the Sally League, which was the Senators' Class-A ball club. I finished the year there, and I had a very good year of playing third base. I hit 15 home runs and hit .325 and came back to Washington at the end of the summer.

The next year, I went to Chattanooga, a Double-A team in the Southern Association. I had a good year there and led the league in home runs, about 29. People say now that 29 home runs is not very many, but it was a lot of home runs then. That was the biggest park in organized baseball, I think. So hitting 29 home runs was a lot, but I only hit 6 at home, and people say that's not very many home runs. It was for a right-handed hitter in the Chattanooga ballpark. It was almost impossible to hit them over that left-field fence there. But I got 6 of them, so that was a great experience for me playing third there. And I got to play for a great manager by the name of Cal Ermer, eventually the manager of the Twins. Cal really worked with me and helped me, not only with playing third base but also with my hitting. Cal Ermer was just all baseball, twenty-four hours a day. He was one of the finest men I've ever met and one of the best baseball people I've ever met. I got to play for him later on in Minnesota, too.

My closest friend, my roomie later on, who I roomed with for ten years in the major leagues, was Bob Allison. So I got to play with Bob at Charlotte and at Chattanooga. And then he was Rookie of the Year in 1959, my first year of playing regularly.

In 1958, they actually farmed me out to Indianapolis. It was a White Sox Triple-A ball club. And the funny thing is that the Washington club didn't have a Triple-A team at that point.

So I went to Indianapolis, and it was kind of like spring training to me. I'd sit on the bench for a month, and going to the minor leagues at that point was tough because the pitching was so good in that league, the American Association at that time, and it took me a while to get going. Well, I was just starting to get going and they said, "We're sending you back to Chattanooga." So I was at kind of a crossroads in my career where I had to make a decision about what I was going to do. I decided that I had to prove to them that I could hit in the major leagues, so I went back to Chattanooga and had a good year the rest of the year. I went back to Washington in 1958 and stayed.

In the minor leagues in those years, I think it was a great time to play baseball. Not only was the caliber of baseball good, but the attitude of the players was wonderful. I enjoyed those years that I had the experience of playing there, and I developed a lot of relationships with the players that probably I wouldn't have had if I had not gone to the minor leagues. I really did enjoy those years that I spent there.

Baseball is really what I wanted to do, and I knew that I could, having been there for the little bit of time that I was. I knew I could hit in the major leagues, and finally I had to prove it to the owner of the ball club and to the manager up there that I could hit. What tipped the decision toward staying was the fact that I loved baseball so much. That's what I enjoyed doing more than anything else, playing baseball.

In 1959, I opened up the season at third base, hit a home run opening day. I hit one the last day of the season, too. It was my first home-run championship—tied with Rocky Colavito. Forty-two home runs.

I made my first All-Star team that year. Played in Pittsburgh at old Forbes Field. That was a great experience. Casey Stengel was the manager of the ball club that year because the Yankees had won the pennant the year before. To be on a club with Mickey Mantle and Al Kaline and Rocky Colavito and Whitey Ford and Yogi Berra, that was a quite a great experience.

The first thing I heard about Griffith Stadium when I walked in the ballpark is that's where Mickey Mantle hit that long home run, 568 feet or something like that, over left field. He hit it to the top of a sign and it bounced out on the street. It was a big park. High fence in right field that was maybe 345 down the line and about a 35-foot-high fence with a scoreboard on the right-field fence; bullpen in center field, it was like 426 to center or off center a little bit with a high fence and a flagpole behind and a tree behind that fence. And left field had bleachers—it was 405 down the left-field line with high bleachers. It was a very big ballpark.

It was not a hitter's park. In fact, I was told that one year, during the war years, there was maybe two home runs hit all year in that ballpark.

I liked playing third base. We had a couple of guys on the ball club after we moved to Minnesota that made it interesting for me, because we had Rich Rollins playing third and Don Mincher was a first baseman, and at that point I kept bouncing back and forth between first and third, so they could play in the lineup. Third base was a tough position to play in the major leagues. I always heard the expression "Knock them down and throw them out," and that's about the way it is playing third base. You have to have quick actions and quick reflexes and a pretty good arm. At that time, there was a pretty good third baseman with the Orioles, probably the greatest third baseman that ever lived, Brooks Robinson. Brooks won sixteen Gold Gloves at third base, so I never got an opportunity to win a Gold Glove at third, but I helped him win a few of those by hitting a lot of balls at him. But that was a great experience. I liked playing third.

I actually think that Calvin Griffith was responsible for me playing regularly that year. He insisted to Cookie Lavagetto that I play

Calvin Griffith

third base or start the season anyway, and so I'll always be thankful and beholden to Calvin Griffith for that opportunity to play. Calvin was a good judge of talent. The Washington Senators and the Twins always had good farm systems, and I think one of the reasons was because Calvin knew baseball talent and was able to suggest certain players to play.

In those days, we always dealt one-on-one with the general manager or president of the ball club in the contract negotiations. No one had agents in those days, and so that was an experience dealing with Calvin. Calvin was good to me that first year when I hit 42 home runs. I was making $9,000 a year. I led the league in home runs with 42 and drove in 105 runs. And the next year, I jumped all the way up to $21,000, so I more than doubled my salary, which was pretty good for the Washington Senators in those days.

But we just weren't drawing people. We just did not have good attendance in those days. And even though we were a pretty good ball club, people weren't coming out to watch us play. The old story, I think, it could have been true. Somebody called the ballpark one night, and they said, "What time is the game?" And then the voice on the other end said, "What time can you get here?" And that's about the way it was. There were days when we had just several hundred people come to the games, and that was not good.

After the season was over in 1960, in the fall, I got a phone call at home. I can't remember now who made the phone call to me, but they said that we were going to move to Minnesota. And I thought, boy, I really hated to see that because two things: I loved playing in the nation's capital. It was nice and warm to play baseball in, and Minnesota didn't seem like a great place for me to play baseball in that cold weather in the spring and the fall. And I wasn't looking forward to that. I remember in June 1959 when President Eisenhower came out to the ballpark. He called me over to his box seat, and he asked me if I would give him an autographed baseball for his grandson, David. And I said—I wasn't going to refuse the president of course—and I said, "Sure will, Mr. President, if you'll give me one in return." Which he did. A few years after that, I met David and asked him if he still had the baseball that his grandfather gave him. And he said yes, he did. And that was the thing that was unique about playing with the Washington Senators in the nation's capital, because you never knew who was going to come out to the ballpark, whether it's going to be a president or a vice president, a member of the cabinet, senators, congressmen. That was a great place to play.

In 1960, I moved to first base and played there some. I was a little apprehensive because I never played first base before. Just a change of the glove from third to first was a big change, and catching the ball in a first-base glove was different than catching it in a fielder's glove in the palm of your hand. You had to catch it out more in the webbing. I liked first base very much because you had the second baseman and the pitcher to help you on plays, and you didn't have to make as many throws, and you got to talk to the players when they'd come down to first base. Another thing I liked was it was a lot closer to the dugout. I remember trying to strike up a conversation with Frank Robinson. Frank was the most serious player, I think, I can remember playing against over those years. He didn't want to have any conversations with the opponents. He wouldn't even answer me when I talked to him. He wouldn't say anything. Now we've become real good friends. Brooks Robinson, on the other hand, was a very big talker. He'd come down and he'd carry on a conversation with you.

I thought the Yankees had maybe one of the greatest ball clubs that I ever saw in the early 1960s—'60 and '61 certainly were great. Early 1960s were great years for the Yankees. I don't think there was a player that I ever saw that had more physical ability than Mickey Mantle. He could hit the ball harder and farther than any player I ever saw and could run faster than anybody I ever saw, early on in his career. He was the only player I ever saw that bunted with two strikes—who hit for power, anyway—and beat out the bunt most of the time. We were hoping he'd bunt every time we came up there. He didn't do that.

I remember opening day in 1956, Mickey hit two home runs over the center-field fence in Griffith Park. I think he hit one right-handed and one left-handed. I was amazed at the kind of power that he had. I was playing second base the day that he hit one that was about three feet from going out of the ballpark in Yankee Stadium. I'll never forget that one. That was a tremendous shot.

Roger Maris, I thought, was a very underrated ballplayer. He did everything very, very well. He was a fine defensive outfielder, an excellent base runner, and had a good arm. Roger probably was his own worst enemy with the press, but he had certainly made the point in Yankee Stadium with that right-field fence. That was a great park for him, but I thought, for the single thing that he did by hitting 61 home runs, he should have been in the Hall of Fame.

Whitey Ford—if I had a one-on-one ball game, I'd like Whitey Ford to pitch it for me. I think Whitey Ford was one of the greatest pitchers I ever saw. He was a great competitor. And to me, the last two years I faced him, he was even tougher than he was early on in

Roger Maris

my career. He changed his style of pitching. When I first saw him, it was a good, hard fastball and a lot of curveballs at different speeds. In the last couple of years he pitched, he threw sinkers and sliders. He was really tough on right-handed hitters.

Yankee Stadium to me was almost like a museum because of the great tradition that the Yankees had, the great players that played in Yankee Stadium from Ruth right on down. And in those days, of course when I played, the monuments were inside of the fences, and they had a speaker in center field that made it interesting. But left field and the center field were like Death Valley out there; the longest center field and left field in organized baseball, I guess, and very difficult for a right-handed hitter unless you hit the ball to right field. Moose Skowron learned to hit the ball to right field pretty well in those days, as I recall. But it was a lot of fun to play in Yankee Stadium, although difficult, because the Yankees had such great ball clubs to play against. Our club surprisingly played quite well against the Yankees.

• • •

We didn't really know what to think about going to Minnesota. We opened on the road that particular year in Yankee Stadium against the Yankees. Then we went home to Minnesota, to snow. They had actually shoveled snow off the field to play the first game in Metropolitan Stadium in Bloomington. I had pulled a muscle before we got back to Minnesota, so I actually did not play in the first game that was played in Minnesota. It took me a while to get back in the lineup. But I thought, "Boy, if this is the way it's going to be in Minnesota, I don't know why they moved the club here." But we got through that season. It was a park that they built for the Minneapolis Millers. And I think that park was built in 1956, and then they expanded it, put in more seating through the years. It became a ballpark that not only the players liked to play in, but the fans loved. It seemed like it was good for everybody. The wind in that ballpark was a factor both in the spring and the fall. I remember the wind blowing in, in the spring and the fall, and in the middle of summer, the ball carried better throughout, so I liked playing in the park. That was a good park for me.

The fans were absolutely wonderful. As cold as the weather was, the fans' hearts were warm, and I just grew to love the years that I played in Minnesota. I think I grew up in Minnesota. I was twenty-four, I believe, when we moved to Minnesota, and I played parts of seven years in Washington and fourteen years in Minnesota. Those were fourteen of the greatest years that I've ever had in my life. I loved playing there. We did become a good ball club. And we won a pennant, and played in the World Series, and we finished high up in the standings several years; it was great playing there. I had 46 home runs in 1961. So it was a good year for me and a good year for the Twins.

That was an interesting year. I thought the feat of Mantle hitting 54 home runs may have been better than Maris hitting 61, because Mickey hit behind Roger and he wasn't in the best of health at that time with his legs. At the end of that season, I ended up with

46 and Jim Gentile also had 46. We tied for third place that year. After that season, we went on a home-run-hitting tour with Roger, down through North Carolina, which was an interesting thing. They didn't want to talk to Gentile or me. They wanted to talk to Roger, of course, about hitting the 61 home runs. And I remember Roger saying he wished that he had brought his clippings with him. They had written everything in the New York papers that they could write about him.

He was a very quiet guy. He grew up, of course, in Fargo, North Dakota. And I think playing in Yankee Stadium and in New York was a tough thing for Roger to do.

Tony Oliva came to our club in 1962 and led the league in hitting as a rookie in 1964. Tony was absolutely fabulous, just a wonderful young player. You could see right away that he was going to be a great hitter. He was one of the finest hitters I've ever seen. He was a Rod Carew–type hitter with power; he hit the ball all over the ballpark, and was the best off-speed hitter I've ever seen. You could throw him ninety-nine fastballs and one changeup and he would crush it. He developed into a very good outfielder. He was pretty rough when he first came up to the major leagues. He couldn't speak any English, and I've kidded Tony over the years that after forty years here, he still can't speak any English. Just an excellent hitter. You'll never see a finer hitter than Tony Oliva.

In 1964, I led the league in home runs, with 49. First time I hit 49 home runs. I really had an opportunity to hit up in the 50s that year, and I think I put more pressure on myself than the pitchers put on me. In those days, 50 home runs was kind of a magical number. Then, in '69, I hit a ball into the center-field bleachers in Fenway Park. And I was on my way to second, rounding the base, and the umpire at second base, who was Larry Barnett, said the ball hit the wall. So I held up at second and I said, "No, that ball went into the center-field bleachers." He said, "No, it hit the wall." The next day, I went out and talked to the center fielder, who was Reggie

Smith. And I said, "Reggie, didn't that ball go into the bleachers?" And he said, "Yes, it did." And so that year, I did hit 50 home runs, but I only ended up with 49 officially.

Mudcat Grant was a pitcher that probably beat us more than anybody else in the American League when he faced us. I think because he beat us so much, they traded for him. And when he came over, we weren't very good friends. As it turned out, though, Mudcat Grant and I are the best of friends. We became very good friends. In '65, he went on to a 20-game season for us, and then won two games in the World Series and even hit a home run to help us win one of the games. And he's just been a great friend and a great guy.

Nineteen sixty-five was an interesting year for me, because on August 2 of that year, I completely dislocated my left elbow in a play at first base. We were playing the Orioles in Met Stadium, and Russ Snyder of the Orioles bunted a ball down the third-base line. Rich Rollins fielded the ball, threw the ball inside the line, toward home plate. I came off the bag at first, to catch the ball, and then I was hit, on my forearm, by Russ Snyder. Not intentionally; it just happened. That completely dislocated that elbow. It felt like it broke my arm off. I was afraid to look at my arm. They carried me off the field. We had a doctor in those days on the club who was not an orthopedic doctor. He was just a general practitioner. And he put my arm back in place. And as it turned out, that was the best thing that ever happened to me, because it wasn't broken, and the quicker he got it back into place, the better. They took me to the hospital, x-rayed it, and there was no broken bones, but I was out for the rest of the season until the last ten games, which I played at third base. I played in the World Series at third base, too.

In 1965, the World Series opened in the American League city that year, Minnesota. In the first game of the World Series, Sandy Koufax was supposed to start. It was a Jewish holiday, so Sandy didn't start the game. Don Drysdale did; we beat Drysdale. And the next day, Koufax pitched; we beat Koufax. And we thought, "Gosh, we may have a chance to sweep the Series here." We went to the West

Coast for the next three games. They won three straight in Dodger Stadium. Then we came back to Minnesota, where we won the sixth game. And then I think I saw one of the greatest pitching performances I've ever seen, with Koufax pitching on two days' rest, throwing mostly fastballs. He shut us out 2–0. That was really a great, great job that he did there. And I'll never forget that Series, because I got the last hit off Sandy in that Series and was on first base when Bob Allison struck out with two out, took his bat, hit the ground, broke his bat. And after the game, I said, "Bob, if you had swung at the ball as hard as you had swung at the ground, we might have won the Series." But we didn't.

Not only did Koufax have a great fastball and a wonderful curve; he had pinpoint control. I always thought that maybe he was lucky. We got John Roseboro in a trade from the Dodgers later on. After that, I said, "Rosie, was Koufax really that good or was he was lucky?" And he said, "No, he was really that great."

Don Drysdale was one of the toughest right-handed pitchers that I've ever seen. He wasn't afraid to pitch inside. I got lucky in one of the games and hit a home run off Don. Two strikes and no balls, but he was tough.

The Dodgers had a complete infield of switch-hitters. Wes Parker at first base, Jim Lefebvre at second, Maury Wills at short, and Jim Gilliam at third base, all switch-hitters, pretty unusual.

We had Bob Allison, Jimmie Hall, and Tony Oliva, which was a pretty darn good outfield and good hitting outfield. In our pitching staff, we had Camilo Pascual, Jim Merritt, Jim Kaat. Jim Kaat was one of the finest-fielding pitchers, and he was a good hitter. Back then, pitchers hit in the American League. He was a fine hitter, great fielder, won sixteen Gold Gloves as a pitcher. I remember playing first base one night, and Jim took a one-hop line drive in the mouth. The ball ricocheted over to Rich Rollins at third. Rich fielded the ball, threw it to first base for the final out of the inning. Like I always did, I looked at the ball to see if there was any scuff marks or anything. I looked at the ball, and there were Jim's teeth—part of his

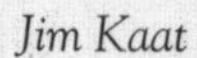
Jim Kaat

teeth—in the ball. Of course, I gave him the ball. And he probably still has it. But he didn't miss a turn. He had oral surgery, and he was back in the lineup his next turn, which not many pitchers would have done.

Jim changed his style of pitching over the years, but he was pretty much a fastball, curveball type of pitcher. He learned to pitch inside to right-handed hitters, and he just became an outstanding pitcher.

In those days, when I played, it was just part of the game for the pitchers to brush the hitters back, and we thought nothing about it. I got hit an awful lot. Fortunately, I never got hit in the head, but I got hit all over my body. And I never really thought much about it, because it was part of the game. And I think that pitchers had to do that in order to help control the game, because if you can't pitch inside, hitters are going to get on top of that plate and it's going to be very, very tough to pitch. Then the game went through a dramatic change where pitchers weren't allowed to throw inside much. In fact, they were ejected from the game a lot because of pitching inside. I certainly don't condone pitchers throwing at hitters' heads, but I think in order to be a good pitcher, you have to move the hitters back away from the plate. A lot of times when you hit a home run, they would throw at the next hitter behind you. That happened a lot. I don't know why they picked on the next hitter after someone hit a home run, but they used to do that.

I batted mostly third and fourth, and that was fun. I remember in 1969, we had Cesar Tovar leading off; he got 154 hits. Rod Carew hit second; he got 152 hits. And most of the time, Tony Oliva, who hit third, got a couple of hundred hits. I hit behind those guys and it was fun, because there was always somebody on base to drive in, and I had my best year that year.

In the 1968 All-Star Game in the Astrodome in Houston, I was playing first base. Curt Flood was the batter. He hit a ground ball to shortstop to Jim Fregosi of the Angels. Jim threw a low throw to first base. It was not a bad throw, just a low throw. I stretched out, caught the ball. A lot of people don't remember this, that Curt Flood was out at first base. Then my foot gave way. And in the Astrodome, there was no sunlight or rain on the soil. It was kind of like dead soil around the bases. And my foot gave way and I couldn't go left or right. I had to go right over my leg. And I completely did a split. I'd never done a split before, but I did it that day, or that night. That was really a freak injury, and it tore some things below my knee—my left knee. It tore the fascia, the covering of my hamstring muscle, and it tore the muscle itself. And it pulled a small piece of bone away from the pelvis where the hamstring was attached. I was out until September. Had it completely torn away from the pelvis, I probably wouldn't have been able to play again. But I worked really hard that winter and came back. In 1969, I had the best year I ever had in baseball. And maybe it was a blessing in disguise that I worked so hard that winter to get back in shape and be able to play. I did a lot of running, lifting, strengthening that hamstring muscle up. I think that's what really helped me.

• • •

Billy Martin was I think one of the finest managers on the field that I've ever seen. He knew the game better than a lot of other managers. But it was the stuff outside the lines with Billy that always got him in trouble. But he was a tough manager. Some managers manage different ways. Sam Mele was a very quiet guy; he let the guys play and kept the guys on the bench that weren't playing happy. Billy was, I think, a manager who ruled the game with fear. He intimidated a lot of the younger players. A lot of veteran players like myself, it didn't bother us. But the younger players he had—he struck some fear in their hearts. I think the thing that I remember about Billy managing was that he didn't let the players beat themselves. He was very strict on fundamentals and the little things that were important.

I walked more later on in my career because I think I was more patient and looked for better pitches to hit than I did early on. And I was more of a free swinger when I was younger. I developed a better attitude at the plate, as far as being more patient and having a better strike zone. Physically, I was in good condition in 1969. I think that it takes a long time to learn to be a good hitter. It took me a long time. I never really became the hitter that I wanted to be. Even then, it's just—it's tough. And hitting a baseball, said Ted Williams—and I have to agree—is the single most difficult thing to do in all of sports. Hitting a baseball consistently is really tough to do.

As a young hitter, I was a pretty high-average hitter, believe it or not. I used to hit the ball all over the ballpark. When I was about eighteen, I talked to a great hitter by the name of Ralph Kiner. Ralph, of course, was a great long-ball hitter. He said he thought that if I would move up on the plate and pull the ball more, I'd hit more home runs consistently. He said that you can't hit for a high average and hit the ball all over the ballpark and still hit a lot of home runs. It was just physically impossible. And Ralph was right. So I tried to move up on the plate a little more and pull more. And I hit more home runs, which I thought did help the ball club more because home runs do drive in runs. And it worked out pretty well.

Mr. Griffith rewarded me after that good year that I had in 1969. I made the most money I ever made in baseball the next year, which was $120,000. And boy, when I look back, I was one of the better-paid players, I guess, at that time.

Marvin Miller, when he first came in—I can't remember what year that was—but when Marvin Miller came in as head of the players' union, that was when things started to dramatically turn around. The year after I was out of baseball is when the free agency came in, which was 1976. That was really the big turnaround of baseball, when players started making the big salaries and long-term contracts came into existence.

I used to hear hitters say they never hit a home run when they were trying to. And I never did believe that because I hit a lot of them when I was trying to. But, of course, I struck out a lot. I popped up a lot. I hit a lot of weak ground balls when I was trying to hit home runs, too. But believe it or not, I tried to play the game as the game developed. If a single would help win a game, I wasn't trying to hit the ball out of the ballpark. Sometimes I did on those occasions, but I wasn't necessarily trying to do that. Just trying to get a base hit or sometimes a walk will help you win a game, too. My most memorable home runs were the first one, the last one, and a lot of them in between. I guess the last one I'll always remember because it was against the Minnesota Twins. I played my last year with the Kansas City Royals and hit a home run off a little left-hander by the name of Eddie Bane. I'll never forget that one.

Nolan Ryan was a great, great pitcher. There's no question about that. Had a great fastball that you heard of. But not only did he have a great fastball, he had a great curveball, too. He probably struck out as many hitters with his curveball as he did his fastball. He's the only pitcher that I ever struck out four times against in one game. That happened opening day of 1975 when I was with the Royals, and that's not a very good way to start off the season. Not a very good way to start off an experience with a new ball club. I think he ended up getting me eleven times. I got him a couple of times. But he certainly was one of the really great pitchers of that era.

Herb Score threw harder than any pitcher that I ever saw. And it was unfortunate he got hit in the eye. It didn't hurt his arm, but he never was able to develop after that, to become the pitcher that he could have been. I think he would have been one of the greatest pitchers of all time, with the arm that he had. He threw extremely hard and had that great overhand curveball. He was the hardest pitcher I ever saw.

I thought Denny McLain for a couple of years was about as good as any pitcher that you'd ever want to see. And while we're talking, he's the last pitcher that won 30 games in a season in major-league baseball. Denny McLain had a pitching coach during that time, Johnny Sain. And Johnny Sain taught him what Johnny called a quick curveball. It was bigger than a slider but faster than a regular curveball, and broke about that much, but it was very quick. And I think that quick curveball really made him an excellent pitcher.

I always tried to watch the pitcher and his complete windup from the moment he had the ball in his glove, all the way through his motion, and tried to follow it all the way out of his hand, all the way to home plate. I've heard some hitters say that they tried to pick the ball up in an area where the pitcher threw from. But you're leaving a lot to chance there, because he might vary the area where he throws the pitch from. So I think to me it's important to follow the pitcher and kind of blot out the body of the pitcher and concentrate on his hand and how he grips the ball. I could tell pretty much when he released the ball what type of pitch it was going to be and where it might end up at the plate.

The rotation on the baseball was important. I could tell what kind of a pitch it was going to be. I guess I was blessed with pretty good eyes. And like a lot of guys, I think that most hitters that are good hitters have pretty good eyesight.

There are different kinds of curveballs, for example. Some that spin a lot and then some that don't spin so much, like the slow curveball Stu Miller used to throw. Sandy Koufax had that great overhand curveball; it would come up and go straight down with real-fast rotation, like Herb Score's. Some pitchers would throw from the side and have a different type of a rotation, or a slider. You'd almost see a red dot in the center of a slider when it would come up there.

The most difficult kind of pitch to hit probably is a knuckleball, because you have no idea what that ball is going to do when it comes up there. I've always thought they should outlaw that pitch because the hitter can't hit it and the catcher can't catch it. The umpire doesn't want to call it a ball or a strike.

The last couple of years I spent in Minnesota were kind of tough for me. I had some physical injuries, my knees were starting to get real bad, and I wasn't playing as much as I would have liked to have played. And our club wasn't winning so much in those days. So it was a little frustrating, the last couple of years that I played there.

In December of 1974, I was at the old Met Stadium, doing a commercial at the ballpark. Mr. Griffith heard I was at the park and asked that after I finished what I was doing, would I come up to his office. It was about the time of the year that contracts were tendered to the players, so I thought rather than him sending it to me, he would probably want me to come up and sign my contract. And, boy, was I wrong. That was the furthest thing from his mind. He actually wanted me to manage a Triple-A club, which was Tacoma at that time, or coach at the major-league level. And I said, "Well, I really appreciate the offer, but I think I can play at least one or two more years." And he said, "Well, that's fine if you'd like to do that, you're welcome to call any other club or talk to any other ball club that you'd like to." And so I did that. I talked to several different ball clubs at the time and had some offers from other clubs, but the one that I really focused on and ended up signing with was the Kansas City Royals, mainly because they were in my kind of area. They were Midwestern-type people and I was from a small town in Idaho and had been playing in Minnesota. I thought Kansas City would fit my personality. And then, too, I thought they had a pretty darn good ball club and had a chance to win. So, I ended up signing a contract with the Kansas City Royals. Mr. Ewing Kauffman, who owned the club at that time, was very nice to me. They were happy to have me over there. They had a manager, Jack McKeon, who had been in the Minnesota Twins organization before. I went over there with the idea that I would be the designated hitter for the Royals. I had had a lot of knee problems up to that point, and in retrospect, if I had stayed in Minnesota playing on grass and dirt, I probably could have played that season and another year, but they had artificial turf in the Royals stadium. That was very difficult on my knees, and I ended up having a lot of problems that year because of my knee situation. I wasn't the designated hitter. All year we alternated, Tony Solaita and myself. Together, we had a pretty good year. We hit 30 home runs and the Royals did well. They ended up seven games out of first place. I hit 14 home runs and didn't hit so well the rest of the year for average or anything. With the knee problems that I had, it was just a long, long, hot summer in Kansas City. And both Kansas City and myself felt it was time to hang them up.

It wasn't too tough because of the way I was feeling physically and the way the year went. I knew it was time to quit playing. So I got on a plane, flew back to Minnesota, went in to Mr. Griffith, and told him I wanted to manage his ball club. He had just fired Frank Quilici and said that he wasn't going to hire another manager who didn't have minor-league experience. So I didn't end up managing the Twins. They hired Gene Mauch as the manager at that time. But I did do their telecast for the next three years. And that was a good experience for me, too.

When I got a phone call in 1984 from Jack Lang, who was the

secretary of the Baseball Writers' Association at that time, he said, "You've been elected to the Hall of Fame." He said, "From this moment on, your life will never be the same." It really didn't sink in as to exactly what Jack meant when he said that, but I've grown to understand that a lot more over the years. When they put "HOF" behind your name, it's something magical. It is a great honor to be selected to the National Baseball Hall of Fame. I'm very proud of that and still don't believe it, and can't believe that I deserve it, or I really am a part of the Hall of Fame, but it's something that has been wonderful. In the induction ceremonies, I wasn't quite sure what to say or how to accept that award, but the one thing that I do remember going through my mind was that I wish my father could have been there. He was the one that helped me get started in sports, and I think he would have been proud. He had passed away when I was sixteen years old. So he never even got to see me play baseball. That's one thing that was really on my mind. And my mother wasn't able to be there. She was at an age where it was difficult for her to travel. And so those two people in my life, the most important people in my life at that time—the years when I became a ballplayer—weren't able to be there. So my mind was in that direction at that time. But it was a very humbling experience. I think one of the things that I remember is I thought, "I'm not going to get emotional about this." And it happened. It's a very emotional experience.

Rod Carew was certainly one of the greatest hitters that I had the opportunity to play with. Seven times American League batting champion. Probably the best bunter that I ever saw. Rod could bunt a ball at third base, and with the speed he had, and the way he could bunt the ball down the third-base line, it was almost impossible to catch him. He used to work at that. He would come out to the ballpark early and bunt for hours, and he became just exceptional at bunting. And with the speed he had, he got an awful lot of infield hits, but he was also a great, great hitter. I was playing when Rod

Rod Carew

came into the American League with the Twins, and then I was broadcasting when he got his 3,000th hit against Minnesota in California. So that was a big thrill for me.

Kirby Puckett was, I guess, everybody's favorite in Minnesota. He brought a special kind of enthusiasm to the game of baseball, a team leader both on the field and off the field. And of course, the years in '87 and '91 when they won the pennants and the World Championships, Kirby was there and was a big part of that. A tremendous player.

Carl Yastrzemski, I think, got more out of the ability that he had than any player that I can remember. He just drove himself to be a great hitter and a good outfielder. Carl was just a winning-type player. He played hard all the time. Very serious guy at the plate.

Tony Conigliaro was the youngest player to win a home-run championship in the American League. It was unfortunate that he had to end his career when he did and what happened to him, but he certainly was a fine young player.

Booger—Boog Powell was great. It seemed like I always got in between Boog Powell and Frank Robinson at the All-Star Games, and I felt like a midget between those two guys. Boog was a mammoth guy, and just as big as he was, his heart was even bigger. He was a great part of those winning years for the Orioles. Not only a great hitter but a great first baseman. Did a great job. Good defensive first baseman.

We kind of started a winning tradition in Minnesota. Took over from the Yankees, it seemed like, and then the A's of the early '70s took over from our ball club. They just had an outstanding group of players that were on that club. Reggie Jackson, of course, was one of the great clutch hitters of all time, I would say. He had that flair for being able to hit in certain situations when the game was on the line. He was an outstanding player.

Of course, Rollie Fingers developed into a great relief pitcher, one of the best you've ever seen. I hit against Rollie Fingers a lot, and he was a great, great pitcher. He kept the ball away from you. He tried to keep the ball in a position where he wouldn't let you beat him.

Al Kaline, I felt, for a period of about ten years may have been the best all-around player in the American League. He could do everything. He could hit and run, he could hit with power, and he was a great defensive player. Just an outstanding, all-around good player.

Rocky Colavito for a few years was one of the better long-ball hitters in baseball, and Rocky had a great arm from the outfield. I always thought he'd probably have been a great pitcher if they put him on the mound.

I don't think there's any question that Willie Mays was one of the greatest players that ever lived. Willie could do everything, and do it with a flair. He hit 660 home runs and was a great defensive outfielder, and a great base runner, and exciting to watch play. There was nobody like Willie Mays. Just great.

Although Hank Aaron hit more home runs than anybody else in the game, and was a great average hitter, and a good defensive—

great defensive—outfielder and a good base runner, he is another player I never felt had the acclaim that he should have gotten. I think that Hank Aaron was one of the greatest players of all time and still didn't get the acclaim. Maybe it was because he played in Milwaukee and Atlanta. But Hank Aaron could do it all. He was a very consistent ballplayer and a great, great player.

I think there's a misconception about the designated hitter. Some people thought it would extend the life of a lot of older players, but having done that for that one year a little bit with the Royals, I know that you can't be a good designated hitter if you've got something physically wrong with you. You got to be able to do everything everybody else does, except throw the ball. And maybe if you've got something wrong with your arm, you can't swing very well, either. Either way, that was a difficult job. It seems to me, you have your mind more in the game if you're out in the field than sitting on the bench just watching the game.

I found it a very difficult job. There are very few really good designated hitters in the game. I do think it did take some dead spots out of the game, made it a little more exciting in some spots. When I played, all the pitchers hit, except for the last couple of years I played, and in those days, the pitchers usually were the best athletes. Growing up as a kid, they were good hitters, too. And those pitchers on our club, like Jim Kaat, Jim Perry, Camilo Pascual, even Pedro Ramos—and you can look at some of the other pitchers, like Drysdale and Warren Spahn—some of the great pitchers were good hitters. Whitey Ford was a good hitter. And then, all of a sudden, younger players stopped hitting. They didn't have to hit, so they weren't as good hitters. So to have the National League have pitchers hit when they hadn't hit all their lives must have been a difficult thing. You don't see too many good-hitting pitchers in the National League like there used to be.

I just think that they ought to have both leagues the same, in my opinion. I'd like to see them go back to the pitchers hitting in the lower leagues—high school, college, and minor leagues—and then I think you'd see some guys that could hit pretty well. It's pretty difficult to hit, and if you don't hit very often, it's almost impossible to be a good hitter.

I think that baseball was meant to be played on grass and dirt and outside, in the sunlight and some of the bad weather. And I think it changes the game completely to play it on AstroTurf. You see a lot of balls go through the infield and through the gaps in the outfield that wouldn't happen if it was on grass and dirt. You see a lot truer hops on AstroTurf. Infielders can play balls one-handed where you—we were always taught to get in front of the ball. On dirt and grass, if you weren't in front of the ball, a lot of times it'd take a bad hop and hit you in your body or bounce over your shoulder or something. I think that changed the game a lot.

Contraction is a word that I don't remember hearing much about before until the commissioner said that they were going to contract baseball and eliminate two teams, and one was possibly Montreal, and the other one, Minnesota. And when I heard Minnesota mentioned in the contraction, it gave me a sick feeling. I was very disappointed that a ball club that had such a tremendous history and won, not so long ago, the world's championship could be eliminated from baseball. And so, I was very disheartened to hear about that. I would feel like a guy without a country if there were no baseball in Minnesota. There's no more Washington Senators where I played, and if they eliminate the Minnesota Twins, I don't know what happens to my history. But the Twins' history goes all the way back to the formation of the American League. Clark Griffith was one of the founders of the American League and over at the Washington Senators, and their history is about a hundred years old. So, for that to happen would be, I think just a terrible, terrible thing.

Baseball is a game of statistics, and I suppose that any ballplayer who plays the game as long as I did, or for any lengthy time, will be remembered for the statistics that he left. And I suppose that to be second to Babe Ruth in the American League in career home runs will be something that it would be nice to be remembered for, or for being the number one right-handed home-run hitter in American League history, but I'm sure that over the years, someone will come along and top that.

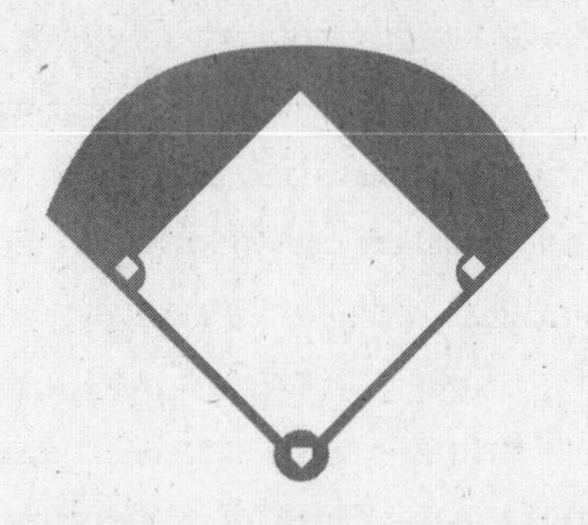

BROOKS ROBINSON

Jim Murray of the Los Angeles Times *couldn't have been more prescient when he once wrote, "In the future, Brooks Robinson will be the standard every third baseman will be measured by."*

Robinson was a fixture at third base for the Baltimore Orioles for twenty-three seasons (1955–77), where he not only won fans but also sixteen Gold Glove Awards for defensive excellence. Nicknamed "The Human Vacuum Cleaner," he set defensive career records for third basemen for games, putouts, assists, chances, double plays, and fielding percentage.

"The baseball park was no place for his performances. He should have played at Carnegie Hall," wrote Atlanta sportswriter Furman Bisher. Another writer, Red Smith of the New York Times, *agreed, "When you see Brooks Robinson walk onto the field you know that nature designed him expressly to play third base."*

Robinson's prowess with a glove was never more evident than in the 1970 World Series against the Cincinnati Reds, where he made a number of sparkling plays in front of a national audience in the five-game triumph.

"We lost the World Series because we made fundamental mistakes,"

said Reds manager Sparky Anderson. "We kept hitting the ball to Brooks." Reds player Pete Rose was equally impressed, stating, "That guy can field a ball with a pair of pliers." Longtime O's PA announcer Rex Barney may have stated it best during Robinson's 1970 Fall Classic heroics: "He's not at his locker yet, but four guys are over there interviewing his glove."

Robinson was more than a defensive stalwart, though, as he finished his career with 2,848 hits and 268 home runs (at the time of his retirement a record for AL third basemen). Robinson also won the 1964 AL MVP Award, when he set career highs in home runs (28), RBIs (118), and batting average (.317), and the 1970 World Series MVP Award, when he hit .429 with two home runs and six RBIs.

Robinson, who was inducted into the National Baseball Hall of Fame in 1983, received glowing remarks from fellow Hall of Fame third baseman Pie Traynor, who was also known for his glove work: "I once thought of giving him some tips but dropped the idea. He's just the best there is."

My dad was a pretty good semipro player back in Little Rock, Arkansas. I ended up going to the same high school, playing on the same American Legion team that he did. He was a good player, and in fact, in 1937, I believe, or could have been '38, he played softball, fast pitch, for International Harvester, and they went to the world's championship in Soldier Field in Chicago. They got beat, 2–1, for the world's championship. He always encouraged me to play. I can remember throwing the ball around and shagging balls, and then when I got to be about eight or nine years old, I was a batboy for several of the teams that he played on. He was a fireman in Little Rock for over thirty years. That was my first love and only love as far as sports go.

I could always catch the ball, of course. When I got higher, professionally, hitting became a little tougher. It took me a while to get the hang of that. I was a good hitter in American Legion baseball,

Brooks Robinson

very average speed, very average arm, but the thing I had going for me was the fact that I could catch the ball. When I signed professionally in 1955, no one wanted to give me a lot of money. That was the time when if you got more than $4,000, you were a bonus player and had to go directly into the major leagues, and no one wanted to offer me a lot of money. I signed for $4,000, and that was my salary for the first year. But I think that benefited me, to go and play with guys my own speed instead of being in the major leagues for two years, which I saw stunt a lot of players' growth for that particular time. So I was fortunate in that respect.

I was ambidextrous to a certain point. I eat left-handed, write left-handed, play Ping-Pong and tennis and shoot left-handed, so from here down, I'm pretty well coordinated. But I can't throw left-handed at all. I do everything else left-handed, and I'm sure that helped me as far as being able to get the glove in the right spot and make the plays.

I was a big baseball fan. In the eighth grade, we had to write a booklet called *My Vocation*—what do you want to do when you grow up? And I wrote it on becoming a professional baseball player. That was my dream, and I had some big decisions to make. I had some scholarships to college to play basketball, and I had to talk my mother and dad out of that to sign professionally. As I say, no one really wanted to give me a lot of money, but they wanted to sign me. I ended up signing with Baltimore through a good friend of my family named Lindsay Deal, a baseball player who played for Paul Richards when Paul managed the Atlanta Crackers. Lindsay's family went to church with my family. And so he wrote Paul Richards a letter saying, "Paul, there's a kid here who we think might be able to make the big league someday. Would you send someone in to scout him?" This was 1955, I guess, the second year the Orioles came to Baltimore. They were the old St. Louis Browns in '53 and then they moved to Baltimore. So Paul Richards took over, and he sent a couple of fellas to look at me. And I ended up signing with the Orioles because that was the quickest way to the major league. That's what he sold me on: we don't have any players, and you're going to get a chance to play early here in your career. Consequently, I got a chance to play when I was eighteen.

I think my mother and dad probably kept me on track better than anyone else—that, and the fact that I played sports. When I played sports, I just knew that you didn't drink—not that I didn't have a drink once in a while—and you didn't smoke. I mean, that was really what sports were all about, and the only way you could compete and be at your best was to do the right thing and be in the best shape. But I think my parents, more than anyone else, were really the guiding light in my life. I had a brother who was five years younger than me. He was a football player; he went to the University of Arkansas and played football. We were into a little mischief, but I think overall we didn't give my mother and dad a lot of problems, simply because we were into sports and we knew that if we wanted to excel in sports, well, we had to do certain things and abide by certain rules. But my parents were very influential in keeping me that way, I think.

I played my first fifty games professionally at York, Pennsylvania, as a second baseman, and then George Staller, who was my manager, and Paul Richards felt in the long run third base might be my best position. Third base is a reflex position, whereas at second base you have to cover a lot more ground. They just saw me as a third baseman, thinking I might get a little stronger and learn to hit. And that was the best thing that ever happened to me, that move to third base.

York, Pennsylvania, was in a Class-B league. I did very well, there, then came back to Baltimore and got to play the last two weeks in 1955. The first game I played in was against the Washington Senators. I think Chuck Stobbs was pitching for the Senators. Anyway, I got two base hits, knocked in a big run. We won the game, and I can remember running back to the Southern Hotel and calling my mom and dad. I said, "Guess what, Mom? I just played my first big-league game, got two hits." I said, "Man, this is my cup of tea. I don't know why I was in the minor league." The next twenty times I went to bat, eighteen to be exact, I went 0-18. I struck out ten times out of those eighteen, and I learned a pretty good lesson right there. These guys are way ahead of me. I got a lot of more work in front of me to be an accomplished major-league baseball player.

After the '55 season was over, the Orioles sent thirteen players out of their organization, all not married, down to Colombia, South America. We played in Barranquilla and Cartagena. They had two teams in Barranquilla and two teams in Cartagena. I was eighteen years old, and I was in South America playing. We lived in a big, big house and had several maids who cooked for us. Tito Francona was there, and he went on to have a very fine major-league career. Also Wayne Causey, who played in the major leagues for a while. So we had a few guys who ended up making it to the majors. I played in South America in '55 and in '56. I came back, knew I was going to be in Double A, which was San Antonio in the Texas League. So I went to San Antonio that year, and after the season was over, I came back to Baltimore and finished the season.

In '57, I made the Oriole team. I was the starting third baseman opening day. In fact, that's when my relationship began with George Kell, another great baseball player, a third baseman, a Hall of Famer. George kind of took me under his wing and showed me the ropes, not only in baseball, but also off the field. I remember he took me to my first stage play in New York, George and his wife. He was kind of my mentor, I guess you could say. And it was his last year. He retired after that year. But opening day of '57, George played first and I played third against the Washington Senators in old Griffith Stadium. And then after that, let's see, about two weeks into the season, I hurt my knee. I had a knee operation. I was out two months, went down for a month, came back, and ended up going to Cuba to play winter baseball. That was really the best winter league at that particular time. So I spent the whole winter in Cuba playing on a team called Cienfuegos. And then in '58, I was back with the Orioles. I was there the whole year. I never really distinguished myself. I played in 145 games. I think I ended up hitting .238. And then I had an Army obligation. I was being drafted for two years, or I could go in the Arkansas National Guard for six months' active duty and five and a half years in the Reserve. So I went into the Arkansas National Guard. I went for six months' active duty, then I spent five and a half years in the National Guard. But anyway, I got out after serving, right when the season started in '59. I missed spring training, of course. But I'd worked out, and I thought I was ready to play. Paul Richards was the manager. About a month into the season, he said, "Well, we're going to send you down to the minor leagues." And that was probably the worst feeling I think I'd ever had. I mean, it probably, ego-wise, I mean, here's someone who spent 1958 in the big leagues and you're saying, "Okay, you got a full year under your belt. Now '59 is your breakout year." And all of a sudden, I'm going to Vancouver. That really took me back a little, but it turned out, honestly, to be the best thing that ever happened to me. Going to Vancouver, I did real well out there. I had hit .330-something. They brought me back right before the All-Star break, and I came back to stay. But when I got back, it was like night and day as far as being a hitter. I ended the season real strong, and I just think probably that confidence-wise, physically, I got a little stronger and I became a better hitter. And that was the key to everything right there. And, of course, 1960 was the first good year that the Orioles had. We had a lot of young players that year and we almost won that year, almost beat the Yankees. But that was the first good year, the first big year that I really had in Baltimore in baseball.

Paul Richards is really the best baseball man I have ever met. I mean, he was like God to me. He just knew more about the game than anyone I've ever met. He knew about each position, and he just was ahead of the game. And I guess the only knock on Paul Richards was, well, you know, he never won. But he put together the White Sox team, back in the 1950s. They won in '59. Paul had left there in 1954, come to Baltimore, and kind of set the tone of what was going to happen. But Paul was a real stickler. He felt like, well, you get good pitching, get good defense, and you're going to be in most of the game and hopefully you'll score some runs. He knew a

Paul Richards

lot about pitching. He was unbelievable. Earl Weaver was a big fan of Paul's. Paul kind of tutored him in his minor-league career as a manager—and, of course, Earl's in the Hall of Fame now.

When I got back after the All-Star Game I played in 1959, I think I ended up hitting close to .290 the rest of the year. I was a much better hitter, a much better player. And then 1960 started, and we had the "Baby Birds." Players like Chuck Estrada, Milt Pappas, Steve Barber, and Jack Fisher. These guys were terrific. There were four guys who could throw hard, they could knock the bat out of your hand. We just had a real good year. Gus Triandos was there, and I'm trying to think who else was on the team. Ronnie Hansen was the Rookie of the Year that year. I came through the minors with Ronnie. We challenged the Yankees. They came to Baltimore on Labor Day in 1960. We were one game behind, and we swept the three-game series. We were two games ahead. Went away for two weeks to play other teams, went back to New York, I think there were about fourteen games left; they beat us four in a row, and that was it. They went on to win the rest of their games. I think they ended up winning fifteen in a row. I finished third for MVP that year behind Maris and Mantle. Maris was the MVP, Mantle was second, and it was the first time that three players, I think, had gotten over two hundred votes for the MVP of the league. But I was thrilled because I had a big year, and it couldn't have been better.

It was my first All-Star Game appearance that year. I was a backup to Frank Malzone of the Red Sox. They had two games that year. Two All-Star Games in '59, '60, '61, and '62. I was a backup to Malzone in '60, but I did win the Gold Glove that year. That was the first of sixteen in a row from '60 through '75.

There were two guys that I always tell people gave me a hard time. They were basically the same type of pitchers. Frank Lary used to pitch for the Detroit Tigers. He was known as "the Yankee Killer." He beat the Yankees with consistency. He was very intimidating, too. Earl Wilson was the same way. There's some pitchers out there—Don Drysdale, for example—they're going to pitch outside, but when they come in sometimes, they don't care if they hit you or not. They just want to let you know that they're out there. Frank Lary was that type of pitcher. He bore inside all the time then. He had those quick little breaking balls, seemed like he was one pitch ahead of you all the time. And Earl Wilson was the same way. In 1955, he pitched for the Barranquilla, Colombia, team. We got to wear batting helmets that year. The first season I played in '55, we had the felt hats with the little plastic inner liner. But we went to South America, and they sent us the helmets. Would you believe that Earl Wilson hit me right in the head with a pitch? He threw hard, too. Hit me right in the head, and it bounced all the way over the backstop. So when I hit off him the rest of my career, I probably had that in the back of my mind. He was very tough on me. Mel Stottlemyre, another guy, sinker or slider, kept the ball down. Two outstanding pitchers.

I always had that little hand-eye coordination. I can't tell you how many times I've been up with a golf ball against the steps, the short hop, taking the tennis ball against the barn or throwing it. And that probably had something to do with me being able to catch the ball, but everyone knew I could catch the ball. The big question mark was, would Brooks Robinson ever hit major-league pitching? Fielding became my forte more than anything else. It was something that I always enjoyed doing. I worked on it. I always felt that the backhand play is probably the toughest play for most fielders because they really don't see the ball well backhand. And so I worked on certain things that I didn't do well, but it pretty much came naturally to me.

There were several things I worked on—the slow hit, the topped balls, or bunts. I used to line up about ten or twelve balls in a row. You just come in and pick one up and you'd make another step and pick one up and throw it, and I worked on it that way. I made a play in the World Series in 1970 that was very unusual. Lee May hit the ball over the third-base bag, which I caught in foul territory, and just got down on and threw it on one hop to Boog Powell and got Lee May out. Most of the time when you make that play, you get the ball, you stop, you plant, you make the long throw. This time, I just got it and threw it. I can't even remember making that play maybe one time like that in my whole career, but it just happened that way.

In 1960, we played two All-Star Games. We played in Kansas City, and then we went to New York. I got on the plane after the first game, and Ted Williams was talking to Nellie Fox and trying to tell Nellie he'd be a better hitter if he stood off the plate a little, and back in the box some. Ted started talking about the slider breaking at 59.6 feet, and I'm listening to this. I'm thinking that I'm never going to be able to hit major-league pitching. He's talking about things I've never heard about. But that was a big thrill being on the team with Ted Williams that year. We didn't win too many games. In fact, one of the records I'm not too proud of, I hold the record for playing in the most losing All-Star Games. I played in eighteen games; we tied one, won two, and lost fifteen.

The American League did struggle, and it's a fact that they didn't sign the black players; they weren't in a hurry to sign them. When the NL signed them, they got the best. Guys like Roy Campanella and Jackie Robinson and Ernie Banks. I don't really know how these guys felt. I never really sat down to talk to them. We'd go to the Sir Walter Raleigh and pick up the black guys and they picked us up at the other hotel. Their primary job was to play baseball, and they probably didn't think a whole lot about it either. I can't say that. Maybe they did think about it. They probably did. But you look back on it now, and you say, "Boy, that was terrible."

Frank Robinson coming over, well that's the greatest thing that ever happened to the Orioles. He made us a real winner coming over. He really fit in well. We had enough good guys on that team,

Frank Robinson

and we had a lot of fun that first year winning the world's championship when he came. But I think we all understood one another a lot better after he got there. He did go through some tough times there in Baltimore, but it made it a lot better for a lot of the other athletes that followed him, I think.

Frank came over in '66. We had a fairly young team that year. We had a rookie catcher, Andy Etchebarren, a rookie second baseman in Davey Johnson, a second-year outfielder in Paul Blair in center field. So we had a young team. Jim Palmer came on board and Dave McNally also. We had a young pitcher named Wally Bunker. I don't think we had over a 15-game winner, but we were basically an offensive team that year. We had three guys that drove in over 100 runs—Frank, Boog Powell, and myself. We just kind of outclassed everyone that year. And, of course, we went to the World Series and played the Dodgers as underdogs, and won four in a row. I think the Series ended where we had the worst team batting average for a winning team, and they had the worst team batting average for a losing team in World Series history. There wasn't much happening after the first inning of the first game. Frank and I hit back-to-back home runs in that first game. Moe Drabowsky came on in relief that first day to strike out seven of the first nine guys he faced, I believe, and then of course the next three games were shutouts. The second game was the last game that Sandy Koufax ever pitched. They made six errors behind him and we won 6–0, I believe. Then we won the last two games, 1–0, 1–0. Frank was the MVP, but that was the start of some nice years for us. In '67, we didn't do well. In '68, Detroit won. Frank got hurt in '67; I believe it was the added concussion that he played with most of the year, and that hurt us a lot. And then, of course, we got in the World Series in '69, '70, and '71. But our pitching really became a force in '69. Mike Cuellar joined us from Houston. And for at least three or four years, you could put Cuellar at the top. He was just as good as anybody who pitched. And, of course, in '71, we had the four 20-game winners. Pat Dobson joined us in '71, and the four guys won 20 games. That will never happen again. They were very competitive; they just wanted the ball every fourth day. Now you got guys who pitch every fifth day or sixth day, but that's just the way the game has changed. These guys, they loved to work on four days, and they wanted to be the best. Those were great teams. We lost two out of three of those World Series. We lost to the Mets in '69, which was a big upset, and then we were the underdogs in '70, and then we're supposed to beat Pittsburgh in '71 and they beat us. In baseball, you get the recognition when you win, and we lost two out of three of those World Series. But just getting to a World Series is exciting. Just look back at all the players in the history of the game who would never get a chance to be there—Ernie Banks or Billy Williams or Ferguson Jenkins or George Kell.

The thing that was so nice about me being with George Kell in the '57 season—and he grew up like sixty miles from me—was his career ended then. Then, in '83, I went into the Hall of Fame through the regular voting and George went in through the old-timers, the Veterans Committee. So here, we're on the stage together going into the Hall of Fame together, which made it that much more exciting. He led the league in hitting one year, beat out Ted Williams. He was a terrific hitter, good fielder. He ended up going to Chicago and Boston, then ended up his career in Baltimore. We became real close during those years.

I think the manager is a major ingredient in a winning ball club, I really do. I think that there is so much a manager can do. After watching the manager for so long, the players begin to see what difference a manager can make. Players recognize in a hurry managers who cannot manage, who cannot run the game the way it's supposed to be run and make the moves. There are certain things that managers do during the season to win ball games, and you've got to be pretty consistent. You've got twenty-five guys, and you've got to be able to make every guy feel important. I think that's what the great managers do. Earl Weaver, whether you'd be the twenty-fifth guy on that team or you were the star of that team, he treated everyone the same. Everyone knew their job, everyone knew when they were going to be called on, everyone knew that they had to be ready. In that respect, a manager can do things to gain the players' confidence.

Paul Richards was a disciplinarian. It was my way or the highway. That's just the way he operated. But he had a lot of young players. He taught me things about the game of baseball that I never even thought about when I was a youngster—rundowns and cutoffs—and he just knew every phase of the game.

He just couldn't put up with mental mistakes. But when you make a bad throw or miss a ground ball, that's part of the game. But he was a terrific judge of talent. He resurrected so many pitchers' careers. Billy Loes, when he came down to Baltimore. Skinny Brown. Connie Johnson, who became an outstanding pitcher with the Orioles. We had guys that he was able just to resurrect their pitching careers, which I thought was phenomenal.

We had catchers Clint Courtney and Gus Triandos, and that's when Paul Richards came up with the large mitt to catch Hoyt

Wilhelm. The day that Gus Triandos would come to the park and Wilhelm was pitching, Gus was in another world. I mean, he just hated it. He knew that he was going to be running back to the backstop many times during the game to pick up the ball because Wilhelm had such a great knuckleball. You're just not going to catch it all the time. And of course, Hoyt Wilhelm's in the Hall of Fame, too. But we had Clint Courtney, and they always used to say when Courtney was going after a pop-up with that big glove, he looked like a guy carrying a pizza trying to catch a ball. Yeah, Paul Richards was very innovative.

A lot of guys drank. No drugs. I can't remember drugs until the 1970s. But there were probably a lot of alcoholics in baseball back in the 1950s, and no one really thought too much about it. No one called it to their attention, but there were a lot of players that I certainly know abused themselves. Today, you're liable to see players go out of their way to really corner certain players that they think are not taking care of themselves, more so than back in the old days. The players today are more attuned to what's going on. And when they see guys not taking care of themselves, and the fact that it might cost them a game—might cost them a championship—guys will say, "Look, this has got to stop. You're costing me money, and this is the way it's got to be." But back in the 1950s and 1960s, I don't think you had that.

I can honestly tell you that Earl Weaver gave me more laughs than anyone that I ever played with or have ever been around in the game. Just to watch him and his antics during the game. For instance, we'd get to a ninth inning or the bottom of the ninth and we needed one out or we were one pitch away from winning. He'd go down in what we call the "hole" there. He didn't want to see the outcome of the pitch. He wanted to listen to the crowd to see if the pitcher got the batter out or not. Things like that. I saw him one time when we were playing in Cleveland. It was a balk or something like that. Here came Earl, and oh, he was at it again. All of a sudden, bang, he was going back to the dugout. I don't know where he went, but he went to the clubhouse. He got the rulebook and came back out and he was running. He said, "This is it." The umpires are shaking their heads. Finally, he just took the rulebook and he tore it up and just pitched it up in the air and said, "Well, if we're not going to play by the rules, we don't need this book." He gave the umpires a hard time, but they really respected him because, I'll tell you, they knew that he knew the rulebook better than they did. And they respected him for that, but they didn't allow it.

I signed twenty-three one-year contracts. That's just the way they operated. They wouldn't give a two-year contract. So you know who had the advantage. The general manager was a professional in negotiating and they always had the answers. I remember when Lee MacPhail [the general manager] was there. Lee MacPhail is the most wonderful guy in the whole world. I remember talking to Lee, and he was saying, "Well, Brooks, I was a general manager with the Yankees. And I didn't pay Mickey Mantle that much money in his third year." And I'm saying, "Well, I don't know. I don't care about Mickey Mantle." He said, "Well, I couldn't give you more than Mickey Mantle got." I'll tell you one more little story here. I held out for a whole week in Florida for $500. And you know, the owners weren't that smart, because they didn't know we would have played for nothing. But anyway, we went to Florida. You're always anxious to get to Florida to get to spring training. You're taking the kids out of school. Put them in school there, maybe. I went down without being signed. I held out for a whole week. Finally, Harry Dalton [the general manager] called me and said, "Well, we got to get this thing straightened out. Come on in now, and sit down here and talk to me." So I went over, and this is in Miami Stadium. I went in and said, "Harry, I deserve $500 more." You know, me being an outstanding defensive player, didn't that mean anything? He says, "Well, how many hits did you get? How many home runs?" Defense was way in the background. Anyway, Harry said, "Well, I just can't pay you that." I said, "Harry, I deserve it." He said, "Okay, I'll tell you what I'm going to do." He said, "I'm going to leave the room for ten minutes, and you sit here and you think about it, and when I come back, we'll make the decision." He left the room. I'm sitting there just waiting for him to come back. Finally, Harry came back and said, "Well, how do you feel?" I said, "Harry, I deserve the $500." He said, "Okay, I'll tell you what I'm going to do." He said, "I'm going to give you that $500. But just remember, when we negotiate next year, you took advantage of me this year." So he made me feel bad, and I don't let Harry forget that. When I talk to him, I said, "Harry, you remember that week I held out for $500?" And he feels bad about it, too. He's seen what has happened in the game of baseball.

I started making $100,000 after the '70 World Series. The most I ever made was like $130,000, and that was in '76. And then the last year, I was player-coach in '77, and the Orioles said, "Well, you're a player-coach. Anybody can be a player-coach. We're going to cut you to $60,000 or $70,000." And that's when Marvin Miller, who was the head of the Players Association, said, "Well, you can only take a 25 percent cut." So anyway, I ended up playing for $100,000 that year. That was the last year I was active.

My wife, God bless her soul, she always thought, "Well, you deserve more. You should get more." And I wish I had been a little more hardheaded. I always see Dave McNally, one of my favorite people and also a great pitcher. Dave was one of those guys that just went in and said, "Well, I'm not signing until I get this." The rest of us, we kind of gave in and wanted to play and wanted to get to spring training. Dave said, "No, I'm not signing." In fact, Dave was one of the guys that became the first players in the history of the game not to sign a contract. They tried to offer him more money later on to sign, but he said, "I'm not signing. The heck with it." But that's another story.

• • •

When the 1960 season was over, I got married. I looked for a job. I worked for a fellow named Larry Willis, I believe. He had a process called Martin Hard Coating. Something they put on the bottom of skis at one time. I worked for him doing some public-relations work. Then I went to work for the Orioles. During the winter, I'd go to about five or six banquets a week for $25 dollars a banquet, I believe it was. So I did have a little job during the wintertime, and that was what I was concerned about more than anything else. Early in my career, I played winter baseball two years, but also went back to college two years, too.

We had an Orioles basketball team that played probably fifteen or twenty games a year in the off-season. I did a little running. Never lifted a weight in my whole life. One day when I was doing the television games, I looked at Scott McGregor, our pitcher, and I said, "You know, I wish I'd just got into some program, a Nautilus program when I was in my early thirties. I could've probably played longer." He started laughing and said, "Well, you played almost twenty-three years. How long do you want to play? You're in the Hall of Fame; what more do you want?" It was almost taboo for players to lift weights. But there's no doubt in my mind that players today are bigger and stronger. They do the right things and they keep in better shape than we were. We went to spring training to get in shape; when they come to spring training now, most of them have really worked out all winter and are in much better physical condition. I think baseball players are probably the worst-conditioned athletes of all the major sports. I was the oldest guy in the league when I retired. I was forty years old, and I could still catch the ball and throw guys out. But where you lose it, you just lose strength. You hit the ball and it doesn't go as far. You just don't have that speed, too. And that was where I lost it. When the hitting left, it was all over for me.

After Frank Robinson came over, he just really fell in love with the Orioles, and we fell in love with him, too. And one of the things we did during the season and the preseasons was these kangaroo courts that we had. We got an old mop and Frank put it over his head here. He was the judge. We had three or four different awards. We had a baserunning award for—I can't think of the fellow's name, but he was the most atrocious base runner in Orioles history. We had an old shoe that we gave away. We had a whoever-had-the-weakest-swing-that-night award. You know, you might break a bat or something and it dribbles to the pitcher. We had a weak-swing award. We had two or three or four awards that we would pass out. We only did this after we won; we didn't do it when we lost. But when we won, we would fine guys for saying crazy things or palling around with the other team or looking up at the scoreboard and saying, "Well, I thought there was two outs and there was only one." Just crazy things that they bring up. And then of course, we would keep these fines, and then I think we donated them to charity when the season was over. I don't know how much money; it wasn't a lot of money. But every time we won, we'd have this kangaroo court. It lasted about fifteen minutes and we got a lot of laughs. It was a good thing to bring the team together. We had a group of guys who really liked one another, which I think is important.

Boog Powell is the only guy in the infield that never won a Gold Glove on our team, and he never let us forget it. Every time we'd make a bad throw, he'd come in and mark it up on the wall. When the season was over, he'd say, "Well, I only saved you fifteen errors, Brooks, on those short hops you threw me over there." Boog was a great target to throw to. He had a great pair of hands. They don't give the big guys enough credit a lot of times, but Boog was outstanding. And, of course, we had Davey Johnson, who was a rookie in 1966. Davey won some Gold Gloves. We had Luis Aparicio at shortstop. He came over in 1963 I believe, in a trade, with the White Sox. We talk about Mark Belanger and the great fielder he was. I have a hard time separating those guys. They were so great. The routine ground ball is an out, and that's really what you want from your shortstop, just make the routine plays every time they hit it to you because you're going to get more ground balls than anyone else. Those guys—Luis and Mark—did it as well as anyone could do it. I was at third, and then we had Paul Blair in center field, who was just as good an outfielder as you'll ever want to see. I'm a little prejudiced because I've played with these guys and seen them day in and day out, but he could do it as well as anyone.

Jim Palmer and Weaver were always at odds. It was unbelievable. They gave us a lot of laughs. It was one of those love-hate relationships. They'd be yelling at one another, and the next day, they'd be playing golf. I remember one game where Palmer came in and told Weaver about the eighth inning, "Look, I've had it. I've had it. I'm not throwing that well." And Weaver said, "What? You're throwing as good as anybody we got in the bullpen, so you're going to go back out there." Palmer went back out, and first pitch he threw to Sal Bando in the ninth inning, Bando hit a home run. So Palmer turned around, he was looking at Weaver. "See, I told you. I don't have it anymore." I saw when Palmer came in one day, he had a little run-in with Weaver. Palmer's locker was right next to Weaver's office. So Palmer just cleaned out his locker and moved down the clubhouse to the other end so he wouldn't have to look Weaver right in the eye.

When I tell people the true superstars of the game, it's Mantle, Aaron, Mays. These guys could do everything the game demands—hit, hit with power, run, field, throw. Do it just about anytime they want to do it. I got to see Roger Maris hit numbers 59 and 60, I believe. Looking back on it now, it's a little sad that he really didn't enjoy it as much as he should have. But these guys just amazed me, and you could always expect the unexpected from them. I hit a home run in Baltimore where Mickey Mantle broke his ankle. And he went under the fence and broke his ankle. I hit that ball. But I saw him when he came back after a layoff and he hit a pinch-hit home run in the ninth inning to win the game for the Yankees. So they just did things that no one else can do. And, of course, Maris, the

MVP in '60 and '61. He is a guy who probably didn't get the recognition that he deserved. Here was a guy who could run. He could throw. A heck of an outfielder and hitting the home runs. I think people look at him as "Well, he just had that one year." But here is a guy who was the MVP twice in a row, ahead of Mickey Mantle. But those guys, they amazed me. The true superstars of the game.

I got to play against Ted Williams his last year, in '60. In fact, I was there when he hit the home run the last time up. They were playing the Orioles in Fenway Park, and that's still a big thrill because I see that little film clip all the time. I'm just kind of standing there. He's looking like this big horse coming around second base. The strange thing about it is that on his previous time up he hit a ball that was actually out of the ballpark. And I think it was Al Pilarcik, playing center field for the Orioles, who jumped up and grabbed the ball, and he was out. The next time up, he hit the home run. And although Boston had three more games, that was his last time up. He didn't go to Yankee Stadium for the last three. He finished the year in Boston.

I would say Williams was the most respected player that I've known in my lifetime. That's a great tribute to him. I guess every generation likes to think their generation is the best. I look at the 1960s and 1970s: to me, I think I played at the best time with the best players. That's just my judgment. We're talking about guys like Koufax, who just dominated the game. Then you think about a guy like Juan Marichal, who dominated the game but wasn't quite Sandy Koufax, although he was right there. If he had been in the American League, he'd probably have won that Cy Young Award four times in a row. I didn't mind hitting off of Koufax as much as I did Drysdale. Drysdale was another one of those intimidating pitchers—it was like he didn't care if he hit you or not sometimes. Koufax had the velocity and the curveball and he came from the same spot all the time, whereas Drysdale kind of sidearmed you and was big and rangy. So I didn't really like to hit off him. Another guy whose career almost paralleled mine is Carl Yastrzemski, just a great day-in-day-out player who worked, worked, worked, and became a superstar. Bob Gibson was another great pitcher. If you had one game to win, this is the guy you'd want to see on the mound. Bob Gibson—he was a competitor.

Whitey Ford was a great pitcher. Whitey kept the ball down. Good curveball. Had a spitter once in a while for you that he could throw anytime. He could throw any pitch, any time for a strike, and that's one of the secrets to pitching: when you're two and nothing, three and nothing, you don't have to lay the fastball in there. You could throw a changeup, a curveball. He had great players behind him, but Whitey Ford was the master. And left-handed hitters against him were almost an automatic out. I don't think Jim Gentile ever got a hit off of Whitey Ford. Whitey was just this consummate pro who went out there every fourth or fifth day.

Tom Seaver was a lot like Denny McLain as far as throwing hard. Smooth. And if you wanted your kid to be a pitcher, I'd say look at Tom Seaver. Look at Robin Roberts. These are the guys you just want to watch throw. They do everything. Their fundamentals are terrific.

Roberto Clemente was a great player. You had to put him with the other great players of the game. Playing in Pittsburgh, he probably never got the publicity the other guys did. The only thing that he didn't do as much of was hit home runs. He was basically a doubles, triples hitter, line drives—that was really his biggest asset. The reason I admire him is because I didn't get to play against him except in spring training, the World Series, All-Star Games. You hear how great these players are. And then you get in the World Series, the showcase of baseball. And you have these players like Roberto do the very things you hear he can do against you. And you just admire a guy like that because that's as good as it gets right there. Roberto was the MVP in the '71 World Series, which we played against Pittsburgh. His arm was better than anyone's. I saw him make a play in that particular series where he caught a ball in the right-field corner. I think Frank Robinson was on second. But he just whirled around and threw the ball like a strike. Just a great arm. I think it bothered

Roberto Clemente

Roberto, God bless his soul, that he didn't get the publicity that the other guys did because, I think, deep down he felt he was on a par with them. He was a great, great player.

I got to hit against Warren Spahn in spring training. And he never forgot it because I hit a home run off him. Spahnie is one of those guys who's got that photographic brain. I'll see him, and he'll say, "I remember the first time I saw you. I threw you a fastball. And I think that's why you hit a home run." He never forgets it. Jim Palmer with the Orioles—he could tell you whoever hit a home run. He can remember back to when he started. He knows what pitch it was, what the count was. And I'm saying, "I don't believe this." But he does it. That's part of what made them the great pitchers that they are.

Mike Schmidt is the greatest who's ever played third base. When you combine power and defense, I mean, here's a guy who won a lot of Gold Gloves and probably his offense has a tendency to overshadow his defense, but he could do it all. And so I put Mike right there at the top.

• • •

I learned a lot of things from failure. When you play 162 games, I don't think any sport emulates life like baseball. You play football once a week or basketball twice. But you start playing baseball, you play every day, day in and day out. And you understand in a hurry that you're going to have bad days and bad nights. You're going to have bad weeks, and you just have to make up your mind that, hey, tomorrow's tomorrow, and you forget about it. You know, when I think about it, I think my love for the game overrode everything else. I'm in the Hall of Fame. I don't think I'm there because of my great ability, but I think my love for the game probably overrode everything else. I was playing big-league baseball every day, and I never wanted to do anything else but be a big-league player. That helped put the bad days in perspective and the good days in perspective.

When things are not going too good, well, you just keep looking up and keep going. And that's really what the game is all about. You got to be able to put things out of your mind and come back the next day and get ready to play. I never really got too excited about things or never got down too deep. My twenty-third birthday, I was 0 for 23. I remember that. I hadn't had a hit in twenty-three times. When we played Oakland, I made three errors in one inning. And the only positive thing that happened that night was Frank Robinson hit a home run in the ninth inning off Rollie Fingers and we won the game. But the next day, the headlines were "Robinson Makes Three Errors in One Inning." I said, "Well, if they'd hit me two more balls, I'd have made five errors." If you play this game a long time, somebody's going to get you or you're going to get them. It's not going to be all great things happening to you all the time. And you learn to live with those things. The Mets beating us in '69, that was a real shock because that's really the best team I ever played on, the '69 team. We won 109 games, and we lost our last five out of six, I believe. We could have won 115 or 116 games that year, and we won 109. We won the first game in the World Series and then we lost four in a row. I was a little in shock because we'd only been in one World Series and we'd won four in a row. So you just can't savor things too long in this game. You just enjoy it and let it go, because you know you're going to be back out there the next day.

In the 1969 World Series, we were heavily favored to beat the Mets. But I think most people don't realize or forget that the Mets won 100 games that year. So they had a pretty good ball club. You run Jerry Koosman and Gary Gentry and Tom Seaver out there every three or four days, you're going to win a lot of games. The guy who surprised us more than anything in that series was Gentry. He threw a lot better than we thought he could throw. And, of course, they made a lot of plays. Tommie Agee in center field. I mean, I hit the balls. Ron Swoboda—remember the catch Swoboda made? That would have been a two-run triple. It ended up being a sacrifice fly, but that could have changed the outcome of that game. That was a World Series that I would say was good for baseball. I guess it was good that the Mets won. But it was a real shocker for us to lose that World Series. And then the next year, we came right back and won over 100 games and went into the World Series against Cincinnati. And we really took advantage of Cincinnati's pitching that year. They had a pitching staff that was pretty beat up. People don't re-

Mets 1969 World Series win

member in that World Series that Woody Woodward hit me a little twenty-four-hopper. I got to it and made a high throw to Boog Powell for an error, and I'm saying to myself, "Here we go again." Just like '69, you know what I mean? But everything else after that was pretty upbeat. And after about the third game, I had a chance to make a lot of plays. And I'm saying to myself, boy, this is just unreal. I can't keep this up. I had a lot of plays down there and then made the plays. And I was also hitting well, too. I tell people I played almost twenty-three years professionally and I don't think I ever had five games in a row where I had a chance to do the things that I did in that particular World Series. It was just a once-in-a-lifetime five-game series, and it happened to be the World Series. That's the only way I can explain it. All the writers were waiting on me to come to my locker. And Rex Barney, [the Orioles announcer and] a great man, said, "Well, don't worry about him. Just interview his gloves. They're a lot better, and that's who's doing all the work."

I was happy to see that Series get over because I know that I couldn't keep going and doing the things I was doing with the five-game series it ended up being. In '71, we were favored to beat Pittsburgh. We won the first two in Baltimore. We just blew them away. Went out to Pittsburgh. They won the first game, and then the second game was the first night game in World Series history. They won that game, and then they won the third game. We came back to Baltimore, and I hit a sacrifice fly in the tenth inning to win that game, 3–2. Frank scored from third base. And then the next day, they beat us 2–1. Clemente had a home run, Steve Blass pitched a great game, and they were the world's champions.

Earl Weaver, our manager, was always a proponent of the three-run homer. He disdained the bunt. He thought that was a terrible play. He thought hitting and running was a terrible play. And we had a few guys on that team that could hit and run. But he just didn't like that because there was too many negative things that can come out of bunting a guy over. And also you're giving away an out. "You only get three outs an inning," he said. "You're giving away one. I don't like it." Same for hitting and running. So anyway, we just felt like we could've won a lot of games if we got a guy over, got him in scoring position. So we had a meeting at Paul Blair's. We'd decided, "Well, let's go to Blair's house and talk about it." So all the players came to Blair's house and we said, "Well, we've got to get guys in scoring position, move them over where they have a chance to score." So we decided that when we got a guy on first from then on, we'd just bunt him over. If Earl gave you the hit sign, just bunt him over. It took Earl about three or four games to finally figure out what the heck we were doing in that situation. And I think he ended up saying, "Well, you'd better be right. If you don't follow these signs, you'd better be right." That was one of the times that, I think, the guys got a little upset at Earl. But it worked out well. And Earl loved us all anyway.

The umpires that you probably don't hear a lot about are usually the ones that are the best umpires. And it's pretty unanimous around the league with all the players; they all know the best umpires. They know which umpire gives you the best job behind the plate. A fellow who's in the Hall of Fame, Nestor Chylak, in my time was probably the best umpire that I've seen. Ed Runge was another. We all knew that he had a monstrous strike zone. If it's close, you better swing. He just wanted the game to be speeded along. But Nestor Chylak was really the best umpire in my days. Ed Hurley, another umpire, was a little confrontational, I guess with a lot of the players. But you knew which umpires you could say something to.

Al Barlick, it was this unanimous. You talk to any player and they'd say, "Al Barlick's the best." Jocko Conlan was one of the best. You get a reputation and deservedly so. You earn it. Everyone really knows who the best umpires are. And then consequently, most of them are in the Hall of Fame.

• • •

Today's players have the same dream that I did, to be a big-league player. Their philosophy is "Look, with all this money out there, I'm just asking for it." If we lived in a society where the importance of your job dictated how much you're going to make, then the baseball player would be at the bottom of the heap, I think. People who work in cancer research or AIDS research or teachers or policemen or firemen would make the most money. But that's not reality. We live in a society where entertainers and athletes are going to make more than anyone else; it's just a fact of life. They know it's crazy. They make these humongous salaries and they just kind of laugh. Can you believe it? But I'm happy I played. It worked out great for me. I do think that back when I played, the owners should have been a little more enlightened. But their philosophy when I played was "Look, this reserve clause has been around for a hundred years. You'd better like it, because that's the way it's going to be." I think there's many times that deals could have been struck that would have been much better for the game economically and for the players, too, as opposed to what's going on now.

I was a part of the first baseball strike in 1972, which lasted three or four days of spring training and three or four days during the season. It's like comparing apples and oranges now. But Marvin Miller came on board, I guess a few years before I really got interested in the players' association. Robin Roberts and Bob Feller and a couple of other players were instrumental in getting Marvin. But I thought Marvin had pretty good insight into what was going on. Marvin saw that there was some inequities, that the players should be getting a little more of the pie, I guess you could say. I don't know the criteria for the Hall of Fame, but if you're looking for someone who had a real impact on the game, Marvin Miller would certainly be a gentleman who should be considered. He got the confidence of the players, and he said, "Well, this is right and this wrong," and they believed him. So he had a big impact on the game of baseball.

• • •

This is a controversial question that comes up all the time—when the guys play too long. I've looked through the record books, and I'll tell you that just about every player played too long. Everyone thinks that they can still do it. Everyone thinks that they've found a fountain of youth, or everyone thinks they've made some adjustments in their swing and they're going to come back and do it. And I thought so, too. I probably played too long. But I loved it, and I never want to do anything else. In that respect, my answer to that question is "Look, I think it is such a business now, I think that you should play as long as you can. And they will let you know when you should retire." In 1975, I didn't play well. Didn't hit at all. So I came back thinking I could still play, but I couldn't. I called Seattle, I called Toronto—this was in '77—thinking that I might make a move up there, might be able to do something in the organization when I did retire. And the best thing that happened to me was to get no response from those two teams, and come back to Baltimore and finish up my career. I came back as a player-coach, but I really came back to play. About the middle of the season, I was not playing, and I said, "Well this is it, you know, my career is over." And I just kind of lost interest, which I never thought I would, but I couldn't wait until the season was over and I got out. I retired probably around the first of September when we had to have a final roster.

There's some differences in the game today as opposed to when I played. There seems to be more offense. These things all run in cycles, I guess, but we've certainly seen offense in the last ten or fifteen years. In my opinion, the ball has juiced up some, the players are stronger, the ballparks are smaller, and you just got more guys hitting home runs. What's happening in the game is unbelievable. Mark McGwire, Barry Bonds—it's hard to keep up with. But as I've said before, the guys all had the same dream that I had. But I think the game has changed. The money has changed the game a great deal.

Now, with the designated hitter, you don't see bunting, which should be the easiest art form there is, just to reach out and bunt the ball. It's kind of a lost art. You don't see a lot of hitting and running anymore. And in that way, the game has changed a certain degree. The way that the pitchers are used now, every fifth or sixth day, you have the middle reliever, you have the left-handed specialist, the right-handed specialist, the short relievers. So, in those respects the game has changed.

I don't have any problem with the designated hitter. Look at all the other sports; it's offense, offense, offense. People are geared for seeing teams score. Personally, I have kind of been for the designated hitter, because I think it gives you more runs, more hits, more everything. Whatever it is, it should be uniform. That's the thing that I say. If you're going to go back the old way, that's fine. But for one league to have one set of rules and the other league have another set of rules—just crazy. I don't understand it, but that's the way it is.

I look back and I can't believe that I played that long, and I can't believe that I went to bat over 10,000 times. It just doesn't seem like that happened, really. I honestly believed that I overcame a lot of things just by my love of the game.

I'd like to be remembered as someone who had a dream and never wanted to do anything in his whole life except be a professional baseball player, someone who loved the game with all his heart. That's the way I want to be remembered. I'm in the Hall of Fame because I think my love for the game overrode everything else. I didn't have the ability that a lot of guys had, but I just think that the fact that I went out there and got better and worked hard and had a love for the game put me in the Hall of Fame.

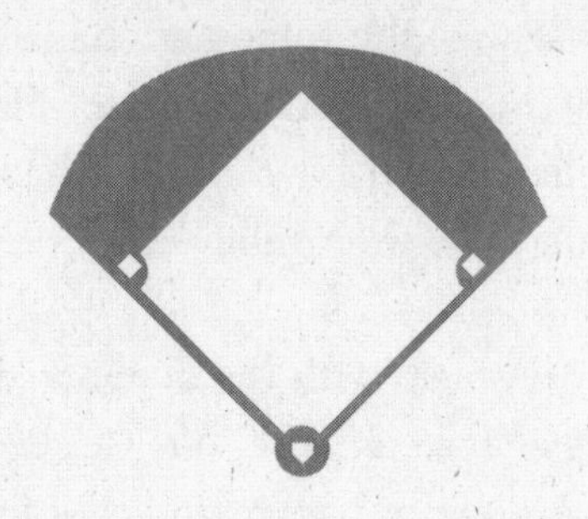

FRANK ROBINSON

Frank Robinson had an impact on the national pastime both on and off the field—first as one of the most feared hitters in the game, later by becoming the first African-American manager in the major leagues.

"But Robinson, perhaps the meanest, hustlingest, most hardnosed of the game's great hitters, deserves even more glory than he gets," wrote Washington Post *writer Thomas Boswell. Pitcher Jim Bouton's scouting report: "Going over the hitters it was decided that we should pitch Frank Robinson underground."*

Robinson came up as a slugging outfielder with the Cincinnati Reds, winning the 1956 NL Rookie of the Year Award after leading the league with 122 runs and finishing second in home runs with 38. He would play with the Reds for ten seasons, winning the NL MVP Award in 1961 as the team won the National League pennant.

Robinson was traded to the Baltimore Orioles in 1966 in one of the game's most lopsided deals. Before long, his leadership was helping the O's to four American League pennants and two World Series titles during his six seasons with the team. Included in this stretch was Robinson's Triple Crown season of 1966, a season in which he led the league with 49 home runs, 122 RBIs, a .316 batting average, and was named league MVP, becoming the only player to win MVP awards in both leagues.

"I don't think we'll have another leader of Frank's type," said Mark Belanger, a Baltimore teammate. Another teammate, Dave McNally, said, "If any of the young guys had hitting problems he had an open ear for them, and they felt they could go to him. Just that meant something."

After short stints with the Los Angeles Dodgers and California Angels, Robinson found himself with the Cleveland Indians. He was named the Tribe's player-manager prior to the 1975 season, thus breaking down a long-standing racial barrier in the game. Robinson, who would eventually gain induction into the National Baseball Hall of Fame in 1982, would finish his twenty-one-year playing career with 2,943 hits, 586 home runs, and a .294 batting average.

"He was perhaps the best all-around batter in the majors in his era," said pitcher Gaylord Perry, a fellow Hall of Famer. "There wasn't a way to get him out, either. Just about everybody has a weak spot. Some guys can't hit down and out curveballs. Some can't hit sliders. Frank could hit everything and he knew that you knew that. It gave him the advantage almost all of the time. People say they are amazed that in the 1960s and 1970s he hit 586 home runs. I'm amazed that's all he hit."

I was born in Texas and it wasn't a great time for baseball in the early 1940s, around 1941 or 1942. There were no minorities in the major leagues at that time. I first came into contact with baseball when I moved to California. There was a recreation center that taught kids. The recreation director in that area in Oakland was Mary Lou Russo. And she really got me on the track of playing baseball and understanding the game.

Baseball to me was the Pacific Coast League. I wanted to play for the Oakland team, the home team when I grew up. That was my introduction to professional baseball.

Frank Robinson

My mother didn't let me play football, organized football. I could play on the playgrounds and things like that, but in high school, junior high school, I could not play football. I was pretty good at basketball. I was the right size at that time for basketball, because I was about five eleven. Now, you're a midget at five eleven in the NBA. But baseball was it. That was the sport that I wanted to play and that I was pretty good at. I just played the other sports in high school to fill my time until the baseball season would start. No one pointed me to baseball, no one said go to basketball, and even when I played with Bill Russell in high school—we had a very good basketball team—I still didn't feel like I could go and play professional basketball. I didn't want to, I had no desire to. I told my teachers in school that I was going to be a major-league baseball player. I was going to sign a bonus contract, big bonus contract, for $75,000, and I was going to be on my way. And I realized most of that—but the bonus fell a little short. I got $3,500. But I wanted to play baseball and I just felt like that's the sport that I would excel in.

One person did teach me the skills and the fundamentals of

baseball that I still rely on today. I was always, I guess, a natural athlete but I wasn't really polished. I had the ability to play—hit a baseball, catch a baseball, throw a baseball, run—but I wasn't polished. A young man at that time was my high school coach. He came in contact with me when I was like eight years old and in the youth league. He managed about five or six youth league teams of different ages. So he got hold of me at eight years old and taught me the basic fundamentals of the game of baseball that a lot of kids didn't know about, the infield fly rule, you know, those kinds of things. How to play offensively and defensively, hit behind the runner, those type of things, hit the cutoff man, and how to approach the game itself. You give it all you have. You play 100 percent at all times. You can go out and hit a home run occasionally, win a ball game with a catch or making a play. But you can't do that every day. What you can do is give the effort day in and day out. There's only one way to play the game and that was to give 100 percent. That's what I live by today. George Powles was the man that really influenced my baseball career, and even now has an influence on my life as far as baseball is concerned.

I am the last one of ten in the family, but I didn't grow up with all of my brothers and sisters because they were out and gone; there was an age gap in there. I grew up with two brothers at home. My mother laid down the law. She never put a hand on any of the kids, never laid a hand on us. All she had to do was look at us and we got the message. And the one thing growing up, I'm not saying I was a saint growing up, because I did get into a little trouble here and there, but nothing serious because I didn't want to embarrass my mother, that's number one, and I didn't want to go home if I had gotten into trouble. I wasn't what you call a great student, but I worked hard at it because I wanted to try to be the best I could probably be, and that's another thing. She gave me that phrase. She said, "You may not always be the best, but you always strive to try to be the best. And if you're not the best, you shouldn't be ashamed." The other thing she used to tell me when I was a youngster was, "You have been given a God-given talent to play the game of baseball. But always remember, you are no better than anyone else, and just remember that, and treat people the same way that you would like to be treated." And that's what I've always done.

She passed away in 1980. She got a chance to see me in basically all phases of the game on the field. She didn't get a chance to see me go into the front office of a Major League Baseball club, but she saw me as a player, as a coach, and as a manager, and she got to enjoy that. She wasn't a baseball fan because she rarely came to the games. She would get me, scold me once in a while when I'd come back out to the West Coast to play the Giants or somebody like that or Oakland. She would say, "I heard the announcers talking about you on the radio, that you were out there arguing and yelling. You're making a fool of yourself." That's the way she put it. She would say, "I don't want that. I don't want that." So, I think that's one thing, that I approached the game, played it hard, played it fair, and pretty rough, you know, but I always looked at it that I wasn't going to get thrown out of the ball games. Once in a while, I would get thrown out, but nothing excessive because I just remember what she'd say, "Don't be out there making a fool out of yourself."

She worked very hard to keep the family going and give us what she had given us. People say, "Were you poor?" I said, "I don't know what you mean by poor because I always had shoes. I always had clothes." I could do some things, and there were a lot of things I couldn't do, couldn't afford to do, but I wasn't poor. I was rich right here inside, and I wasn't rich in the pocket, but I was rich right here. She gave us what she could give us. And when I did sign a contract, got the bonus, it was given to her. And everything that I could do for her as long as she was living, I tried to do.

There was racism when I was growing up in Oakland, California. It was all over the country, but just a lesser degree than down in the South, really. And there was prejudice. I didn't know it existed at that time because it was never spoken of in our household. My mother never made a difference in the color of someone's skin in our household. We grew up in a neighborhood that was mixed, Latinos, blacks, and whites, and we went to a school that was mixed. So I had friends that were white. We brought them to the house, but there was never anything in the household mentioned about prejudice or racism, anything like that. So I grew up really not feeling that. And the friends that I didn't like were black friends. I used to fight against the black kids because they were always fighting against my friends who were white and Latino. So it was a mixture there. I didn't really run into prejudice and segregation until I headed into professional baseball. Then I found out real quick what it was. But living in Oakland, California, I didn't come across it.

Jackie Robinson meant, at that time in 1947, that if I had the ability to play Major League Baseball, or professional baseball, that I could have the opportunity. That's what it meant at that time. I think Jackie Robinson's contribution to baseball was tremendous, there's no doubt about that. But I think his contribution off the field, in our society, was even more because he brought this country together at that time with his baseball play and the way he conducted himself. People said, "Well, do you think you could have done that, what he went through?" I said, "No way." There's no way that I could put up with it and then do what he did. I don't know how he did it, but he was the right man.

The Negro Leagues came out barnstorming. They played in Oakland against the Bob Feller–led team, a Satchel Paige–led team, and that's the only way the Negro Leagues touched me. But I didn't know any history about the Negro Leagues until I grew up into professional baseball. A lot of people say, "Did you play in the Negro League?" I did not. They were back east and they played their baseball mostly back east and in the Midwest.

We had a very good team in high school, but we didn't play very many games in those days. We played only ten league games and four or five exhibition games. So it wasn't a big schedule. It wasn't a big sport in high school because it wasn't a moneymaker or anything like that. I played on an American Legion team. My first year in high school, I was the youngest to ever play American Legion baseball at fourteen years old. My high school coach, George Powles, had coached the American Legion team in another area. So, I joined that team and we became the first American Legion team to win back-to-back championships. I was a third baseman, believe it or not. That's when I was aware of scouts on the American Legion team, because they were scouting a catcher with tremendous abilities whom I still admire to this day named J.W. Porter. He signed for one of the biggest bonuses at that time, $50,000, with the Chicago White Sox. And I still didn't understand what being scouted meant at that time. So, I didn't pay much attention to it. He was signed by Bobby Maddox when he graduated from high school. And Bobby used to come around my last year in high school. When I was getting ready to graduate, I figured, "Ooh, I want to be a White Sox. I want to be signed by the White Sox." But Bobby changed from the White Sox to the Reds. And he was the only one personally to come talk to me and my family about signing. The difference in the offers was not the money but the classifications. The Reds said, "We'll give you the $3,500 and we'll start you at Class C." And I felt the loyalty and personal attachment to Bobby Maddox because he had not only shown an interest in me as a player, but he showed an interest in me as a person, and that made the difference in me signing. I said then, "I have someone I think will look out for me." When I graduated in June, I didn't even get a ticket or a flight. He drove me to the minor-league team.

My first full year in baseball was in 1953. I was living out in Utah and then I went to Tulsa, Oklahoma, to play. I didn't want to be there, I didn't want to go. I only played eight games at Tulsa and they demoted me to Columbia, South Carolina, in 1954. I was very unhappy there because, number one, I couldn't go to the movies unless I sat upstairs only. And you can't eat in a restaurant unless you ate in the black area, and I was upset about that. It was, kind of, you were in prison. I just made myself a promise. I said I want to have the best year that I can possibly have and get the hell out of there. And I had a good year, but then I came up with an injury late in the season to my shoulder, and I couldn't throw in spring training. I had made the Cincinnati Reds in 1955 but I couldn't throw, so I had to go back. And they said, "We're sending you back to Tulsa." I said, "No, you're not." They said, "Well, where do you want to go?" I said, "I will go back to Columbia because they wanted me." Tulsa didn't want me the year before so I went back to Columbia for a second year, but only because I was familiar with the area and the territory and the people down there. I felt more comfortable down there. I went down and had a pretty good year and came back the next year and made the major leagues and never looked back.

When I got to the minor leagues, it was in the middle of the year, in June 1953, when I graduated. I went to Utah and we won the championship. I played in 72 games. And I hit .348 with 17 home runs and 83 RBIs in the 72 games. I signed as a third baseman, but after a few ball games, I said to the manager, "Look, does Cincinnati have any ideas of where to put me in the major league? You better get me out of here. You noticed that no one buys tickets behind the first baseman? That's because I am throwing the ball there instead." I said, "Get me in the outfield," and he did that. Next year, I opened the season in Tulsa as the second baseman. And the first thing that the manager wants to do, Joe Schultz, was to change my swing. I had the hitch, as they call it. He said, "You can't hit like that. You got to keep the bat still," or whatever. So, okay, in those days, you did what the manager said. So I did, and I had eight hits in eight games, all singles to right field. I couldn't pull anything. We finished up the eight-game road trip and we went home to Tulsa, and we had an off day the next day. And I got a call from the manager, "Come out to the ballpark." And I thought that was kind of strange for an off day. They sent me down because they didn't like how I played second base.

So I said, "Okay. I'll go down. But I'll tell you what; I'm going back to hitting the way I used to hit with my hitch, the heck with this stuff. And I'm not gonna play second base; I'm going to the outfield." I went to the outfield, and I had a good year. I hit .336 with 110 RBIs, 25 home runs. Ernie White was the manager. And toward the end of the year, I started to feel every time I threw that someone was sticking a pin in my shoulder. And he says, "That's all in your head. Don't worry about it, kid." So, you listen. I went to play winter ball that year in Puerto Rico. And I was down there a month in Ponce, and we came to play Santurce one rainy, damp night. And I had to throw from right field and I threw the runner out, but it felt like everything broke loose in my arm.

Basketball took some of the better athletes away because it was a little easier to play. You get a pair of sneakers and go down and play, the courts are there, and you don't have to buy anything other than a pair of sneakers. The baseball scouts stopped going into the inner cities, and high school teams stopped having the sport of baseball because it generated no income. I think probably in the '60s it started to decline like that. The kids had to turn to other sports. Are they as prepared today as we were then? No, because they don't play as much baseball as we used to. The kids want to get to the major leagues as soon as they can. They don't spend as much time in the minor-leagues learning their skills and the rules and regulations of baseball and honing their craft for a number of reasons. "I'm signing this contract now"—they haven't seen one field, one curveball, one slider, or anything. "I will be called up in September to the major-league team, and I will go to spring training with the major-league team," and they have no experience under their belt.

When I was coming along, the rule of thumb was a hitter had to have at least 1,500 at bats under his belt before they felt like you were ready for the big leagues, or should be ready for the big leagues. The pitcher had to have 500 innings under his belt. And also, you know, when I was coming along, we talked baseball and we listened to baseball, and we breathed and we ate baseball, and we took time to listen to elders talk about baseball and respected them for that.

But you don't see kids now spending much time learning and talking about their craft. I don't blame the kids or the players for it. A lot has to do with management, too, the way we go about promoting these kids. It used to be you had to earn your promotion to the major leagues. Now, they're just not ready to play the game and haven't been associated with it long enough to understand it fully. Playing the game is more than just putting on the uniform, catching the ball, throwing the ball. Instincts have a lot to do with it. Understand what the situation calls for before it happens, you know.

A perfect example from a teammate of mine is Brooks Robinson. Brooks is one of the most outstanding defensive players that ever played the game. One of his patented plays is where he'd go over the third-base line, catch the ball, and throw to second for the force out on a double play. You'd swear that he didn't even look at second base, and everybody goes, "How could he make that throw when he didn't see where he was throwing?" I said, instincts, number one, but also he's worked at that, he's prepared himself for that, and he anticipates going on over there, and he has a feel for that throw. He knows where he is and he knows what he has to do on that throw. Does he have a play there? He goes out and works at it, practices, and does it, and prepares himself for those instances instead of reacting. You have to be prepared before you make a play, before the play comes to you. All of that is thought out before it happens. And after a ball game, we used to spend a lot of time in the clubhouse sitting around, talking about not only that game last night, but the games coming up. I used to get up in the mornings and I couldn't wait to get the newspaper to see who was pitching, because we weren't given all this advance information you get today. Now you know who's pitching against you two weeks in advance because the PR guys get it out and everybody wants to know. The media wants to know who is pitching. But we didn't know who was pitching the following day because the managers wouldn't tell you who was pitching until you read the paper the next day or got to the ballpark. I wanted to spend that time of day, when I was at home getting ready to go to the ballpark, going over how they pitched me that time before, what success I'd had against the opposing pitcher, what success he had against me, what pitches he threw in certain situations. That's the way we used to do it. And now, these kids, they know it all. We have created what I call zombies, because the player today doesn't have to think for himself. We got a coach for everything. Infield coach, outfield coach, hitting coach, pitching coach, bullpen coach, and we even have a bench coach. A guy that comes out and makes sure the bench is there, right? The players don't think for themselves.

You go over where you want to play these guys defensively before the game starts, right? You say, "You're going to play Frank to pull to the left fielder." And the left fielder is a little toward the line. So now the right fielder is over at right-center field. But against some pitchers, maybe I can't get around, right? Today, they stand right there. They don't move and think unless the coach—an outfield coach or the bench coach—goes, "Move." But in our day, if I saw that myself, if I'm playing in right field, I would say to my center fielder, "I'm moving over toward the line because this guy is not getting around on the ball." We had to think for ourselves and make adjustments to win in the course of a game. You don't see that today. It's not the players' fault. It's just that we developed all these things to help them, but what we're forgetting and not understanding is we are not allowing them to use their own mind and their own instincts, and we're just making them, like I say, depend on us too much in the dugout before they do anything and know how to do it. And it's not as good a brand of baseball as it should be.

We did things that we felt like we had to do to survive. We studied the game. We analyzed the game. We used to sit around and talk about the game, ride on the trains. The ride on the trains, you were together as a team. We used to talk baseball. I don't care where baseball players go. If you go as a group, you can go to a bar, you can go to a restaurant, you can go on a picnic or whatever you want to do, eventually, you're going to be talking baseball. It's going to come around to where you're talking baseball. And that's what we used to do on the train, we used to sit in the parlor car and talk baseball. It used to be in the hotel because you could come down to the lobby during the day, sit around, and you would talk baseball. We didn't have the video games you have today. We didn't have TV at that time. Back then, it all came from what you would see, observe, and what you would remember to do.

When I went from the National League to the American League, people said, "Well, it's gonna be tough over there. You don't know the pitchers and whatever." Well, I didn't have to know the pitchers. When I went to Baltimore, I could have drawn from a lot of knowledge that was there, Brooks, Boog, Aparicio, those guys were there. But all I asked them was one thing, does this pitcher have a trick pitch that he throws when he's got two strikes on the batter? It didn't matter to me because with me sitting on the bench, I'm hitting maybe third or fourth in the lineup, watching what was going on, I understood how hard he would throw, what his curveball would do, if he was throwing it for strikes, if he wasn't throwing for strikes, if he's getting a slider over or whatever. That's all I wanted to do. I could see it for myself. The radar gun is one of the worst tools that came into baseball. I don't need a radar gun to tell how hard a pitcher is throwing. I just have to see three or four pitches, good fastballs, to tell you within a couple of miles what it is. I've done it with the radar gun. They'll say, "Well, what was that?" And I'll say, "That was 95." They say, "No, it was 94." I said, "Well, one mile an hour. It doesn't make any difference." And I think this is what we did in the old days. We learned by passing on information, by talking, we learned by observing. I hate the words, "He's a natural." I hate that. Sure, you're a natural, but everybody has to work and polish those skills to be as good as you possibly can be. You can't just be a natural and go out there and play this game. And I think this is what a lot of players rely on a little bit too much in the modern era of the game of baseball: their own natural ability. And also, one of the things, I think, missing in baseball today is pride, to be the best you possibly can be. "I did the best I could. Yeah, I can't do any better." Yes, you can. You can do better. Every year, after the season was over, I would go back home and analyze my year. Where could I be better, where did I maximize my ability? Okay, home runs. I hit 49 home runs last year. If I do that again, that would be fine. If I don't do it, but I can improve on my batting average, I can improve on my runs scored, I can improve on driving runs in. That would be my goal going to spring training the next year, to improve on the areas that I was down in the year before, knowing that I can be better.

When I came to Cincinnati my first year, in 1956, that's when I first ran into a manager that cared about players. That was Birdie Tebbetts. He was excellent with young players. He'd walk up and down the dugout in spring training and say, "What's the count?" And, "How many outs," you know, this type of thing. Kept you on your toes. He was concerned about you and just talked baseball with you. I learned an awful lot. On opening day in Cincinnati, I went two for three, just missed a home run my first at bat. We lost the ball game to the Cardinals. Stan Musial had a home run and beat us in the ninth inning. After the ball game, reporters asked me, "Frank, what's the difference between minor-league ball and the major leagues?" I said, "None. None. Not much different." I probably went 0 for 23 after that.

I became the regular left fielder the rest of the year. Birdie would hit me anywhere from seventh to second. One time, I hit first in the lineup and I had a good month. And then, after that, I said, "That's enough of that, Birdie, put me back down."

We hit 221 home runs that year. We won ball games 15 to 14, 13 to 12, you know, that type of thing. I started off hitting seventh in that lineup, which was a good position for me because no one paid any attention to me. And I got good pitches to hit. I had a good year, Rookie of the Year. They always told me to get three swings every time up. And that's what I tried to get. I was the youngest guy on the team at twenty years old.

I could hit the fastball. I didn't care how hard you threw it, I could hit the fastball. I had trouble with the off-speed balls because even when I was in sandlot baseball in Oakland, I had trouble with curveballs. But no one tried to correct that because, I guess, in those days, they just felt like if you were a good hitter, they didn't want to fool around. In amateur baseball, not too many guys could throw curveballs anyway.

To correct that you would take extra hitting and you'd have whoever was throwing, if it was a coach or whoever, throw you a curveball. Today, you don't see that. In a regular batting practice, everything is straight. The hitters just want everything right there. At times the coach wouldn't even tell you, he would spin one up there to you. And if you complained, he'd say, "Hey, do they tell you what's coming in the game?"

You have to make adjustments. So, if you can't adjust in batting practice, how are you going to adjust in the game?

If you're patient enough at the plate, each time up there, you're going to get your pitch to hit. And sure enough, you know, if you are patient enough, they're going to throw you a pitch to hit. And this is how I survived. I survived until I saw enough curveballs, saw enough of them because everybody thought that was my weakness, so that's all I was getting until the point where I was working at it. And seeing enough of them and playing enough that I became accustomed to doing it. What it was is timing, that's all. I didn't know the timing mechanism there until talking to some of the older guys, the pitchers especially, and they told me that. They said, "You got to wait on that pitch soon as you see the curveball coming out."

The slider was a tough pitch, but it didn't give me that much trouble because it was strong—like a fastball. It didn't give me as much trouble as the curveball or the changeup. I hit the sliders pretty good because I was right on top of the plate. So, a slider out on the outside corner, it's right down the middle to me.

Koufax was just unbelievable. You know, he had trouble in his first few years in the big leagues throwing the ball over the plate. Then about the middle of the '58 or '59 season, he started getting the ball over the plate, and he took off from there. He was unbelievable.

His fastball came up, and I didn't see any other pitcher do that. I still haven't seen any other pitcher throw a fastball down about knee-high and the ball comes up, rises up. He would always go to his fastball on 2–0 or 3–1 or 3–2, until he could get his curveball over. So you just had to wait for it. But to this day, he was a tough pitcher to hit against, although, like I said, you knew what was coming. I had good success when Bob Gibson first came up. A matter of fact, he came to Cincinnati in his first game, he was called up and pitched in Cincinnati, and the first time up it was two men on, and he tried to throw the fastball by some kid and the kid hit a double. And then it went downhill a little bit. Over the years, he started to get me out. Bob threw what we called a heavy ball. He had a hard slider. He was just mean enough, you know, he was up under your chin and that type of thing. So he was tougher to hit against than Sandy Koufax. But Koufax was tougher to get hits off of. They were both outstanding pitchers.

Don Drysdale was a mean pitcher. He said half the plate was his and half the plate was the hitter's. The only difference was the hitter didn't know which half Drysdale wanted at the time. He didn't mind hitting you. He didn't mind throwing at you. And you know, I was right on top of the plate and he was this long, lanky guy. He had good control when he wanted to have it. His fastball would tail in on you, slide away, and would be on top of the plate. It was very difficult with the fastball that slid away, trying to protect that area. When I would finish four at bats against Drysdale, it was like wrestling a horse or a mule, or being in a fight. That's how tired I would be after the ball game. One time, I was up and the manager signaled for Drysdale to put me on. And the first pitch, he hit me in the ribs. After the ball game, he said, "Why waste three pitches? I put him on." He was the toughest pitcher for me to hit off of in my career, toughest pitcher. In ten years, I had two home runs off him in the

Don Drysdale

National League and in the World Series. I respected him and I think he respected me as a hitter. The way I was taught was not to let the pitcher intimidate you. And when they would knock me down or hit me, that just made me more determined. I always had to tell myself, "Don't get upset because now he has you not really focused in your thinking." So, it just made me focus better and be more determined that you weren't going to get me out.

In 1965, Dick Sisler was managing the Reds. And I was having a pretty good year. And then I went 0 for 22 and I didn't know if I was going to get another hit at all. This is the first time I was booed by the home fans, and it really hurt. I just wanted out. I didn't say it, but I wanted out. I said, "They don't respect me. What the heck. Well, I don't want to be here." Bill DeWitt was the Cincinnati general manager. I was used to going into the office because I stayed in Cincinnati in the off-season. I could see DeWitt just like that, in a second, because he would make the time. "Come on in, sit down and talk." I was used to that. So I went in to talk about my contract before I left to go to California before the holidays. And he made me wait an hour and a half. The first thing he said to me when I walked in there, after I sat down, he said, "I hear that you don't always hustle."

I said, "What?"

"I hear your reputation, you don't always hustle."

I said, "I don't know who you heard that from but I give it my all every time." I said, "I don't go from the outfield at 100 percent because what does that prove? But when there's a play to be made or whatever, I give 100 percent."

"Well, that's not what I heard." So he said, "I'm gonna have to cut your salary."

And I said, "Wait a minute. Wait a minute." I said, "I hit very well in 1965, you know, almost 300, 113 RBIs, 33 home runs."

He said, "I don't care. I'm cutting it."

In my MVP year, 1961, I was making $30,000 going into the year. I felt like I would get a raise to $40,000, at least, you know, and maybe fifty, but they offered me a $5,000 raise. And I had to battle. I had to battle and not threaten to hold out because, you know, you couldn't go to spring training unless you had signed your contract. And that's what they would hold over your head. They would sit and wait and wait and because they felt like you weren't making a lot of money in those days, and that's before taxes, the $30,000. And then you had to play for that—to get that salary the next year. And they would just sit and wait and wait and wait until you signed the contract and, usually, you didn't want to go to spring training halfway through. You wanted to go and get yourself in shape, to go have the good year the next year. And so, I battled with them for quite a while and wound up getting the $20,000 raise on that. But it was tough. It was tough.

I became kind of the spokesperson for the players on the team in those days, when you're with troublemakers, when you would speak out against management or whatever, speak up for what you felt like was right. Most of the time, it wasn't my problems that I was speaking out; it was a teammate's problem. They would come to me. "Frank, you're the big guy on the club, you know, you could go talk to them and they're not doing this, I'm unhappy with this or that." And I would always take the problems of my teammates to management as my own problem. I would never say, "Fay said, Fay wants"; it was always like it was my problem. When you would speak up or speak out against management, they would classify you as a troublemaker. And this is what I became, a troublemaker. I was also bad for the young players. Vada Pinson came along, and I influenced him. He wasn't getting his proper rest and that kind of stuff or whatever, they said.

So Cincinnati traded me to Baltimore for a pitcher, one of Baltimore's better pitchers at that time, they said, Milt Pappas. Also, Jack Baldschun, who had been with the Phillies for a number of years as a reliever, and was just traded to Baltimore that winter. And Dicky Simpson, who had been with the Angels until then. And those are the three players who were traded to Cincinnati for me. Simpson and Baldschun had not played a game in the Baltimore uniform.

This happened in '66. I knew I was going to a good team because in the two previous years, they had wound up third, only a few games behind. I knew some of the names. I knew Brooks Robinson was there. I got the call. It came from Phil Seghi, Cincinnati's assistant general manager at the time. I was eating dinner, getting ready to go bowling, and my wife said, "Telephone." I said, "Who is it?" She said, "Phil Seghi." This is December 1965. I thought I was safe. "This is Phil Seghi. I just want to call you and tell you you've been traded to Baltimore." I said, "Where?" "Baltimore." "For who?" "Milt Pappas, Jack Baldschun, Dick Simpson." "Okay. I wanna thank you." Click. So my wife said, "What is it?" I said, "We've just been traded." She said, "To where?" I said, "To Baltimore." That killed my dinner. I went bowling that night, bowled my worst three games I ever bowled in my life. For three or four days, I didn't leave the house. I just couldn't leave the house.

Brooks was the big guy there in Baltimore. My wife went with a real estate broker to look at houses. She liked a couple. "Well, this is a very nice place. How much does this cost?" The broker said, "Oh,

Mrs. Robinson, yeah, you will be glad to have it. Your husband, Brooks, will be happy here, too." And she said, "No, my husband is Frank." And all of a sudden that place wasn't available. It was not available. My wife called me and said, "I'm not gonna stay here when I can't find a place to stay." I went to Jerry Hoffberger, the owner, and I said, "I have to leave spring training to go to Baltimore and get my family. I'm going home."

He said, "Just give me a couple of days. We'll get this thing straight." So he finally found a house, but when I got back to Baltimore, she said, "Oh, this thing was filthy when we the first went in. It just took us three or four days to get it cleaned up." Even the next year, looking for a better area to live in, we ran into the same thing again. Next-door neighbor, they want to know who was moving in. "Frank Robinson, the Baltimore ballplayer." They said, "Okay, that's fine." But when I moved in there, they'd have nothing to do with me, never talked to me. They never talked with the family or whatever. It was a little tough, yeah, at the beginning in that respect. But overall, it was pretty good.

Brooks and I hit it off from the beginning. We never had a cross word, our lockers were next to each other. And we are friends to this day. And coming in, I knew that was a good ball club because they'd been close the two years before. I said, "If I can go over there and have the type of year that I'm capable of having, we have a good chance to win." And sure enough, we won. It was a great bunch of guys there. Brooks, Luis Aparicio, and Jerry Adair were there. I was in right field; Curt Blefary was in left field; Paul Blair was in center.

Great pitching, young pitching. Steve Barber, Dave McNally, Wally Bunker, guys like that. Everything just jelled from the beginning with Hank Bauer, the big rough, tough Marine-type manager.

There was good chemistry in there. I didn't go in there to be a leader. I just went out and led by example as far as the way I played the game. They took to me as a team. I didn't go out there and tell anyone, "I'm the leader," or anything like that. I just let Brooks have his space just like the rest of his team. I just did my thing and then they started to gravitate to me.

Some guys looked at me as a leader of the team. And I just wanted to take some of the load off of the manager. We took things to the back room and we laid it out on the line. We pointed fingers at each other. We didn't just go in and gloss it over and say, "Well, some of us are not running out the ball." No, "Hey, *you're* not running the ball out. Don't you get that, you are taking money out of my pocket, babe? Get down the line and don't be worried about your stats or whatever. You should've been on second base, should've been on first base." It was important because if we hadn't had that meeting, I think the team would've probably not responded the way we did that year and had the year we had. It was Brooks's idea in a way, but he came to me before he called the meeting and said, "I think we"—not him—"we should call a meeting." And I said, "You know, you're right. I think that'd be good."

Brooks and I and Boog were in quite a battle for RBIs, home

Brooks Robinson

runs, and that type of thing. And I kind of pulled away going into September and had the RBI and the home run thing kind of locked up. The only thing I had to do was battle for the batting average. Tony Oliva and I were battling. We were up and down. So, it came right down to the last series of the year. We were playing each other. Our pitchers were doing a great job against Tony in the series, and I happened to get a few hits and go ahead of him or stay ahead of him. So the question came up, would I want to play the last game. I was leading Oliva in batting, and I didn't have to play. But I said, "I played in 161 games. I didn't take any time off. Why would I want to take off, be sitting over there, and watch Tony take the lead?" I said, "No, I've gone this far and if I'm gonna win it, I'm gonna win it on the field. If not, I'm gonna lose it on the field." And I wound up winning the batting title and winning the Triple Crown. And then, we went into the World Series to play the mighty Dodgers. A lot of people said we don't belong on the same field with the Dodgers. I said to our players, "I think we have the pitching and I think we have the offense. I think we can beat them." And a great start, I had a two-run homer in the first inning off Drysdale. Brooks followed it up with one behind me. So we're leading three to nothing. McNally, who was pitching for us, had a tough time. They started to come back a little bit, three to two. So, Hank Bauer brought in Moe Drabowsky, and he had a great stretch of five or six innings of shutout baseball, eleven strikeouts. We won the ball game 5–2.

In game two, Koufax was on the mound, but we won that one six to nothing. We go back home, for game three. Paul Blair hit a home run in the fifth inning. We wound up beating Claude Osteen one to nothing. The next ball game, Drysdale's back on the mound. I'm going to the plate in the fourth inning. The first two hitters hit the first two pitches, made outs. I'm saying, well, I should take a pitch. Don't let them get out of the inning with three pitches. And I'm walking up to home plate and I said, "No, I'm gonna look for a fastball in my area that I can hit, and if I get it, I'm gonna swing." And

Sandy Koufax

sure enough, he threw me a fastball and then boom, I hit it out. And we won that ball game one to nothing.

So, we won the last two ball games one to nothing. We swept the series. There was a great celebration and Baltimore had a great year; everything just fell into place for me personally and as a ballplayer. I think that was the first time I got full recognition across the country that I was a pretty good player. I didn't get that in Cincinnati, but I think it started coming.

Winning the Triple Crown is the single most difficult thing for one individual to do in baseball. With all the players in the league, you have to win or tie in those three categories. You're battling against all the other players in the league in those three categories. That is very difficult to do. It's not something you go into a season thinking about.

But the proudest thing in that season was winning the World Series and getting the ring. In those days, that's what it was all about, a ring. And the paycheck coming out of the Series was a lot more sometimes than guys made all year.

• • •

I knew I couldn't continue to play for the rest of my life, although I'd love to. What would I want to do in baseball; what job would I want to stay in? I like the competition. The closest thing to being a player is managing the baseball club. So that was what I wanted to do.

In 1968, Earl Weaver came along, middle of the season. He was in the dugout, and the owner of the Santurce ball club in Puerto Rico was talking to Earl. I was coming out of the clubhouse to get ready to play the game. I was walking by them, and I heard Earl say, "Well, I can't go back to manage this year because I'm the manager now and I'm going to be the manager next year." And I just turned and said, "Well, why not me?" And Earl looked at me. After the game, he said, "Were you serious about it?" I said, "Yes. I was serious." So he made an appointment for me to talk to the owner when we got back to Baltimore. And I was to manage in the '68–'69 season down there in Puerto Rico. I went back for seven more years after that to manage down there and to try to prepare myself. And one year, Gabe Paul was down there. He had gone to the Yankees as their general manager. He was my first general manager back in Cincinnati. He said to me, "You know, if you just had a little bit of experience, I would hire you as the manager of the Yankees." And I said, "What is this? What is it?" He said, "This doesn't count." That bothered me. But it did help me prepare for the opportunity that came along when Cleveland offered me the job in '74.

In July 1974, the Angels—whom I'd played for since '73—put me back on waivers. I said to myself, "Evidently, they don't want me here, and whoever claims me next, I'm out of here." Cleveland claimed me. So, I called and talked to Phil Seghi, who was the general manager there, and I told him what I wanted. He said, "Okay, you got it." I was told that I was going to be the manager at the end of the year. But I went there, and there was turmoil at the end of the season. Phil Seghi called me. We were getting ready to go to Boston, the end of season, the last three games. Phil offered me the manager's job, and I accepted. Then I said, "What are you going to pay me?" I had a contract to play for the following year. He said, "Well, we want you to be a player-manager." I said, "Oh, I prefer not to be. I'd rather concentrate on the managing part of it." He said, "No, we want you to be a player-manager." I said, "Okay, but on one condition." I said, "I'm going to manage the ball club first, then I'm going to handle Frank Robinson the player second, just like any other manager would handle him. I'll play when I feel I should play." He said, "Okay." I said, "Well, what are you going to pay me to manage?" He said, "We're going to give you $200,000." I said, "Well, wait, wait a minute. I'm going to make $180,000 next year as a player. You give me $20,000 to manage this ball club?" And that was the offer. My agent was there, and he said, "Let's go out in the hallway and talk." Well, we go out in the hallway and he says, "Hey, look, do you want to manage or not?" I said, "Yeah." He said, "Well, here's the opportunity. If you close the door here, who knows?" So I went back and told them I'd take it. So I managed my first year for $20,000.

I did it because I knew I was making history. Absolutely. That's why I did it. First minority manager in the history of baseball. I said, "If I don't take it, who knows when the door would open again." They could say, "Hey, we offered one of the most qualified minorities in baseball and he refused." So, not for myself, but whoever might be in line for the next opportunity to come.

I wasn't going to go in the field at thirty-nine years old to play. So before that first ball game, I went to the office that morning and before the game, Phil said to me, "You want to put yourself in the lineup. You want to put yourself in the lineup because you know you do some real good things when the pressure's on." I said, "You got to be crazy." But I went downstairs and I thought about it, and I said, "Hmm. Okay." So I put myself in the second spot in the lineup.

Photographers were all over the on-deck circle. I couldn't move. When it was my turn to hit, I was trying to find the way to home plate with all the flashbulbs going off and whatever. My mind was really blank. I didn't think so at the time, but it was. The first pitch comes in, strike one. Second pitch comes in, breaking ball. I thought it was low. I turned around and the umpire said, "You didn't think that was a strike?" I said, "No, I don't think so." But it was a strike. Now it's oh and two. So, now I just happened to just flick the bat like that and fouled it off. I stepped out and I said, "This man is not reading the press clippings. This is my big day and he's trying to embarrass me by striking me out on three pitches."

I thought, he's going to waste a pitch. So I worked the count to two and two, and I hit a slider, a line drive to left field, and I was running. And I'm running and watching the play, and I tripped and almost fell on my face, I'm watching, and then almost tripped again and fell on my face. I finally got my legs under me. The ball went clear to the fence. And I'm running around, and I get to third base and the third-base coach is waving me home. And I'm coming home, and I make it.

I get to the dugout, then I turn to managing. We won the game 5–3. It was a great moment and a great moment in the history of baseball. I thought about the comment that Jackie had mentioned about wanting to be alive to see an African American in the dugout, managing.

What does it take to be a good manager? Number one, you have to try to be your own self. Don't try to imitate anybody else, to be someone else or be worried about what someone would be thinking about your moves before you make them. The one thing that makes a good manager is good players, really. If you have the players and they perform where they're supposed to play, it makes it easy to manage. And as a hitter, I knew hitting, I knew position players. The toughest thing, I think, for anyone in this game, and it still is today for me, is when do you take a pitcher out and when do you leave him in?

It's very important to communicate with your players on a daily basis now. That's how it has changed. Everybody says, "I want to know my role." In the old days, there was no such thing. If you weren't a starter, you were on the bench. If you weren't a starting pitcher, you were in the bullpen. Nowadays, you have to spell it out in spring training. This is your role. And when the season starts, you have to spell it out again. And during the first month of the season, you have to spell it out again. Everybody wants to know their role and continues to ask about their role throughout. Communicating and dealing with the press are probably the two toughest things about being a good manager. I was low maintenance throughout my career. You didn't have to talk to me. Today you almost have to talk to the players every day. I might talk to a player about last night's game, a little bit about his pitching performance. That's communicating a little bit. Some of the other ones you got to go and pump up a little bit because he had a tough night or whatever. You have to know who needs that hands-on type of thing. But you have to do a little bit each day. And I make sure that I walk through the clubhouse each day just to say hello to some of the guys. I'll let them see me and talk to them, I'll joke and kid with them.

I had a good career, you know? Five hundred and eighty-six home runs.

It doesn't look as important anymore when these guys are going by me, you know, Barry Bonds and Sammy Sosa and those guys. In the end, you know what's going to happen? Down the road, people are going to say, "Well, you're talking about Frank Robinson—a great home-run hitter? Oh, why is he fifty-second on the all-time home-run list?" People say, "Do you resent Barry Bonds and these guys passing you?" I say, "No. I passed a lot of people on my way up."

In the days when there were Aaron and Mays and Clemente, I never led the National League at anything because if I hit 37 home runs, somebody hit 38. If I hit .342, someone hit .345. I won the Most Valuable Player Award in 1961. I came close another time but I never led any category until I went to the American League. Then I led the league in all three categories that year. I not only got the recognition on the field, I think, but also personally. People started to understand Frank Robinson as a person also. That's what that year

1966 did for me. I started to get more respect from baseball people, even to this day. But I've enjoyed baseball. I don't know what I would've done otherwise. People ask me, "What would you have done if you weren't a baseball player?" I have no idea. I don't even think about those things because what I'm doing at the time gets my full attention. What I am going to do next will get my attention when I feel like it's time to move on to something else. And as long as I'm healthy and feel like I have something to contribute to baseball, I'd like to stay in baseball to some capacity because this gets in your blood. People don't understand what that means unless you've been in this game.

I would just like people to think of me and say he was a winner. He played the game the way it's supposed to be played, and he was a team player. And if they think of me that way, that would be great.

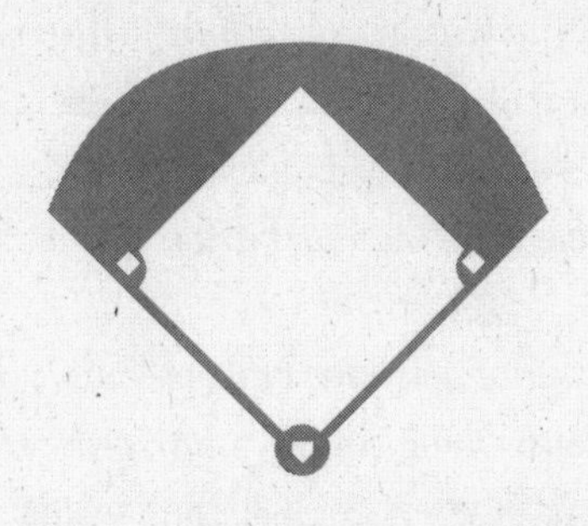

BILLY WILLIAMS

Known for his sweet swing, quick wrists, and quiet disposition, Billy Williams may have been overshadowed by a few of his higher-profile Chicago Cubs teammates, but he was never overlooked. The lefty-swinging left fielder, six-time All-Star, and 1961 National League Rookie of the Year ended his eighteen-year big-league career with 2,711 hits, 426 home runs, and the senior circuit mark for consecutive games played (1,117) until surpassed by Steve Garvey.

"This man never gets excited," said Cubs manager Leo Durocher referring to Williams. "He never gets mad. He never blows up. All you do is write his name down in the same spot every day. Put him in left field, bat him third, and be thankful that you don't have to worry about him. All I know about him is that he does his job. And he does it every day. He's some player. He does the job and he never says a word."

Hall of Famer Rogers Hornsby, upon seeing Williams as a minor leaguer in 1960, called the Cubs, his employers at the time, to report some exciting news: "I suggest you get this kid Williams to Chicago as rapidly as possible because there isn't anybody on the Cubs right now who can swing a bat as well as he does. It's silly to keep him in the minors any longer when you need help as desperately as you do."

In 1964, when Williams was an established big leaguer, Cincinnati Reds manager Fred Hutchinson called him the best-looking hitter in the league. "Mays just overpowers the ball, but Williams is an artist up there," Hutchinson added. "Quick hands and lightning wrists give Billy the fastest bat in the National League. And maybe you can make that in both major leagues."

Longtime teammate and fellow Hall of Famer Ernie Banks said in 1962 that "Billy has everything going for him—the stance, the swing, the eye, the disposition. His swing is compact and he has a real good eye to go along with it. That makes him hard to fool. He has no weaknesses either. Now the average batter usually has one weakness at least. It may be on an inside pitch or a high one. If that's the case, that's the pitch he'll see most of all. But the pitcher doesn't have that advantage with Billy. He can hit anything and hit it anywhere."

The soft-spoken Williams preferred to let his bat do the talking for him. As someone once said, "Billy is both friendly and cooperative, but he'll never talk himself hoarse."

I was going to say I'm from Mobile, but if I say Mobile, a lot of people from Whistler will get mad, so I'm going to say Whistler, Alabama. I was surrounded by a lot of baseball. My father played in the Negro League. He played first base. They used to call him Suzy. They say he was pretty smooth around first base and, of course, along with my three brothers, we would sit around and just look at baseball. And, of course, playing baseball in Whistler, as I say, I was surrounded by guys like twenty-five, twenty-six, twenty-seven years old; anywhere you'd go on a Saturday or Sunday, you could see a doubleheader. And when you're playing with individuals that old, they've been around the game a long time and, of course, they know how to play the game, and if you being sixteen to seventeen years old, if you make a mistake, they'll grab you by the back of the shirt and say,

Billy Williams

"Hey, you don't play baseball like that." I just had a lot of fun playing, and that's how I got started. I saw the old guys playing, and this is the one thing I wanted to do.

My father would go out and play catch and do things like that—"This is how you do it"—and so it was the thing that he always put an interest in us. I know that my mother, she was a strong personality—used to take us swimming and fishing and stuff like that—but when it came to playing sports, my father would always take the three boys out, along with myself, and we would play baseball. I would go down and see the Mobile Bears play, and I just took an interest in baseball because it was all around me.

I was the youngest of the family, and I would tag along with the brother that's in Sacramento now. He was the guy that signed to play in the Pirates organization. His name is Franklin Williams. He got up to Triple-A baseball in the Pirates organization. And it's a strange thing. When I got a chance to come to the big league, a lot of people in Whistler thought it was him because a lot of people said, "That Williams kid made the big league." Franklin was the best athlete. I just happened to be at the right place at the right time, and, of course, my older brother, he was a pitcher on the same club that Henry Aaron was on. So when they would play—I was a little bit too young to play at that time—but I would go watch them. This is when Henry Aaron played infield, and you know the story. He was a cross-handed hitter and a second baseman, and all of a sudden you don't see Henry Aaron playing. When he left, he went with the Indianapolis Clowns. He had to go to the outfield because there was a lady by the name of Toni Stone playing second base. So I guess this was something in his behalf, when he went to the outfield, because Bobby Thomson broke his ankle in 1954, and Aaron came to the big league. And the other brother, Adolph, Adolph Williams, he was a good left-handed hitter because he used to tell me, "This is what you got to do to hit the baseball." I think my father and all my brothers had a little interest in trying to get me to be that ballplayer.

Something happened, I guess on my eleventh or twelfth birthday. My brother had some new shiny baseball shoes, and I thought this was a beautiful pair of shoes. So he went to work, he was doing something, so I sneaked these baseball shoes out, and I guess this was the start of hook sliding because I was sliding on the grass. And I took these baseball shoes, and I wore them, and when I came back, he knew I had worn his shoes because I put them somewhere, and I think that started a little fight. But it was enjoyable. We had a good time.

You start there, in the home, with your mother and father. And, of course, the school, the principal. I remembered Miss Lily A. Dixon, when I made my Hall of Fame speech. This was when we come in in the morning, we have assembly on Wednesday morning, and after the assembly, she always said, Good, better, best, never let it rest until the good is better and the better is best. And this is what I repeated in my Hall of Fame speech. Because when I was playing in Atlanta, a lot of people used to come there to see me. I would come down with the Cubs, so there was two or three busloads that come to Atlanta to see us play. And, of course, she had a bus ticket to come.

And she passed away before she could make that trip. And I wanted to bring her name up because my mother went to that school. She was the principal when my mother was there. And my sisters and my brothers were there, and she was a great inspiration to a lot of people who went to that school, Whistler Elementary School, in Whistler, Alabama.

I remember going to see Cleveland and the Dodgers when they came to play an exhibition game, but then they came back at the end of the season, during the barnstorming tour. They played at—I think it was Metro Field in Mobile. You see these guys get off the bus, seeming like they're ten feet tall. These were major-league guys here. So they were getting dressed, and I remember the guy that sponsored them, a guy by the name of Ed Tucker. My brother and myself, we were the two best ballplayers, I guess, at that time in the area, and he wanted us to play with these major-league people. So we walked in the clubhouse, and you can imagine a kid fifteen or sixteen years old, walking in a clubhouse with guys who've played major-league baseball for a while, and you've read about them, you've looked up to them. So when I walked in the clubhouse—we're getting dressed over in the corner, and you see all these guys: you see Jackie Robinson; you see Junior Gilliam; you see Don Newcombe, Joe Black, and these individuals. So we got a chance to play with those guys. I remember I got in the game about the sixth inning and Joe Black was pitching, and it seemed like he was throwing the ball hard as anybody in the big league. It seemed like he was throwing the ball a hundred miles an hour. I'd never seen that before. But when I came up to the plate I was a skinny kid, 165 straight up. I was like 6'1½" and hadn't put on any weight at that time. I was 165 pounds. So I got up to get in the batter's box against Joe Black, and I said, "Jesus Christ, this guy is playing major-league baseball." I remember he threw a couple of pitches, and I said, "I can't hit that. He's too good." But I finally wind up. He got behind or something. He threw me a fastball. I couldn't pull it, so I hit it to left field. But just to hit the ball—it made me excited about doing something against a major-league baseball player. I mean, you read about these people, you watched them on television, and all of a sudden you're in their company playing baseball. It was exciting to be there with them.

I was signed in 1956 right out of high school. I was signed by a guy by the name of Ivy Griffin, who was a scout for the Chicago Cubs at the time. And somebody asked me the other day, when you first got signed, did you recognize that eventually you might play in the big league? And I said no. I was just out having fun. It was a way to make a buck. The buck wasn't that big, because I was making $225 a month.

A lot of my friends were enlisting in the service. That was a way out of Whistler, Alabama. And I remember going around playing with the Mobile Bears; I was playing with Henry Aaron's brother, Tommie Aaron. This is before I finished high school. I'm traveling with Tommie, going from city to city playing baseball. So we go in Prichard, Alabama, to Mitchell Field, where we had a game that Sunday, and the officer that day—they always had a policeman at these ballparks—he came up and said there was a scout from the Chicago Cubs in the stands. I didn't know who the Chicago Cubs were. I knew who the Dodgers were. So in my mind, I thought he was talking about Tommie Aaron. This scout followed us to a couple of cities, and Tommie and I were there. Later on, we probably were in Moss Point, Mississippi, and Tommie couldn't make the trip, but the scout was still there. So I got kind of itchy then, and thought he might be looking at me to play the game of baseball. So just before I was finishing high school, he approached my father and asked whether I would like to play organized ball. In the meantime, Franklin had signed with the Pirates. So I said that this is exactly what I want to do. Because I didn't want to go in the service; I wanted to do something else.

When the scout came to Whistler, he came by this grocery store and asked, "Does anybody know where the Williams family lives,

Billy Williams's family lives?" Nobody would tell him because they thought I was in some kind of trouble. He had to show people and reassure them that he wasn't looking for me because I was in trouble. He said, "I want to sign him to a contract to play professional baseball for the Chicago Cubs." Somebody told him where I lived, and I could hear him tapping on the screen door. Everybody had screen doors in Whistler because of the mosquitoes down there. So he tapped on the door and my father answered, and they were sitting there and talking about contracts and talking about playing professional baseball. So this was a thing my father wanted me to do, too, because he had one other son playing; if we get them all playing baseball, they'll leave home. But I heard him in there talking, and at the time, I guess, $4,000 or $5,000 was big money to sign and play professional baseball, so I didn't get it. I didn't get the $4,000, but as I heard him talking, Mr. Griffin said, "Your son would like to play professional baseball?" And I said, "Sure, sure." I'm hollering in there, I said, "Sign the contract. Sign it." I got $1,500 to sign, and my father got a couple of cigars, but the most important thing was I signed a contract to play baseball. It was something I wanted to do all my life, because this was what I was doing since I knew about baseball. I played the game and enjoyed the game, but just signing that contract and to go off to play ball . . . Two days after I finished high school, I was on my way to a little town called Ponca City, Oklahoma, to play professional baseball. I rode the Greyhound bus for like two and a half days; and when I got off the bus, that was one of my first times away from home, because my mother always said, "Be in about 11:30 because night doesn't have any eyes." She always wanted me to come home. Two and a half days of riding this bus, and I got off to find this black individual, Mr. White, had come to pick me up to take me to his house, because we had to stay in a private home. We couldn't stay at the hotel, but he made me comfortable. Two and a half days after high school, I was on my way to play baseball. And it was a great time of my life.

I was scared. I was nearly eighteen at the time, and this was one of my first times away from home, so quite naturally I was going to be afraid. I think Buck O'Neil had called Mr. White and said that he's going to come in, that he's going to arrive at a certain time, so be over there to pick him up. When he took me to his house, other guys had the back rooms, I had the front room, so I had a big bed that made me feel comfortable.

I knew I could hit. I could put the bat on the ball, but I was a terrible outfielder. When I first went to Ponca City that year, 1956, I joined the club to fill out the roster of the Class-D league team. But that first year, the only thing I did was go up and pinch-hit. I think I got about five straight pinch hits. The first year, that was it. The team would go on the road, they would leave me in Ponca City. I didn't know exactly what was going to happen at that time, but I guess the ball team knew that I could hit the ball, but that I couldn't catch it in the outfield. I signed to play baseball as a third baseman, and I imagine when they saw me catching balls in there, they said, "You better go to the outfield." They put me in the outfield, and I had to learn to play there. Through hard work and time, I became a decent outfielder.

I was in my second year at Ponca City, and we were playing a team from Ardmore. I think it was in the Cardinals' organization. I got the base hit to win the ball game. I was the only black person on the team. As a matter of fact, I was the only black person in the whole ballpark. There were a lot of Osage Indians there, but I was the only black player on the ball club at this time. A few of the Ardmore guys went back to the hotel, and they had this black guy running the elevator, and I guess they were pissed off at me so much, they wanted to take it out on somebody. And they beat this guy, they kicked this guy. The guy told them, "I will get you guys tomorrow, okay?" I was playing left field. I looked in the stands, and I see this guy sitting there. And I see this guy walk down to the dugout, and he looked around and said, "Where's Corey Smith?" Corey Smith was one of the guys playing on the ball club. And Corey Smith looked up and saw him, and Corey Smith started running. This guy pulled out his .38 and started shooting at Corey Smith. You could see the bullets hitting the ground. This is at the ballpark. Our second baseman is trying to hide behind second base. Our center fielder jumped the fence and as the manager jumped up, J. C. Dunn, he hit J. C., in the side. I'm standing in left field. I'm looking at this, and all of a sudden, the officer came out and got me and took me in the clubhouse because they thought somebody was going to mess me up. So I sat around in the clubhouse, and the game was called off. They put the guy in jail. We had to go to another city to play, and I said I wasn't going. So the Chamber of Commerce in that city wrote a letter to Ponca City and reassured me that everything would be all right. This was my second year in baseball, and I witnessed this.

I was quick with the bat, but when I got to Double-A baseball, I think that my nickname, "Sweet-Swinging Billy," came because I had an opportunity at that time to work with one of the greatest right-handed hitters in the game of baseball, Rogers Hornsby. He and I and Ron Santo spent a lot of time together. I remember when going to spring training in 1957 or 1958, Rogers would tell me to come down in the batting cage. He would sit there in a chair, and he would watch me swing the bat. He just watched and watched, and he talked about the strike zone. I think the polish, the final thing of the swing I had, was done through Rogers Hornsby because we used to work all the time. He was a great man, and I think at the time he had five friends. Don Zimmer was his friend, because he used to take him out to the Arlington racetrack; and, of course, there was Santo.

I'll tell you a little story about Rogers Hornsby when he was the hitting coach for the Chicago Cubs. Mr. John Holland, who was the general manager of the ball club, told Roger to go through the organization to see what kind of players that we had. At that time, you had D, B, C, Double A. He went through all the organization, and he finally wound up down in San Antonio, where Ron Santo and I were playing. He took us all out, and we had batting practice—guys

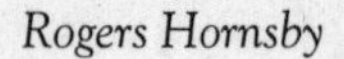
Rogers Hornsby

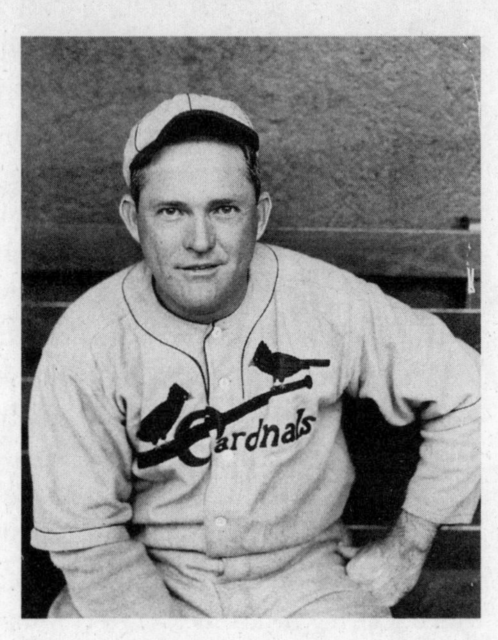

took the field. And he sat us all in the stands, and as he was going down the line, he told this one kid, "Listen, you could go get a job at this time. Leave, because you can't play baseball." So he got to Santo and me, and we were sitting here with our shoulders crunched like this. He said, "You two guys could play in the big league right now. You could hit in the big league, and you could catch the ball. You guys are practically better than anything in Chicago right now. You could play major-league baseball." So after going around, he went back to Chicago and he sat down with Mr. Holland, and he said, "When I reached Double-A baseball, you got two players down there. You got Williams and Santo, who could play in the big league right now. You could bring them up right now. But the other fellows you had in the minor league, you could release everybody down there because you don't have any players." This is how he was. He was a straightforward guy.

Rogers was, I guess, about sixty years old. He would do a little show-and-tell. He would get in the batter's box. If you know the batter's box, it's practically six feet. He was standing all the way back in the corner, the farthest away from the plate, and he always stepped into the baseball. He got a lot of base hits, but he got a lot of home runs, too. I think Joe Morgan broke Rogers's career home-run record for second basemen and I think eventually Ryne Sandberg did it in Chicago. But he hit a lot of home runs for a second baseman in the dead-ball era. He was such a great hitter; he could see the ball and read the pitch. We just had a good time together in conversation, talking about hitting. When you get a guy like that—once you start talking about hitting, you could draw a great conversation.

He often said, "You're going to get one good ball to hit. One good ball to hit—don't miss it." He said, "Try to see the baseball hit the bat." For eighteen years, I tried to do that. I couldn't do it, but I knew what he was saying later on in life: he was trying to get me to follow the ball as close as you can to the bat. The only way you could do it was if you had a right-handed pitcher, a sidearm guy like a Rollie Fingers throwing to a left-handed hitter—and Rollie used to backdoor a lot of left-handed hitters, backdoor meaning to start the breaking ball out and let it come to the outside corner. You've got to hit that ball to left field. And I think that's the only way that you will see the ball hit the bat. But I knew what he was trying to say after I thought about it for a while in the game of baseball. He often talked about that strike zone, and this was implanted in my mind: make sure the ball was over home plate, seventeen inches wide, and between your armpit and your knees. You're going to get one good ball to hit up there. I tried to stay with the baseball as long as I could. Later on, when Rogers came up to the big league, he used to sit right behind the batters behind home plate. When I missed a ball, when I swung and missed a ball, I knew what he meant when he said, "Just keep your eye on the baseball." So he was always with me—in Double A, when we first met, and all through those years in the big league.

I was playing with the San Antonio Missions in Double-A baseball. Grady Hatton was the manager. I remember San Antonio—it was hot and I didn't want to be there. I was hitting .325; that was the only reason I was still playing, I guess I got back to the hotel, and I didn't unpack my bag. I had talked to my brother the day before. I said, "What are you doing?" He said, "I'm home. I'm fishing. I'm enjoying life." I said, "I'll be there tomorrow." So I told J. C. Hartman, my roommate, "J., take me to the train station." J. said, "Where are you going?" I said, "I'm going home. I'm tired of baseball." He said, "You can't do that." I said, "Yes, I can." I said, "Come on, take me to the train station." He tried to find millions of ways not to do it. Finally, he said, "You're serious, aren't you?" I said, "Yeah. I'm going home." So he took me to the train station. I rode the train into Mobile, and I left the ball club. J. went to the ballpark that evening—he and I used to go there together. When he walked in the clubhouse, Grady Hatton looked around and said, "Where's Billy?" And J. said, "Billy's going home." "Going home? Why is he going home?" Grady Hatton called John Holland. John Holland called Buck O'Neil and said, "Somebody's got to get Billy back somehow."

So I got home and stayed two or three days. and I was sitting on the porch—my father built a house, it was way back. You looked down, you had to drive in, and you came back there. I was sitting on the porch, just cooling out. Buck always had a Fury—you know, the Plymouth Fury? And I was sitting on the porch getting ready to go swimming or something, and I saw this thing coming up in the yard. I said, "Oh no, I'm in trouble now." So Buck came, and we just started talking. He said, "You know, you're swinging the bat pretty good. Why'd you come home?" I said, "Buck, I just wanted to come home." And he said, "You going to play again?" I said, "No, I don't want to play baseball no more." And I was making all kinds of progress. And he said, "Man, that's just too bad, because we were looking forward to you coming to Chicago because you swing the bat real good." That's all he said. He said, "Well, I'll be around here a couple days, and we'll talk and stuff." Then he went down to Prichard Park. He said, "You want to ride down to Prichard Park?" I said, "I'll go down there." Buck and I rode down there. He took me down to the

Buck O'Neil

park and we walked around. He introduced himself as the scout for the Cubs and everything. And a lot of guys came up to me and said, "Billy, where've you been?" I said, "I've been off to play baseball." "Off to play baseball. Man, that's a great thing." And everybody started talking about how good it was. Buck saw all this. Guys would come up and say, "Man, you playing professional baseball. That's great, man. That's what I want to do." And I was hearing all this stuff, and Buck and I started talking. Buck said, "You're ready to go back now?" I said, "Yeah, I'm ready to go back."

So I went back with the ball club. I played about five more days, and I got called up to Triple-A baseball. In five games, I hit about .600 and hit about four or five home runs. Later on, I was called up to the big league.

So, this is how I got called up to the big league in 1959. And I pinch myself sometimes. I say, "I could have been a released ballplayer." It was just an opportunity to come back and do so well, so when I got back, I was pretty satisfied, and I went on to play and didn't get homesick anymore.

I didn't play for Buck in the Negro League, but he knew who I was, he knew all of my family because he used to come to Mobile maybe every three or four weeks. It seemed like Buck was always around every time somebody needed him in the Cubs' organization. He was always there. When they first signed Ernie Banks to play from the Kansas City Monarchs, he was wanting to go home all the time. Buck was the inspiration to him, just staying in the game of baseball and just doing good.

When you played in the Negro League, you played baseball. They played hard baseball, and that's what they brought to the major league. They slid hard. They ran the ball hard. Because if you didn't, they would get somebody else right away. They used to have a thing they called Dutch. When you went to different places, you pitched in money, and you went to grocery store and bought a lot of stuff and you came back on the bus and you started eating. So if one player didn't do all the right things, many times, they would give him money—enough to get home. They would give him money and tell him to go into the store and buy the stuff. If he hadn't been the ballplayer they expected, they would send him in the store, and all of a sudden he would look out and see that the bus was just taking off. So you had to play hard. You had to do the right thing to play on these teams.

When I first came to Chicago, because the Chicago Bears used to play their games in Wrigley Field every year, they had to put new sod in there. When they put this new sod in there, and we came from spring training in April, this sod was so new that it could slip out from under you. So the first year I came to the big league, I made eleven errors in the outfield. That's a lot for an outfielder. I was the Rookie of the Year, of course, in 1961: 25 home runs for the ball club. I knew I could swing the bat, but I wanted to make myself a complete baseball player. After those eleven errors, the following year I went to spring training and got help from Bob Kennedy, Lou Klein, and those other individuals. They hit me a lot of fly balls, a lot of ground balls, and I made myself a pretty good outfielder. I cut it down to three errors a year pretty consistently. If I wanted to do something, if I wanted to play major-league baseball, I wanted to be one of the best ballplayers.

I also had to do a lot of throwing. Each time that I played catch with an individual—with the Cubs uniform, you had a nice circle up there. I always tried to hit the "C" on the Cubs. I didn't have a really strong arm, but I knew I had to charge the ball and be accurate. They always talked about catching on your throwing side, with your throwing hand right close to the glove, the reason being that when you reach in to get the ball, when you come out, you will be cross seam. That was always what they talked about: grabbing the ball across the seam and throwing it where you get a rotation stitch over stitch.

When I got to Chicago in 1959, one of the first things I did was pick up the telephone and inform my father that I had made it to the major league. He was very excited. He really was, because my other brother had been released and had stopped playing baseball. When we used to sit on a Saturday afternoon and watch baseball, we talked about the game. I remember we were looking at the Braves one time. Lew Burdette was pitching. My father pointed out, and said, "Look there." He said, "He threw a ball right down the middle, the first strike." He said, "If you ever get to the big league, you make sure you hit that first pitch." And I thought about that. I think we were playing the Milwaukee Braves and Lew Burdette was pitching. The whole time I was walking up to the batter's box, I was thinking about this. I said, "If he gives me a good ball to hit, I will swing the bat." But as all that stuff passed through my mind, my knees were shaking and everything. Lew Burdette wound up and threw the ball right there. And guess what I did? I took the darn thing, because I wasn't ready to hit. I was so enjoying being in the big league.

In 1960, I went back and played Triple-A baseball in Houston. That was before Houston was major league. I came up to play regularly in 1961. After having a year in Triple A, maybe 24 home runs and hitting over .300 and playing in a whole bunch of ball games in that heat down there, they said, "Well, if you could do that there, you possibly could play in the big league." But it didn't happen like clockwork. I guess somehow I didn't relax myself. I wasn't hitting the baseball. I played and my batting average kept going down and down and down. I remember a night playing in Philadelphia, I went 0 for 4. After going 0 for 10, 12, something like that, I sat on the bench. Everybody had gone in the clubhouse, and I could see the lights were going off. I sat on that bench for about twenty-five or thirty minutes in old Shibe Park. I wasn't swinging the bat real well. So the following day, I was taken out of the lineup, and while I was sitting on the bench, I said, "If I ever get back in the lineup, they are going to have to tear the uniform off before they get me out of there again." So we were playing in the Coliseum and Bob Will came up with a sore neck or something, and I got a chance to play. And from that time, that's when I went on to hit the 25 home runs, win Rookie of the Year. Coming up from Triple A and having the numbers I had was enough to win the Rookie of the Year.

I think most of all it was just relaxing, putting things in perspective. You got to see the ball before you hit it. I was visualizing the base hit before I even saw the ball. But I was relaxing, just doing the things I did when I was in Double A, when I was in Triple A. When I first came to the big league, I thought everybody threw the ball 90 miles an hour, 100 miles an hour, but they didn't; they pitched to your weakness. Sitting on the bench and thinking about this, I said, "I got to correct my weakness, because that's what they're going to throw to." It wasn't that hard. I had to get back to the old way, hitting strikes. This is when the Rogers Hornsby thing started coming into my head: "Get a good ball to hit."

Going back to Rogers Hornsby, my hitting coach, one other thing he said that always stuck is that when you got two strikes on you, you got to be like a goalie. You got to protect the outside. You got to protect the inside. You got to protect everything. So that's what you did; you shortened your stroke up, shortened your swing, and you wanted to make contact. You didn't swing for the fences. If you get your pitch on the first pitch, you swing for the home run, and that's what I did. When I got a good ball I could hit on the first pitch, I swung. But each time you swung you should try to make contact a little bit more. Nobody likes a strikeout. I went to the plate 600 times for about six or seven years in a row, and every tenth time I'd strike out. So I struck out about sixty or seventy times a year, and that was great. I was hitting home runs, too. I think the pride is gone from a guy striking out a lot. They don't care about it too much now.

My home runs were still opposite field because I still couldn't pull a ball then. I remember that when I was in Double A or Triple A, somebody talked about how you hit the ball out of the catcher's mitt, meaning that you wait until the ball's right here. Then I hit the ball to left field. The ability to be quick allowed me to wait to see the baseball a little longer. When you're hitting good, you see the ball good, you make good contact, you always have balance. A lot of times, people will ask me, "Did you know what was coming?" A lot of times I didn't. My weight was always back. I had the ability to get the bat head to the ball. So I waited a long time just because I was quick. I could wait and see what the pitcher was going to do.

Don Drysdale was one of those kind of guys—his ball ran into the right-handed hitters. And he was pretty rough on the mound. But Drysdale's ball would tail away from a lefty; I got some hits off of him. And Bob Gibson—I can say this now because I'm not playing. I tell people this, but I didn't believe it until somebody brought it to my attention. I remember a couple of balls I hit out of the ballpark on Gibson in one game, but he was one of those guys; he'd always challenge you. And I was fortunate enough to hit eleven home runs off of him.

The guy who gave me the most trouble was Sandy Koufax. Everybody knows him. But another guy, you won't read about him, he's not in the Hall of Fame: Ray Sadecki. He pitched with the Cardinals. When he first came up, he went straight over the top, and I was an aggressive hitter and wanted the guy to bring it on. I didn't care how hard you'd throw, I could challenge you. But he started dropping down, throwing everything, keeping me off balance. This is what a pitcher should do, keep the hitter off balance. But I couldn't hit him. I remember when I went with the Oakland A's, he was traded to Kansas City. I was playing for Chuck Tanner then, I was a DH, and we got in a ball game that we needed to win. This was one of the first times I ever did this, because experience told me I couldn't hit this guy. So I went to Chuck, and I said, "Chuck, we need a base hit here. You better get me out of the game, because I don't have no kind of numbers off this guy." But there's a guy in the major league, I don't care who he is, if he's a good hitter, there's one pitcher out there, and he doesn't have to be a Hall of Famer, he'll get him out. Curt Simmons didn't throw hard; Henry Aaron couldn't touch him. One night, he was pitching, and he threw Aaron a curveball, and it stayed on the outside part of the plate. Aaron stepped across the plate and hit a home run on him. Because he couldn't hit him, he said, "I got to do it somehow." But once a guy established that he

Henry Aaron

could get you out, I don't care who it is. I was watching a game the other night, Sammy Sosa—he hit a lot of home runs off a lot of people. Good hitter, but John Smoltz always got him. When I was the hitting coach with the Cubs, he always had trouble with Smoltz.

I think the thing started turning, I guess, when Leo Durocher came in 1966. We had Santo, Banks, and myself. We were each hitting around 30 home runs a year, driving in maybe 100 runs. I remember Leo saying when he first came to the club in '66, "This is not an eighth-place club." And we finished tenth. But things started looking up because in 1966, he got Fergie Jenkins. Fergie was a relief pitcher for the Phillies. So right away, Leo said, "You're not going to relieve for me. You're going to be one of my starting pitchers." That's because he had been around baseball and because when he came here, Mr. Wrigley gave him carte blanche. "You make the trades. You do what you want to do here. I want to win." And he went to San Francisco and got Bill Hands and Randy Hundley, who called a lot of ball games for us here. I don't know who he gave up, but we got

Ernie Banks

Ferguson Jenkins

those two players, great baseball players. Bill Hands became a starter along with Fergie and won a lot of ball games. We had a kid named Kenny Holtzman who was throwing the ball good. I remember, we were playing in Long Beach that year, Long Beach, California. That's one of the first times we trained there, the only time, the one year. Leo and I were standing behind the cage, and Leo said, "This kid can win in the big league right now." He was in the service at the time. He went in the service, spent his time during the week. He pitched on Saturdays and Sundays. He was 9-0. He was a good athlete. He pitched a no-hitter in Wrigley Field. Actually, he pitched two no-hitters, I think, one of them in Wrigley Field. He had one when Henry Aaron hit a ball that was out of the ballpark, but the wind in Chicago brought it back so heavily. I caught the ball facing away from home. He was a good pitcher, but Fergie was the leader of that pitching staff. He won 20 ball games six years in a row. Fergie didn't walk anybody. He had control. If you hit a home run off of him, it was a solo home run.

You know, we were pretty solid at every position. Randy Hundley was the catcher, and, of course, Ernie was playing first base at the time. We had Glenn Beckert after Kenny Hubbs, who passed away in an airplane crash. Beckert came from Boston, and we had Don Kessinger, who was drafted in several sports. He chose baseball to play. A lot of people say he was like Marty Marion—a tall, lanky guy. And, of course, we had Santo, used to be a catcher. So he was at third base, and I was in left field. Jim Hickman came over. We had Adolfo Phillips here. So we had a good baseball team. We were a pretty solid team.

Leo had been out of the game for ten years. But Mr. Wrigley wanted a strong person to come with the ball club. That was one trait of Leo's. He was a strong individual. And he wanted a guy that knew the game of baseball. When Leo joined us in Long Beach, California, he made it known that he was in charge. But Leo was a guy that knew the game. He was the guy that took a young club and molded a winning attitude. We were a good team, but we never could get over the hump. Matter of fact, we still didn't get over the hump, because we didn't win the World Series. But we played good,

Leo Durocher

sound baseball. Leo fought for his players. I remember Tom Gorman, Jocko Conlan, all those great umpires. When they made a call against us, they always looked over at Leo. They knew that if it was wrong, he would be right there for his player. Leo was always about three innings ahead of every manager. He knew what was going to happen about three innings down the road. Leo didn't beat you down when you were losing. When you started winning, that's when he brought your mistakes to your attention.

I remember an incident that happened in the '60s, when Curt Flood was with the Cardinals. Next to Willie Mays, and close to Willie Mays, Curt Flood was one of the best outfielders in baseball. Curt Flood charged a ball real well. Curt had something wrong with his arm. I imagine at that time it was his rotator cuff, but nobody came up with that. I was on first base and a ball was hit to center field. I played baseball instinct, and when Curt Flood came in, he charged the ball real well, and somehow I forgot that he didn't have a good arm. His arm was sore, but I didn't go to third base. Leo was on the top step of the dugout at that time, because we were at the tail end of the season. We wanted to win ball games. And that's when Leo and I had some words. He wanted me to go to third base, and we started shouting at each other. But that was it. Those were the only harsh words Leo and I ever had on the ball club. He challenged you to be a better ballplayer.

I could be a little prejudiced about Ron Santo, because we were in Double A together and in the big league. Santo had a lifetime batting average of .277; a few times he hit over .300, and he got some home runs. He has five Gold Gloves. I saw a lot of great plays at third base. I know this might sound corny, but I think Santo is not in the Hall of Fame because we were never in postseason play. At the end of the year, because we didn't win, a lot of people didn't know what kind of player Santo was. But I know. And I think that for what he has done for the game of baseball and how he played, he should be in the Hall of Fame.

• • •

Ron Santo

I wanted to be on the field. That was where I relaxed, that was where I thought I could play the game and really enjoy the game. So after I got to a certain point, after I started reaching numbers of consecutive games, I remembered Richie Ashburn's 730, and it was a mark I wanted to get to. And then I got close to Stan Musial. I think Musial had 895 or something like that. And then, after I got those games under my belt, I would say, "I want to go to a thousand and see what happens." I knew I wasn't going to make two thousand. I knew that. But after I got to one thousand, I wanted to just see how far I could go. I remember we were playing on the road. I told Leo some little things I wasn't doing to win ball games. Maybe somebody'd get a base hit and I wanted to be sure I could make it to third, but I didn't do it. I said, "I'm not playing the game that I should be playing now." I said to Leo, "I got to have some rest after eleven hundred. I got to have a day off." So we talked, and Leo said, "Well, we're going to do that. We'll do that." We got to Chicago, and I remember going to the clubhouse that morning. For one of the first times in all those games, I don't see my name in the third slot because we had talked the day before. And Joey Amalfitano approached me and said, "You could go back home if you want to." I elected to stay. After the game was over, and luckily we won that day, it was just like somebody just took a piano or something off my back. When you're on a streak, you know you got to play. A couple of times, fouling a ball off my foot—I fouled the ball off my ankle in Cincinnati. So I come to the plate in about the fifth inning and hit the ball out of the ballpark and that thing was stiffened up. I practically walked around the ballpark. I said, "Leo, you got to get me out of this game." So I went to the clubhouse. We had a day off the next day, and Al Schunneman, who was the trainer for the Cubs for many years, had me going back and forth—whirlpool, heat, whirlpool, ice, whirlpool, heat, whirlpool, ice. Luckily, within about a couple of days, I was back playing. This was coming up to the day that they were going to have in Chicago to celebrate my streak. Of course, you get wrapped up in numbers. There is just a lot of weight on your back, knowing you got to go out there and play. And once I took a day or two off, I felt stronger. I felt more at ease on the baseball field, so a lot of things began to work in my favor at that time. Of course, I think I was like about thirty-two then, so a day off at that time would do me good. But to set that streak and have the National League record. When Steve Garvey played in the 1,118 games, I think the 1,119th, or next game, he slid into home plate and hurt his finger.

I've talked to Cal Ripken many times. It takes a person like me or Steve Garvey to recognize what he'd gone through. The whole while I'm out there playing in the streak, the other players are saying, "Why are you doing this? You should take a day off every now and then." But it's not in your vocabulary to take a day off. You want to be on the baseball field. You relax. You're enjoying it out there. And a lot of people don't recognize that. You're just having fun playing. But I grant you, playing in Chicago, playing all day games, it was rough. It was rough. But I enjoyed the game. I enjoyed being out there when I was on the baseball field, it relaxed me. That's what pulled me through a lot of baseball games.

• • •

In 1969, I remember we were down one run in the opening game, and Leo looked down the bench. He called Willie Smith up to hit. Willie Smith hit a home run, and the Chicago Cubs won the first game, opening day of the season. From that moment on, we never did look back. We were always winning ball games. We were in first place. Everybody was having a pretty decent year. It was so exciting. We would go to the ballpark, get there by 9:30. I wanted to get there before everybody got there, and still about ten to fifteen thousand people were waiting to get into the ballpark at that time. It was a fun summer. We played good baseball. As I said, we were beating everybody. And around August 9, we were leading the league by about nine games. Early in September, Pittsburgh came in. I remember a game that Phil Regan was pitching, and there was a base open, and Willie Stargell was the hitter. We elected to pitch to Willie Stargell, and he hit a home run. We lost the game that particular day. And we started to lose games. We never did think about the Mets that year. The Cardinals were the team to beat. Nobody looked at the Mets. But the Mets played better than .700 baseball, I think, from about twenty-five or thirty games to go. They played great because they had the pitching. The Cubs didn't lose it, as I look at it, quite so much as the Mets won it. Because they had the great pitching and they came on at the right time. The one thing I hated when they won—two of those guys were from my hometown. They played against us, then they used to come here and my wife used to cook a lot of food and made them strong. At one time, the Mets could've had three guys from Mobile in the outfield. They had Cleon Jones from Plateau, where my wife was from. They had Tommie Agee, the late Tommie Agee, playing great center field. And, of course, Amos Otis was playing center field at the time. So they had to get rid of one center fielder, Otis, but they played real good. They had great pitching.

I wanted to do everything I could to win ball games. And I know there was a lot of cases that guys weren't catching the ball, guys weren't hitting the baseball, but I did everything I could to kind of inspire guys. In the old clubhouse, I went around at the time and got some soap, and I wrote "$10,000" on every mirror, saying, "This is what we could get if we go all the way, guys." I tried to do everything I could to inspire the guys, but as I said, the Mets, they were playing good baseball.

When I first came to the big league, the minimum salary was about $6,500, I think it was. And now it's like $400,000, or something like that, I don't know what it is. But when you played, it was a year-to-year contract. You signed a contract and that was it until you went in to negotiate just before spring training. Nobody talked about two-year contracts. Nobody had an agent. When I was with the Cubs, I remember hitting .322, driving in 129 runs, and hitting 42 home runs. And I had to stay home, I didn't go to spring training for like five days, because I wanted $100,000. I wanted to be the first Cub to make $100,000. So me and John Holland, we were negotiating by phone. And I said, "I'm not going to spring training unless I get the money, because a lot of people had made that much. I want to be the first Cub to make $100,000." I finally wound up getting it. And Mr. Wrigley wrote a long letter—I still have the letter at home now—saying how much he appreciated what I'd done with the ball club, that they would have given me $99,990, but they don't want to go to $100,000. The last year I was there, I wanted two years at $150,000 each or one year at $180,000, I think it was. And when I spoke to Mr. Holland, he said, "I can't do that. I can't do that. I can't pay you that kind of money." So he said, "You're going to have to go down and talk to Mr. Wrigley." This had to be 1974. So I said, "Make the appointment. I'll go down there." So I went to the Wrigley Building. I went up the elevator, and I got off on the tenth floor. A lot of people recognized me, and I signed autographs for the secretaries and stuff like that. So after signing the autographs, the secretary said, "Mr. Wrigley's ready to see you now." So the door swung open. There was Mr. Wrigley, sitting behind a long table, I guess about twenty feet long with chairs all around where he had the board meeting. He was on one end; I was on the other. I wished I could've had an agent with me, but I didn't. He said, "What can I do for you, son?" I said, "Mr. Wrigley, I didn't get a bonus." I said, "I got $1,500. And my father got a couple of cigars." And I said, "Every year, I'm driving in runs, I'm having a good season, I'm putting people in the ballpark, I'm putting a lot of those six thousand to twenty-five thousand people in the ballpark." But he said, "I can't give you that kind of money." He said, "I can't do that." He finally gave me $150,000 for one year. And he said, "Billy, you guys are going to price yourself right out of baseball." This is what he told me. And I said, "Mr. Wrigley, baseball was here before you and me, and it'll still be here when we are both gone." And I think I pinched a nerve with that remark. "Sign up that contract and get out of here." But he was a good owner. Mr. Wrigley was an old handshake guy. If he told you something, you didn't have to put it on paper.

I think the individuals who play a sport inspire people to do certain things. Jackie Robinson inspired a lot of black kids to say, "You know, let's play baseball." Later on, you get a guy like Michael Jordan playing basketball. Every time you turn on the TV, you see Michael Jordan, and kids say, "I want to do that." I think Michael and basketball took a lot of players from the game of baseball. They wanted to play basketball. Just like Pelé, when Pelé came over here, playing soccer. A lot of publicity, and now a lot of kids, they're getting involved in soccer. If I went back to Whistler today to go see baseball on Sunday evening, I don't think I would see any. People are involved in so many things to do now: basketball, hockey, soccer, golf. Tiger Woods has inspired a lot of young kids to play golf. But if I went back to Whistler now to see a doubleheader on Sunday, or a doubleheader on Saturday, you couldn't now because people don't play baseball as they used to.

The old saying is everything I have, everything I've gotten, every person who I've met, I owe it to the great game of baseball. I've enjoyed playing it. Baseball has been a great game. It gave me an opportunity to travel around the world. I don't know whether I would have done that if I hadn't been involved in baseball. I met some great people in baseball. As I said, everything I own, every person I met, I think I owe it to this great game of baseball.

INDEX

Page numbers in *italics* refer to illustrations.